£6.50

C000063394

# Criminal
# Behaviour

*An introduction to criminology
and the penal system*

**SECOND EDITION**

# HERSCHEL PRINS

Tavistock Publications
London and New York

Second edition first published in 1982 by
Tavistock Publications Ltd
11 New Fetter Lane, London EC4P 4EE

Published in the USA by
Tavistock Publications
in association with Methuen, Inc.
733 Third Avenue, New York, NY 10017

First edition published by
Pitman House Ltd 1973

Photoset by
Rowland Phototypesetting Ltd,
Bury St Edmunds, Suffolk
Printed in Great Britain by
Richard Clay (The Chaucer Press) Ltd,
Bungay, Suffolk

*British Library Cataloguing in Publication Data*

Prins, Herschel
Criminal behaviour. – 2nd ed.
1. Crime and criminals – Great Britain
I. Title
364.941      HV6947

*Library of Congress Cataloging in Publication Data*

Prins, Herschel A.
Criminal behaviour.
Includes indexes.
1. Crime and criminals.    2. Criminal psychology.
3. Corrections. I. Title.
HV6025.P67 1982      364.2      82-5691
ISBN 0-422-77680-7              AACR2
ISBN 0-422-77690-4 (pbk.)

Every act of authority of one man over another, for which there is not an absolute necessity, is tyrannical.

CESARE BECCARIA

*For my family*

# *Contents*

# Acknowledgements

I am grateful to various colleagues and others who made useful criticisms of the first edition of this book. In the preparation of this second, and much revised, edition, I have been greatly helped by my colleague David Webb, Lecturer in Sociology, for his assistance with Chapter 3. He has brought me to a much better appreciation of sociological perspectives on criminal behaviour. My friend and colleague, Professor Edward Griew, of our Faculty of Law, advised me on certain legal questions. If I have misunderstood or misrepresented him, the responsibility for any error is mine entirely. My thanks are also due to David Atkinson of the Prison Department of the Home Office for updating my information on the organization of prison services and of Prison Department Headquarters. My most grateful thanks are due also to Mrs Janet Kirkwood who, despite the demands of the latest arrival in the Kirkwood household, has once again managed, with her customary calm and efficiency, to produce order out of my chaotic and barely decipherable drafts. Despite the recent traumatic effects of the cuts in university expenditure, the University of Leicester has endeavoured to continue its practice of affording staff regular periods of study leave. Without such relief from more routine duties, this book might never have appeared or, at the least, its production would have been long delayed; my thanks are therefore due to the University for granting me study leave for the Autumn term, 1981, and to my colleagues (and in particular, Martin Shaw) for coping with my duties under difficult circumstances. Finally, as always, I must acknowledge my great debt to my wife, Norma, who, in her usual selfless way, makes everything possible.

HERSCHEL PRINS
*June 1982*

# Introduction

In the introduction to the first edition of this book (published by Messrs Pitman in 1973) I posed the question: 'Why another book on the study and treatment of crime?' That question is still relevant some eight years later and worthy of the same answer, namely that there are still very few introductory texts that deal with the explanations and management of criminal behaviour in a reasonably concise and yet fairly fully documented form. As then, the present work is intended *merely as a guide and an introduction* to a very complex territory. It should be regarded as a skeleton upon which the reader may add the flesh of his or her further reading and enquiry. To this end I have supplied specific references for each chapter and general guidance for further reading. Reviews of the first edition indicated that the book would be found useful by a wide range of readers, for example local authority social workers, probation officers, students in these fields of activity, teachers, medical and law undergraduates, and others. I have no reason to believe that the need for such a book on the part of these groups has diminished over the years. In addition, the book is intended to meet the needs of a variety of other people whose work brings them into regular contact with offenders, for example sentencers, both professional and lay, police and prison officers in training, wardens of after-care and other hostels, staff working in the field of residential care of young offenders (such as community homes – formerly known as approved schools), and the growing numbers of volunteers and auxiliary workers.

It is also hoped that the book will be particularly useful to medical postgraduates studying forensic psychiatry as part of the examination requirements of the Royal College of Psychiatrists, and the growing numbers of clinical psychologists in training – both groups should find Parts Three and Four useful. More detailed discussion of these matters may be found in my book *Offenders, Deviants, or Patients?* (1980).

In producing this second edition, I have kept to the same outline and format in the main, but have substantially revised certain parts of the book by the inclusion of recent literature, research findings, and changes in law and practice. Although a number of proposals for changes in penal provisions are now before Parliament, the law as stated in this text is that currently in force at 1 June 1982.

# PART ONE
# Defining and Measuring Criminal Behaviour

# CHAPTER ONE

# *Defining crime and those who study it*

The state of the criminal law continues to be as it should – a decisive reflection of the social consciousness of a society. What kind of conduct an organised community considers at a given time sufficiently condemnable to impose official sanctions, impairing the life, liberty, or property of the offender, is a barometer of the moral and social thinking of a community. Hence, the criminal law is particularly sensitive to changes in social structure and social thinking.

WOLFGANG FRIEDMANN

## What is crime?

I begin this book by making some brief attempt to define what we mean by the terms 'crime' and 'delinquency'. Such an attempt must, of necessity, also include some discussion of crime in relation to sin, criminal responsibility, and criminal liability. I then discuss the subject matter of criminology, and give some indication of where those who study the crime problem are most likely to be found.

According to Mannheim: 'Crime is, first of all, a legal conception, human behaviour punishable under the criminal law' (Mannheim 1965: 22). He suggests, however, that for criminologists crime is much more than this, because in the first place the legal term 'crime' is too wide, as it can describe behaviour ranging from murder at one end of the scale, to minor infringements of the road traffic or food and drugs regulations at the other.[1] In the second place, it is not always easy to distinguish *crime* from *civil* wrongs, or *torts*, as they are called in English law (in this book I shall be dealing with English law only, the law and procedure in Eire and Scotland being different).

Some authorities define civil offences (*torts*) as wrongs against individuals, in contrast to criminal offences, which are offences against the community as a whole. Such a distinction is unsatisfactory for two reasons. First, a criminal offence can well be both a crime against individuals *and* against the community (as for example in the case of a bank robbery involving serious personal injury to bank staff and the theft of many customers' money). Second, there is in general no bar to the initiation of civil proceedings by the injured party in cases where the accused has been convicted of and sentenced for the offence under the criminal law.

In English law, a distinction is sometimes made between crimes that are *mala in se* (bad in themselves) and those that are *mala prohibita* (created under some statute). Although this distinction may be interesting to academic lawyers and moral philosophers, from a practical point of view it is not particularly relevant for students of the crime problem. In his discussion of this issue Mannheim quotes the legal authority Blackstone as stating that there were offences against 'those whose rights which God and nature have established' as compared with 'violations of laws which enjoin only positive duties and forbid any such things as are not *mala in se*' (Mannheim 1965: 29).

Mannheim concludes that:

'The essential points of [the] discussion are, first, that the term "crime" should be used in technical language only with reference to conduct that is legally "crime". Secondly, such conduct, if fully proved, is crime, regardless of whether it actually leads to a conviction before a criminal court, or whether it is dealt with by other agencies, or not at all.'

(Mannheim 1965: 34)

---

[1]  History provides some interesting illustrations of forms of behaviour that were at one time regarded as criminal, for example printing a book, professing the medical doctrine of circulation of the blood, driving with reins, and having gold in the house. See Sutherland and Cressey (1960: 15) for a fuller discussion of these examples.

Traditionally, lawyers have divided crimes into three classes: treasons, felonies, and misdemeanours. Briefly, at the risk of over-simplifying a very complex subject, I shall say that treasons are defined as crimes against the Sovereign or the State; felonies as crimes of a serious nature, which at one time occasioned the forfeiture of the convicted person's lands and goods; misdemeanours as lesser crimes, not involving forfeiture. The anachronistic distinction between felonies and misdemeanours has now been abandoned, and replaced by a new distinction between 'arrestable' and 'non-arrestable' offences. (See also Chapter 6.)

I now consider what constitutes the ingredients of criminal behaviour from the point of view of the criminal law.

## What constitutes criminal behaviour?

Sutherland and Cressey indicate that there are a number of factors that must be present before a piece of behaviour may be labelled as 'criminal' (Sutherland and Cressey 1960: 12–13). Some of these can best be summarized as follows:

(1) 'Before behaviour can be called crime, there must be certain external consequences of *harm* [my italics] . . . even if one decides to commit a crime, but changes one's mind before doing anything about it, no crime has been committed. The intention is not taken for the deed.'

(2) The harm must be legally forbidden; antisocial behaviour is not crime unless it is prohibited by law.

(3) There must be 'conduct', i.e. there must be an intentional or reckless action or inaction, which brings the harmful consequences about. (But see discussion under 'liability' below.)

(4) There must be *mens rea* (criminal intent). The issues of intent, liability (at law) for the consequences of one's actions, and *mens rea* are all important controversial subjects to those who study jurisprudence. (See also Prins 1980: Chapter 2.)

Suffice it to say at this stage that, for behaviour to be labelled 'criminal', there must be (i) harm, (ii) conduct (intentional or unintentional), (iii) *mens rea*, and (iv) prescribed punishment (that is, not only must the harm be prescribed by law, but there must be a threat of punishment for those who violate it). In English law, this is embodied in the principle of *nulla poena sine lege*. In effect, this means that an offender should not be punished for any action without a clear and definite legal basis.

## The purposes of the criminal law

Friedmann (1964: 374)·quotes an eminent American authority as stating that 'the purpose of the penal (criminal) law is to express a formal social condemnation of forbidden conduct, buttressed by sanctions calculated to prevent it'. Although he accepts this definition, Friedmann admits that it poses three important questions 'to which different societies give very different answers'. First, what kind of conduct is forbidden? Second, what kind of formal social condemnation is considered appropriate to prevent such conduct? Third, what kind of sanctions are best calculated to prevent officially outlawed conduct? I make some attempt to answer the first of Fried-mann's questions in this chapter, and I discuss the implications arising from questions two and three in Parts Three and Four.

In examining what kind of conduct should be forbidden, we are forced to examine, by implication, the purposes of the criminal law. Walker (1969) lists a number of purposes, of which the following seem to be the most important for our present discussion.

(a) The protection of the human person (and in some cases of animals) from intentional violence, cruelty, or unwelcome sexual approaches.

(b) The protection of people against some forms of unintended harm (for example from traffic, poisons, or infections).

(c) The protection of particularly vulnerable individuals (for example the young, the mentally ill, and the subnormal) against abuse of their persons or property. The protection of individuals (even if they be willing partners) from certain sexual acts, for example sodomy and incest.

(d) The defence of the Realm (for example from espionage).

(e) The prevention of certain forms of behaviour which, if performed in public, might shock, corrupt, or deprave. (As some recent court decisions show, this is a highly controver-

sial area for the intervention of the criminal law; witness the
heated and emotional comment over the famous trial of *OZ*
and the blasphemy case concerning the poem about Christ
and His crucifixion.)

(f) The protection of property (for example, against theft or
damage).

(g) The protection of certain social institutions (such as marriage and the family); the collection of various revenues, the
enforcement of certain criminal-civil sanctions (as for example attendance at school); the prevention of inconvenience (for example the offences of causing obstruction of the
public highway with a motor vehicle; and offences concerning pollution or noise).

It can be seen from the foregoing that criminal law serves a
wide variety of purposes, some of them controversial, and that it
seeks to control and regulate behaviour extending from the most
serious and antisocial at one end of the scale to minor pecula-
tions and infringements at the other. Moreover, its purposes
serve to illustrate further the problem of drawing a hard-and-
fast dividing line between the civil and criminal wrongs referred
to earlier.

It is also obvious that the purposes of criminal law will reflect
changes in the attitudes of society towards crime and 'sin'.[2] In
this context:

'It is of particular importance to note the ways in which
offences "come and go" – a (further) reminder that crime is
only what the law says it is. For example, incest did not
become a specific criminal offence until 1908; and the law
relating to infanticide was not finally clarified until the late
1930s. Attempted suicide has now disappeared from the
statute book. In the reverse direction, the laws concerning

[2] Limitations of space preclude a detailed discussion of this issue. The case for
the criminal law's concern with 'sin' has been argued by Devlin in his
Maccabean lecture *The Enforcement of Morals* (1959); the case against the
intervention of the criminal law has been argued by Hart (1963). Much of the
controversy at that time centred around the question of sexual offences,
particularly consenting adult homosexual acts committed in private. More
recent discussions have been concerned with other forms of sexual behaviour,
notably incest, sexual relations with children, and the possession and ingestion
of 'soft' drugs such as cannabis.

gaming, drinking in relation to driving, and drugs have all been tightened up. These issues reflect the see-saw elements in law enforcement, and the ambivalence of our society towards those who deviate.'                    (Prins 1970: 47)

Walker (1969) also gives a number of instances in which new offences have been created in response to social pressures; he cites the depositing of litter, and the control of public perform-ances of hypnotism. Obviously, such changes have important implications for interpretations of the crime rate, as reflected in the criminal statistics. These are dealt with in Chapter 2.

## Crime, delinquency, and deviancy

Many writers prefer to use the term 'crime' when they are discussing adult offenders and offences, and reserve the term 'delinquency' to describe offences committed by young persons (juveniles) and of a less serious nature. However, one of the problems of using the term 'delinquency' is that it

'is so broad that it embraces practically all manifestations of juvenile behaviour . . . thus, disobedience, stubborness, lack of respect, being incorrigible, smoking without permission . . . hawking and the like, are considered juvenile delin-quency.'                              (Middendorff 1960: 17)

Deviancy is sometimes used as an umbrella term to include such behaviour as crime and delinquency; in certain circum-stances this is appropriate if the dictionary definition of the word 'deviation' is applied (i.e. turning away from, deflection, varia-tion from some line or standard of reference). However, there are forms of behaviour which society regards as deviant, but not necessarily as delinquent or criminal. From a theoretical point of view, there is some merit in considering all three as appropri-ate subjects for criminological study, as is evidenced by the full title of the *British Journal of Criminology*, which is *The British Journal of Criminology, Delinquency, and Deviant Social Behaviour*.[3]

---

[3] See the first issue of the *British Journal of Criminology* (1960) Editorial, **1**: 1–2, for a discussion of the factors that influenced the Editors in their decision to change the title of the journal from the *British Journal of Delinquency* to that of *Criminology*. For a useful account of some of the problems involved in defining deviancy see Taylor (1971: Chapter 2).

## Criminal responsibility and liability

It has already been stated that one of the essential ingredients in criminal conduct is *mens rea*. Implicit in the concept of *mens rea* is the presumption that men are responsible in law for their actions. 'All normal persons are responsible for their actions unless they can show good reason why this is untrue for the particular act of which they are accused' (Whitlock 1963: 3). The key issue here is that of 'normality' in relation to responsibility; the history of the criminal law in this country, and in the United States, contains many fascinating illustrations of the problems involved in determining 'responsibility'. These problems arise most frequently in relation to crimes committed by the mentally disordered or those of 'unsound mind' and are dealt with in more detail in Chapter 9.

Of equal importance and interest, from our point of view, are the problems associated with the concept of 'strict liability'. Hogan, in his inaugural lecture *Criminal Liability Without Fault* (1969), provides us with a number of interesting illustrations of cases in which persons have been convicted of offences, notwithstanding that at the time of their commission they were unaware of the fact that their acts were criminal. In such cases we find the concept of strict liability being applied as, for example, in the case of the butcher who inadvertently sells unsound meat, an offence which in law is sometimes regarded as 'absolute'. The concept has been challenged in the courts from time to time, a fairly recent instance being the case of Sweet.[4] This young lady, the tenant of a farmhouse in Oxfordshire which she sublet to various other tenants, was charged with being concerned in the management of premises which the prosecution alleged were being used for the purposes of smoking cannabis. At the time of the offences alleged, Miss Sweet was in fact no longer living in the farmhouse. Nevertheless she was convicted. Her conviction, after appeal, was eventually overturned as a result of a decision of the House of Lords. This was one of the fairly rare instances of a case being sent to the House of Lords on a question of exceptional legal importance. Miss Sweet's case and the cases of many others before her illustrate the important point 'that the courts need to determine whether the defendant acted know-

[4] Sweet v. Parsley [1969] 1 All E.R. (347).

ingly or recklessly, as opposed to merely inadvertently' (Hogan 1969: 17).

Perhaps enough has been said at this stage to indicate that the interpretation and application of the criminal law are complex matters and are constantly changing. It now remains to consider the subject matter of criminology, and to say something about those who study the subject, and where they are to be found.

## The scope of criminology

Criminology in its narrowest sense simply means 'the study of crime' (Mannheim 1965: 3). Defined a little more widely, it 'is the body of knowledge regarding crime as a social phenomenon. It includes within its scope the processes of making laws, and of reacting towards the breaking of laws' (Sutherland and Cressey 1960: 3). Sutherland and Cressey also state that there are three principal divisions of criminology, (i) the sociology of law, (ii) the study of the causes of crime, and (iii) penology, which is concerned with the control and treatment of crime.

Some writers prefer to treat penology as a subject in its own right, distinct from criminology: I share this preference. On this basis therefore, Parts One and Two of this book are mainly criminological, and Parts Three and Four are penological in content.

To what extent can criminology be described as a 'pure' science, compared with the sciences of chemistry or physics for example? Are there known 'laws' and proven 'theories' that have a universal application and validity in the criminological field as there are in chemistry and physics? The honest answer to these questions must be 'no'. There has always been much dispute about the claims of the 'human' sciences to be regarded as sciences in the pure sense. Much of the argument centres around the methods used to study phenomena, and the inability of those who study the human situation or condition to simulate the controlled experimental laboratory situations of the pure scientists. However, Guntrip holds that the antithesis between a 'scientific' and a 'human' approach is false. Discussing psychology and psycho-analysis, he argues convincingly that both can be scientific while proceeding by different approaches:

'Psycho-dynamics studies its objects basically as "subjects", while traditional science studies whatever it does study as "objects only". It is this excessively objective approach of classical science that fails to do justice to persons as subjects of experience. Psycho-dynamic studies pose a genuinely new problem for science, which cannot be handled by the classical scientific modes of conceptualization.'

(Guntrip 1967: 32)

Admittedly, Guntrip is writing of psycho-dynamics and psycho-analysis, but much of what he says holds true for other sciences that study aspects of human behaviour, such as criminology. Guntrip's views are echoed by more recent writers such as Kelk (1977) and Will (1980). As Radzinowicz has pointed out:

'Criminology is not a primary and self-contained discipline, but enters into the provinces of many other sciences which treat of human nature and society. Indeed, any advance made in causative research into crime must arise out of advances achieved in those other departments of knowledge.'

(Radzinowicz 1961: 115)

In other words, criminology is very much an 'applied' science, and heavily dependent upon, and interconnected with, other disciplines. I have tried to illustrate aspects of this interconnectedness in *Figure 1 (1)*.

Since criminology is so dependent upon, and interconnected with, other disciplines, it is understandable that many criminologists have their origins in, and major affiliations with, one or other of the major fields shown in *Figure 1 (1)*. Some authorities see criminology as a specialist branch of law, others, like Polsky (1971), take the view that it is a sub-field of sociology. Many of our younger criminologists are primarily sociologists, and it is from the perspective of sociology that they have provided a useful corrective to a tendency on the part of some to over-pathologize criminal behaviour.

In the years immediately preceding the Second World War the subject of criminology in this country gained immeasurably from the work of refugees from Nazi persecution such as Mann-heim, who was primarily a lawyer and a judge. At that time,

*Figure 1 (1)*    Inter-disciplinary nature of criminology and penology

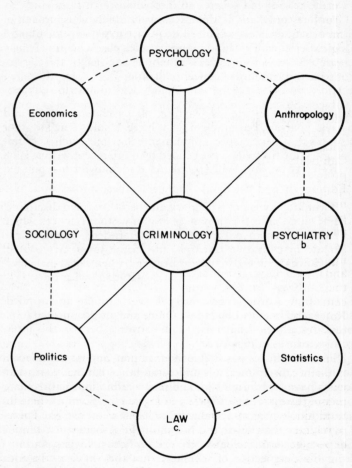

*Notes to Figure 1 (1)*
Double lines and capital letters indicate close subject links.
Single lines indicate less close association.
Broken lines indicate overall subject association.
a. is abnormal psychology.
b. is forensic psychiatry.
c. is criminal law, law enforcement, and police science.

and almost up to the end of the war, the only other specialists were Grunhut of Oxford and Radzinowicz of Cambridge (see Grunhut (1948) and Radzinowicz (1961)). Between them these three great teachers produced many of our present-day criminological authorities, who are now working in a variety of fields, both academic and applied. Before the Second World War, outside the London School of Economics and the Universities of Oxford and Cambridge criminology was almost an unknown subject. Since then more and more universities have gradually added it to their courses and curricula.

There are now a number of chairs in criminology, the most notable perhaps being those at the Institute of Criminology at Cambridge University, but there are also other significant professorial departments, for example at the Universities of Edinburgh and Sheffield. Alongside these professorial posts many universities have criminologists on their staff, some examples being Birmingham, Keele, Leeds, Manchester, and Southampton. In addition, a number of lecturers in sociology, psychology, and social administration in other universities and in the polytechnics are concerned primarily with research in, and the teaching of, criminology. Through the Home Office and the DHSS, central government has also made a significant contribution to the field by the work of the Home Office Research Unit, and by Home Office and DHSS sponsorship of research in other centres.

Because criminology is an applied subject, there are criminologists operating in what might at first appear to be rather unlikely centres, such as in departments of adult education and extramural studies. Psychologists too can claim more than a passing interest in this field and have made important contributions to the subject. Psychiatry or, to be more precise, forensic psychiatry, has since the beginning of this century supplied experts to swell the ranks of criminologists. Lombroso, one of the founding fathers of criminology, was a psychiatrist; in this country, the names of Prichard and Henry Maudsley were very closely associated with studies of the criminal mind. More recently, the appointment of forensic psychiatrists to work in the regional health authority areas has been a notable development.

The relevance of some of the disciplines associated with

criminology will become more apparent as I deal with their respective contributions in later chapters of this book.

In conclusion it may be said that criminology as an academic discipline draws very heavily on the other social and behavioural sciences (notably sociology and psychology), and on law and psychiatry. There are encouraging signs, however, that criminology is being increasingly recognized as a subject in its own right, worthy of both undergraduate and postgraduate study and application (see Radzinowicz 1961).

## References

Devlin, Lord (1959) *The Enforcement of Morals*. Oxford: Oxford University Press.

Friedmann, W. (1964) *Law in a Changing Society*. Harmondsworth: Penguin Books. (Quoting: Wechsler (1955) The Criteria of Criminal Responsibility. *University of Chicago Law Review* **22**: 374.)

Grunhut, M. (1948) *Penal Reform*. Oxford: Oxford University Press.

Guntrip, H. (1967) The Concept of Psychodynamic Science. *International Journal of Psychoanalysis* **48**: 32–43.

Hart, H.L.A. (1963) *Law, Liberty and Morality*. Oxford: Oxford University Press.

Hogan, T.B. (1969) *Criminal Liability Without Fault*. Leeds: Leeds University Press.

Kelk, N. (1977) Is Psychoanalysis a Science? A Reply to Slater. *British Journal of Psychiatry* **130**: 105–11.

Mannheim, H. (1965) *Comparative Criminology, Volume 1*. London: Routledge and Kegan Paul.

Middendorff, W. (1960) *New Forms of Juvenile Delinquency: Their Origin, Prevention and Treatment*. (Second United Nations Congress on the Prevention of Crime and the Treatment of Offenders.) A/Conf. 17/7: London.

Polsky, N. (1971) *Hustlers, Beats and Others*. Harmondsworth: Penguin Books.

Prins, H.A. (1970) Probation and After-Care: Some Aspects of Casework. *The Howard Journal* **13**: 47–57.

—— (1980) *Offenders, Deviants, or Patients?* London: Tavistock Publications.

Radzinowicz, L. (1961) *In Search of Criminology*. London: Heinemann Educational Books.

Sutherland, E.H. and Cressey, D.R. (1960) *Principles of Criminology (sixth edition)*. New York: J.P. Lippincott and Co.

Taylor, L. (1971) *Deviance and Society*. London: Michael Joseph.

Walker, N. (1969) *Sentencing in a Rational Society*. London: Allen Lane.

Whitlock, F.A. (1963) *Criminal Responsibility and Mental Illness*. London: Butterworths.

Will, D. (1980) Psychoanalysis as a Human Science. *British Journal of Medical Psychology* **53**: 201–11.

FURTHER READING

*The two standard British textbooks are:*

Mannheim, H. (1965) *Comparative Criminology, Volumes 1 and 2*. London: Routledge and Kegan Paul.

Walker, N. (1968) *Crime and Punishment in Britain (revised edition)*. Edinburgh: Edinburgh University Press.

*Two recent and concise accounts of some important general criminological issues may be found in:*

Bottomley, A.K. (1979) *Criminology in Focus: Past Trends and Future Prospects*. Oxford: Martin Robertson.

Hall, Williams, J.E. (1982) *Criminology and Criminal Justice*. London: Butterworths.

# CHAPTER TWO

## *How much crime?*

There are three kinds of lies: lies, damned lies, and statistics.

MARK TWAIN

One of the principal interests of criminologists and penologists is measuring the volume of crime. On this subject there are documents of interest as far back as the seventeenth century, probably even earlier (see Wiles 1971). There is the suggestion of one seventeenth-century writer, William Petty, that the collection of statistics of crime might help in judging the 'moral health' of the nation; then in 1778 Bentham advocated that systematic data should be collected on crime. It was not until 1810, however, that any official statistics were published, and even these were in a very limited form. Social investigators of the nineteenth century, Mayhew and Charles Booth, had drawn attention to the need to know the extent of the crime problem so that appropriate treatment measures could be taken. Even so, the study of statistics, so essential for a thorough understanding of social phenomena, was only in its infancy during the early and middle parts of the nineteenth century. The science of statistics as we know it owes much to the work of a little-known Prussian clergyman called Sussmilch; his early work was followed up by the Belgian scientist Quételet, founding father of the Statistical Society of London.

Most of the early information collected about crime and criminals was of a fairly rudimentary nature; moreover, such information was acquired almost accidentally as a by-product of a study of some other social problem so that even the so-called 'official' statistics lacked breadth and precision. Although our methods of data collection and interpretation have improved in recent years to a considerable degree, it will be apparent from the rest of this chapter that the official statistics relating to the crime problem still give but the barest indication of its extent.

## Information derived from official sources

Information concerning the volume of crime and the numbers of offenders is derived from the annual criminal statistics, from various reports containing police and judicial statistics, and from specialist reports published from time to time by government departments.[1] For the purpose of the following discussion we are concerned mainly with information derived from the criminal statistics, in which the information can be grouped under the following five broad headings.

(a) The number of both indictable and non-indictable offences known to the police.
(b) The percentage of offences 'cleared up'.
(c) The number of persons 'cautioned' (instead of being taken to court).
(d) How the courts dealt with various groups of persons – both in relation to age and the type of offence committed.
(e) Certain other information, such as use of legal aid, use of remands, which are of less immediate concern to us in this discussion.

For the purpose of presenting what is known about the number of offences, the criminal statistics provide a valuable source of information, and the manner in which they are presented has improved very considerably in recent years. However, the conclusions that we may reach about the phenomena we describe as crime from a study of these statistics are very uncertain indeed.

## The increase in the volume of crime

Perusal of the criminal statistics for the last fifty years or so shows that there has been a steady increase in the number of

[1] For example, Reports on the Work of the Probation and After-care Department of the Home Office, certain DHSS statistics, Reports on the Work of the Prison Department, Chief Inspector of Constabulary, and the Commissioner of the Metropolitan Police. Some authors prefer to describe the statistics as criminal, judicial, and penal respectively.

indictable offences known to the police. In the year 1900 there were 77,934, while in 1978 there were some 2,396,000 (Home Office 1979). This rate of increase has shown an accelerating trend; for example, between 1900 and 1935, crimes known to the police trebled, and between 1935 and 1978 they increased more than six-fold. Even if we recalculate the figures to give a rate per million of the population at risk, so taking into account the argument that there is simply a growing number of people available to commit crime, there is an increase from approximately 2557 indictable offences per million in the period 1900–04, to 29,914 per million for the years 1965–68 (Wiles 1971). These figures refer to indictable offences, which are frequently regarded as the most serious. If we examine the number of *indictable* offences recorded by the police and grouped by offence, and express these in percentage terms, the general picture is as follows:

| | | |
|---|---|---|
| Theft and handling stolen goods | 56 | per cent |
| Burglary | 22 | per cent |
| Criminal damage | 12 | per cent |
| Fraud and forgery | 4.8 | per cent |
| Violence against the person | 3.4 | per cent |
| Sexual offences | 0.9 | per cent |
| Robbery | 0.5 | per cent |
| Other offences | 0.1 | per cent |

(Criminal Statistics, Home Office 1979: 39)

However, the number of *non-indictable* offences has also increased from 564,844 in the year 1930 to about 1,500,000 in the year 1978. Although theft, burglary, and handling stolen goods are the commonest indictable offences, in recent years there has been a disturbing increase in the numbers of young persons in the 17–21 age group found guilty of offences of violence against persons (Home Office 1979).

In relation to other types of offences, however, the statistics show that, although many young people may make one or two appearances early on, they do not offend again in later life. It appears that apart from a fairly small group of recidivist offenders, a good many so-called young criminals subsequently develop into law-abiding citizens who do not offend again. Moreover, because indictable offences are officially classified as the most serious, concern about them may well mask the real nature of the problem: many of the juvenile offences that have the greatest social nuisance value are in the non-indictable group – for example certain offences of wilful damage, disorderly conduct, and minor assaults (see also Chapter 6).

## The prevalence of crime

Allowing for the inadequacies of the criminal statistics in providing a useful picture of the real volume of crime, it is still possible to calculate a prevalence rate for recorded delinquency.[2]

Little (1965) concluded that, at least in relation to adolescent offenders, increase in crime could be calculated in the following arithmetical terms: 28 per cent of the increase was due to population increase, 42 per cent was due to increase in the rates of first offenders, 6 per cent was due to the recidivism (repeated offences) of the additional first offenders, and 24 per cent to increased rates of recidivism.

## The seriousness of crime

As will be seen later in this chapter, the published statistics give no true indication of the seriousness of the crimes actually recorded. Using the hypothetical case of a domestic brawl in which a husband hits his wife over the head with a hammer, Walker (1968: 18) shows convincingly just how inadequate are the descriptive terms used in the criminal statistics. The offence could be classified as attempted murder if it could be proved that the husband had said before hitting his wife: 'I'm going to kill you.' If he said nothing, or nobody heard what he said, then his crime might be recorded as one of felonious wounding. If the blow merely rendered the wife unconscious, the offence might be recorded as a malicious wounding. If she dodged it, it might even be treated as a non-indictable assault!

[2] The term *prevalence* is borrowed from the field of epidemiology, and is used to mean the number of persons suffering from a particular disorder, or, as in this case, showing evidence of a 'disorder' at a given time. Prevalence should be distinguished from *incidence*, which is generally taken to mean the number of examples of a disorder which begin during a *specified* period.

A further illustration of the inadequacy of the official classification is the definition of indecent assault. This can cover all
kinds of sexual overtures, from a hand placed lightly on a
female's thigh in a cinema, to a serious attempt at sexual
intercourse that just falls short of attempted rape. Similar
problems exist concerning the official classification of other
forms of crime, serving as a serious stumbling-block to those
who wish to study the clinical and social implications of reported criminal conduct.

The extent to which the criminal statistics reflect accurately
the real volume of crime can perhaps best be seen by reference to
*Figure 2(1)*, in which I have attempted to use an 'iceberg'
analogy.

Various experts have also provided estimates of the percentages of crimes actually known to the police or prosecuted by
them. Radzinowicz (1964) suggested that only about 15 per

*Figure 2(1)*    The 'Iceberg' model

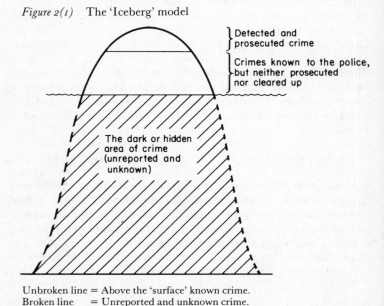

Unbroken line = Above the 'surface' known crime.
Broken line   = Unreported and unknown crime.
Wavy line     = Sea level.

cent of all crimes committed in England are officially recorded, but Jones (1965: 18) estimated a somewhat higher figure – 25 per cent. A German criminologist, Wehner (1970), suggested that the total number of unknown criminal offences, including the unreported, varies between a minimum of twice and a maximum of four and a half times the number shown in the criminal statistics. Rose (1969: 17) estimated that in the United States the proportion of unknown and unreported crime was probably about 50 per cent overall, but that there was a considerable degree of variation between different types of offence. (See also next section.) One does not have to be a criminologist to recognize that the report rate for different types of crime will vary enormously; for example, not many of us would report the loss of a 50p piece to the police, but there is evidence of a report rate of almost 100 per cent for stolen motor vehicles! Recent research by Deane (1981) on tax evasion adds further support to the view that some types of criminality (notably 'white-collar crime') are viewed more sympathetically by the authorities. Deane found that tax evasion was a common activity in the UK and was widely regarded as morally accept-able. Moreover, the chance of detection appeared to be rela-tively low, and even when detected the evader ran small risk of being criminally adjudicated. Deane found that over 100,000 cases each year resulted in a financial settlement, compared with less than 200 criminal convictions. It is very tempting to see class factors at work here; some of these will be examined in Chapter 3.

## Reasons for variation in the reporting of offences

At this stage it is important to ask why it is that from year to year there is such a difference in the number of reported and prosecuted crimes. As was pointed out in Chapter 1, crime is what the law says it is at any moment in time, and of course there is abundant evidence that the law may change from one generation to the next. Moreover, changes in the very classifica-tion of offences may lead to misunderstanding, as for example in the case of manslaughter. The official statistics for this offence may appear to show a decrease in recent years, but we need to remember that the new classification of causing death by dangerous driving is likely to include a number of offences previously reported under the old manslaughter heading.

The Sexual Offences Act of 1967 also removed a whole section of human behaviour from the jurisdiction of the criminal law when it made legal certain forms of male homosexuality committed in private between consenting adults. It is of interest that this change stemmed, not only from the increasingly accepted view that wherever possible the private behaviour of adults should remain private and outside the criminal law, but also from the knowledge that the laws concerning this form of behaviour were being enforced unevenly and perhaps capriciously. Twenty-five years ago the Wolfenden Committee (HMSO 1957) could estimate that only 1 in 2500 cases of indictable homosexual acts reached the ears of the police. After the prosecution of certain well-known persons for offences of the kind just described, the police were directed to be circumspect in bringing future prosecutions and were to consult with the Director of Public Prosecutions in appropriate cases; later it was decided that prosecution should cease and the law be amended as outlined above.

Examining the picture from another angle, we can observe that the apparent vast increase in some property offences is due, as Wilkins (1964) has suggested, to the very obvious fact that there is now more transportable property available for theft. For example, the reporting of thefts of motor cars is quite clearly linked with the increase in the number of motor vehicles registered.

REASONS FOR FAILURE TO REPORT OFFENCES

There are a number of reasons why offences may never be reported to the police. In the first place, the participants may not be aware that an offence has been committed, as for example in the case of some children who in their play may commit various assaults which may strictly speaking constitute offences. Much of the responsibility for such actions has of course been removed from many juveniles by the implementation of the Children and Young Persons Act 1969 which, like the Sexual Offences Act of 1967 mentioned above, is an interesting example of how a whole group of individuals may be placed outside the jurisdiction of the criminal law.

The second reason for failure in reporting crimes is that the parties concerned may be acting illegally but with consent, as in cases of incest and certain sexual offences between youths and girls. A third reason is that, even if a victim is unwilling, he may not wish to involve the offender in the consequences of prosecution. For example, it has been shown that in certain areas it is not considered to be the done thing to report an offender to the police, especially if the police are not popular in the area concerned (see, for example, Parker 1974, especially Chapter 5). Fourth, in cases where minor offences have been committed, the victim may consider the offence too trivial to be worth reporting, or the loser may not think that there is any real likelihood of bringing the offender to book. Fifth, there are certain types of offences that are less likely to be reported than others. There are many reasons for this. For example, the reporting rate for the offence of indecent exposure is very low, which may be due to the fact that the woman is too embarrassed to report her experience (though some people consider that the offence does not shock as much as is frequently supposed). Walker (1968) suggests that some men may refrain from reporting cases of homosexual importuning in case they are themselves suspected of making advances; similarly, in cases where young children have been molested, parents may wish to spare their child the stress of police questioning, and possible court appearance. Sixth, a victim may well be intimidated by threats of blackmail which used to be a very real fear for some male homosexuals before the introduction of the legislation referred to above. Finally, we must ask, how many of us report ourselves for speeding or for depositing litter? It is important to remember that there are many cases in which an offence is unknown to anyone but the offender.

## Crimes reported but not cleared up

The number of crimes reported to the police but not cleared up is considerable – according to some authorities more than 50 per cent. *Table 2(1)*, taken from the criminal statistics for 1978,

Table 2(1)    *Clear-up rates*

| year | clear-up rate percentage |
|------|--------------------------|
| 1975 | 44 |
| 1976 | 43 |
| 1977 | 41 |
| 1978 | 42 |

shows the percentage clear-up rate for the years 1975–78 (Home Office 1979).

The clear-up rates for different types of crime of course vary considerably. Few reported murders are not cleared up; serious assault is said to be cleared up in four cases out of five; in 1978, the clear-up rate for all sexual offences was 76 per cent, being lowest (64 per cent) for indecent assault on a female and for rape (69 per cent). We must therefore keep the percentages expressed in *Table 2(1)* in some perspective. It is worth noting that police performance can vary quite considerably. Paradoxically, however, an increase in police efficiency will not only tend to increase the clear-up rate, it will also increase the number of crimes known to the police, thus making it appear that the crime situation has actually got worse. The expression 'cleared up' requires some comment. It may mean that the offender has been traced, prosecuted and convicted. It may also mean that the offence has been taken into consideration (t.i.c.) when the offender was dealt with for another offence. Moreover, an offence will be regarded as cleared up by the police even if the defendant has subsequently been acquitted by the court. In some instances, more than one person may have been involved in the commission of an offence, but only one person prosecuted and convicted: such cases are still officially regarded as cleared up. For a useful discussion of some of the problems involved in defining the clear-up rate see Walker (1971).

## Police discretion and the practice of cautioning

In this discussion of the volume of crime, account must now be taken of the importance of the exercise of police and other forms of discretion. For example, in certain cases, criminal proceedings may be brought only with the consent of the Director of Public Prosecutions or, more rarely, of the Attorney-General. In some cases the Director may be consulted by a police authority and advise against prosecution. (It will be remembered that this was referred to indirectly in the comments concerning police discretion in cases of homosexual offences.) Unfortunately, until recently, very little detailed information was available as to the manner and circumstances in which the police exercise discretion over the country as a whole, though useful studies have been carried out in the last few years by Landau (1981) and Farrington and Bennett (1981).

There are several ways in which police discretion may be exercised. In the first place, instead of reporting someone for an alleged offence, the police officer on the beat may decide to issue an informal caution on the spot. This must be a daily occurrence, as many motorists will know. Even if a motorist is reported, there is quite a good chance that he will receive a formal (written) caution instead of a summons. Second, let us assume that the commission of a much more serious offence has been alleged: it does not follow necessarily that prosecution will be launched. The officer on the beat will report the offence to his superiors, who may decide that a prosecution would be unwise, either because the evidence is uncertain, or because of the age or circumstances of the alleged offender. If, for instance, a number of mentally disordered persons commit delinquencies when on leave from hospital, the police usually return them to the institution concerned instead of taking any further proceedings.

Another example is the case of a man who had been placed on probation for indecent exposure, and who, as a condition of his probation, was required to undergo psychiatric treatment as an out-patient. The probation order and the psychiatric treatment were both completed satisfactorily, but some years later the man was again reported for (and admitted to) the same offence. During the course of their enquiries, the police discovered that he had been undergoing a fair degree of recent stress. They therefore consulted the psychiatrist who had treated him some years earlier, and he agreed at their request to see the man again. In the years that had followed his earlier conviction the man had established himself as an industrious and respectable citizen in a small community, and had made very great efforts to live down his unfortunate tendency to expose himself; in view of this the police decided to administer a formal caution instead of bringing a prosecution.[3] There must be many similar cases where discretion in favour of the accused is exercised in this way.

*Table 2(2)* (compiled from the criminal statistics 1978) shows the number of men and women formally cautioned by the police for the years 1975–78, as an alternative to court proceedings for indictable offences (other than motoring offences), and *Table 2(3)* depicts the situation in relation to non-indictable offences.

Table 2(2)    *Cautions for indictable offences*

| males | | | | females | | | |
|---|---|---|---|---|---|---|---|
| 1975 | 1976 | 1977 | 1978 | 1975 | 1976 | 1977 | 1978 |
| 76,277 | 72,651 | 84,355 | 77,524 | 25,948 | 25,030 | 30,629 | 29,318 |

Table 2(3)    *Cautions for non-indictable offences*

| males | | | | females | | | |
|---|---|---|---|---|---|---|---|
| 1975 | 1976 | 1977 | 1978 | 1975 | 1976 | 1977 | 1978 |
| 26,695 | 29,461 | 26,786 | 25,526 | 7447 | 8335 | 7642 | 9106 |

Throughout the years 1958–78 the police have tended to use the caution increasingly for juveniles (i.e. those aged ten and under seventeen) and this is particularly marked in relation to young women. There was a marked increase in the use of cautioning by the police for juveniles between the years 1967 and 1971 – for males aged ten and under seventeen the proportion remained at close to 45 per cent from 1971–78, while in the same period for females aged ten and under seventeen it remained close to 70 per cent. For those aged seventeen and over, the proportion cautioned was small (in the region of 3–4 per cent for males and 9–10 per cent for females). This figure has remained fairly constant over a twenty-year period. *Table 2(4)* shows the numbers of offenders cautioned for indictable off-

[3] Informal cautions are not recorded for statistical purposes. Formal cautions are usually administered by a police officer of senior rank.

ences *as a percentage* of persons found guilty or cautioned, by sex
and age for the years 1958, 1968, and 1978 (abstracted from
criminal statistics, Home Office 1979). It is worth noting the
extent to which the use of cautioning declines as the older age
groups are reached.

Table 2(4)   *Percentage cautioning rates*

| year | males | | females | |
|------|-------|---|---------|---|
| | *aged 10 and under 17* | *17 and over* | *aged 10 and under 17* | *17 and over* |
| 1958 | 21 | 3 | 31 | 9 |
| 1968 | 26 | 3 | 39 | 10 |
| 1978 | 44 | 3 | 69 | 9 |

## Attempts to increase our knowledge of the real volume of crime

From the foregoing discussion three conclusions may be
reached. The first is that the information provided in the
criminal statistics, though admirable in many respects, is inadequate for those who wish to make a more detailed study of
the crime problem, particularly from the point of view of
assessing its pervasiveness. In the second place, fewer than 50
per cent of indictable crimes reported to the police are not
cleared up subsequently (*see Table 2(1)*). In the third place, even
when offenders are reported or become known to the police, a
considerable degree of discretion may be exercised in favour of
the accused, the reasons for the exercise of such discretion being
varied. It is therefore apparent that there must be a vast area of
hidden delinquency or a dark area of crime as it is often called
(*see Figure 2(1)*), knowledge of which has obvious and important
implications for theories about the causes and treatment of
delinquent behaviour.

Unfortunately, there have been comparatively few studies
aimed at exploring this hidden area of crime in this country, a
large proportion of them having been carried out mainly in the
United States (Hood and Sparks 1970; Gold 1970; West and
Farrington 1973; Belson 1975; Sparks, Genn, and Dodd 1977).

Some of them are of sufficient importance to merit brief mention here. The first type of exploration is the attempt to measure the amount of undetected crime by questioning selected groups in the population about delinquent acts they have committed, whether or not these have led to a court appearance. Studies of this type have the obvious advantage of providing information about the range and frequency of delinquent acts in any given community and facilitate comparison between groups of official and unofficial delinquents. They are, however, beset by numerous research difficulties, as for example when respondents do not answer questions accurately or honestly about themselves, even though strict anonymity is guaranteed. Also, this type of research would need to be carried out on larger groups of people than has hitherto been the case for the general validity of the results to be assessed.

In the second type of exploration, endeavours are made to measure the amount of hidden crime by questioning victims of crime in selected populations and comparing the data obtained with the number of crimes actually reported to the police. In addition, victims may be asked why they did not report certain cases to the police, and the reasons for this. As with self-report studies, there are research problems to be surmounted: respondents may distort their answers or fail to remember certain offences, and may or may not be able to speak with accuracy about crimes committed against other members of the household. Furthermore, this method does not reveal information about the extent to which consensual crimes may have been committed.

Most of the studies carried out so far have sought information about offences committed against 'victims' during the period of a year or so, and it is likely that this is too long a period for accurate recall. A shorter period might produce more accurate results. But whatever the problems may be in mounting the kind of research just described, it has been a serious attempt to improve upon the previous method, which consisted merely of informed guesses.

## Implications for theories of crime causation

By way of conclusion we must consider briefly the implications of the foregoing discussion for those who are interested in explanatory theories of crime. These theories rest largely on the evidence contained in official statistics concerning those labelled as delinquent. Such labelling has vital implications when we are considering the comparison of a so-called delinquent group with a control group of allegedly innocent people. Self-report and victim studies alert us to the very important fact that for the most part criminals are not a race apart, but are very much like the rest of us. In our discussion of explanatory theories in Part Two, we shall consider carefully the extent to which it is worth continuing to theorize in such explanatory terms, and ask ourselves whether it would instead be more profitable to consider the processes by which people are labelled or label themselves delinquent. Not only does this labelling have important implications for theorizing about crime, but it also has a most important impact upon the way in which criminal acts are construed and the measures taken by society to deal with them.

## References

Belson, W.A. (1975) *Juvenile Theft: The Causal Factors*. London: Harper and Row.

Deane, K.D. (1981) Tax Evasion, Criminality and Sentencing the Tax Offender. *British Journal of Criminology* **21**: 47–57.

Farrington, D.P. and Bennett, T. (1981) Police Cautioning of Juveniles in London. *British Journal of Criminology* **21**: 123–35.

Gold, M. (1970) *Delinquent Behaviour in an American City*. Belmont, California: Brooks-Cole.

Home Office (1979) *Criminal Statistics, England and Wales, 1978*. Cmnd. 7670. London: HMSO.

Hood, R. and Sparks, R. (1970) *Key Issues in Criminology*. World University Library. London: Weidenfeld and Nicolson.

Jones, H. (1965) *Crime in a Changing Society*. Harmondsworth: Penguin Books.

Landau, S.F. (1981) Juveniles and the Police. *British Journal of Criminology* **21**: 27–46.

Little, A. (1965) The Prevalence of Recorded Delinquency and

Recidivism in England and Wales. *American Sociological Review* **30**: 260–63.

Parker, J.J. (1974) *View from the Boys: A Sociology of Down-Town Adolescents*. Newton Abbot: David and Charles.

Radzinowicz, L. (1964) The Criminal in Society. *Journal of the Royal Society of Arts* **112**: 916–29.

Rose, G.N.G. (1969) Crime Statistics – Uses and Abuses. In *Crime – Myths and Reality*. London: Institute for the Study and Treatment of Delinquency.

Sparks, R.F., Genn, H., and Dodd, D. (1977) *Surveying Victims*. London: John Wiley.

Walker, N. (1968) *Crime and Punishment in Britain*. Edinburgh: Edinburgh University Press.

—— (1971) *Crime, Courts and Figures: An Introduction to Criminal Statistics*. Harmondsworth: Penguin Education.

Wehner, B. (1970) Quoted in M. Lopez-Rey *Crime – An Analytical Appraisal*. London: Routledge and Kegan Paul (p. 10).

West, D.J. and Farrington, D.P. (1973) *Who Becomes Delinquent?* London: Heinemann.

Wiles, P. (1971) Criminal Statistics and Sociological Explanations of Crime. In W.G. Carson and P. Wiles (eds) *Crime and Delinquency in Britain*. London: Martin Robertson.

Wilkins, L.T. (1964) *Social Deviance*. London: Tavistock Publications.

Wolfenden Committee (1957) *Report of the Committee on Homosexual Offences and Prostitution*. (Estimate given to the Committee by Doctor D. Parr, p. 18.) Cmnd. 247. London: HMSO.

FURTHER READING

Walker, N. (1969) *Sentencing in a Rational Society*. London: Allen Lane, The Penguin Press.

# PART TWO
# Towards an Understanding of Criminal Behaviour

# CHAPTER THREE

## Society and crime

No Society can surely be flourishing and happy,
of which the far greater part of the members are
poor and miserable.

ADAM SMITH

### Introduction

Those who study the crime problem are acutely aware that
numerous pitfalls abound when they try to separate out for
detailed examination the social, psychological, and physical
factors that are considered to be important in the explanation of
criminal behaviour. If we learn anything at all from our study of
the problem and particularly from what sociologists have to tell
us, it is that crime is due to a complex combination of factors,
and that we are quite unable to pin-point them at all clearly or to
apply satisfactory remedies. In recent years, some sociologists
who have examined the crime problem have been heavily
criticized for indulging in too much generalized theorizing, for
being 'anti-establishment', and for being destructive rather
than constructive. While some of this criticism may well be justified, it needs to be remembered that the task of the sociologist
is, as many of them have pointed out, to ask questions about
society and not to find or recommend immediate remedies. It is
just because sociologists see their task to be to take a wide view
of society, its structure, and its divisions, that their contribution
is important. In this and the following two chapters, the material concerning explanations of criminality is dealt with under
separate sections merely for convenience. *The three chapters should
be read on the clear understanding that their content overlaps, that the
divisions are to some extent arbitrary, and that each chapter is closely
related to the others.* The purpose of this chapter is to examine some

of the earlier attempts at environmental explanations of criminality, to refer to some American and British sociological
studies, and to note the importance of culture and sub-culture
and in particular the phenomenon of the gang. I shall conclude
with some examination of recent and current sociological
approaches, particularly those that examine the significance of
the process by which offenders become labelled. All these
matters are the subject of a vast literature and I make no
attempt to review them exhaustively. Those readers wishing to
fill in on the background and to broaden their knowledge of
current thinking on these matters should consult the references
and further reading given at the end of the chapter.

Throughout history, man has always struggled to know more
about his environment and its effects upon life and behaviour,
hence the perennial search for environmental and social explanations of crime. As I showed in Chapter 2, social historians
have been able to provide us with information about early
attempts to assess the volume and distribution of crime. From
such information, we can reasonably assume that, although
crime has always been present in our society to some extent, it
was not until the period following the Industrial Revolution
that people became particularly concerned about its impact.
One of the first persons to draw attention to this problem was Sir
Thomas Barnard who, in 1796, emphasized the need to investigate all aspects of pauperism including crime. A year later, Sir
Frederick Morton Eden published his book, *The State of the Poor*,
which contained a large compilation of facts concerning poverty
in all its aspects (Woodroofe 1966).

The importance of the social environment was stressed in the
work of various social reformers in the nineteenth century, and
also in the works of various socially conscious novelists such as
Dickens, who depicted in books such as *Oliver Twist* and *Great
Expectations* some of the worst aspects of the crime problem and
the measures then in use to check it. (See also Tobias 1972 and
1974.) Indeed, a useful way of aiding one's understanding of
criminality and social disorder is to supplement the technical
literature by reading the work of socially conscious novelists.
For example, much can be learned about stigma and the
distance that exists between the so-called criminal and other
men (particularly the judiciary) in Chekhov's novel *The Criminal*.

Zola's *La Bête Humaine* also provides insightful glimpses into divisions within the class structure.

At about the time these writers were at work, Marx and Engels were drawing attention to the economic causes of crime and possible political consequences for society as they emerged within Victorian industrial capitalism.

> 'One thing only is astounding, that class prejudice and preconceived opinions can hold a whole class of human beings in such perfect, I might almost say, such mad blindness. Meanwhile the development of the nation goes its way whether the bourgeoisie has eyes for it or not, and will surprise the property-holding classes one day with things not dreamed of in its philosophy.'
>
> (Engels. In Carson and Wiles 1971: 19)

The work of Marx and Engels has undoubtedly had a tremendous influence on generations of commentators on political and social problems. Although Marxist doctrine in its extreme form is unlikely to find favour with the majority of people in this country, the message he and his colleagues propounded concerning inequalities in the class structure and some of the associated dangers of capitalism are both viable and valuable for those who wish to understand the broad background of social disorder and crime, particularly as these manifest themselves in inner-city areas.

At about the same time that Marx and Engels were propounding their theories, another social investigator, Mayhew, was commenting specifically on the crime problem.

> 'In a subject like the crime and vice of the Metropolis [London] and of the country in general, of which so little is known – of which there are many facts but little comprehension – it is evident that we must seek by induction, that is to say by careful classification of the known phenomena, to render the matter more intelligible; in fine, we must, in order to arrive at a comprehensive knowledge of its antecedents, consequences and concomitants, contemplate as large a number of facts as possible.'
>
> (Mayhew 1862. Quoted in Morris 1958: 43)

What Mayhew had to say about a surfeit of facts but little comprehension and also the need for classification is no less true today. One of the purposes of this book is to outline some of the most important facts so that readers may draw their own conclusions on the basis of as much objective evidence as possible. Before turning to examine some of the research carried out on the social environment, brief mention will be made here of the relationship between *physical environment and crime*.

## Climate, season, and crime

For many years students of the crime problem have attempted to demonstrate relationships between physical environment and crime. (See for example, Mannheim 1965: 203–05.) Various studies have shown that in summer there are more crimes against the person, in winter more against property. There have also been reports that crime rates seem to vary with changes in barometric pressure. But although a number of studies have been carried out in this area they do not really advance the practical applications of our knowledge very far (though of course there may well be implications for environmental and town planning). For example, it need not come as any great surprise that crimes against the person seem more common in summer, because it is then that people would seem to have a greater opportunity for proximity to one another.

It would be difficult to prove that there was a human condition as described in the phrase 'in the spring a young man's fancy lightly turns to thoughts of love', though it may be that the human metabolism is affected more than we think by changes in temperature and season, making us at certain times more vulnerable to pressures and stresses. (It is of interest to note in passing that there are a large number of research studies which have explored the onset and duration of certain psychiatric disorders, for example, schizophrenia, in relation to seasonal and climatic variations.) The best we can say about this matter in relation to criminality is that, even if it could be proved that climatic conditions and changes were of importance, it would be difficult to see what could be done to prevent their impact upon the human organism.

## Territorial and areal studies of crime

We must now examine some of the evidence concerning the importance of human environments or territories and their relationship to criminal behaviour. Such studies are usually described as ecological. According to Morris:

'Human or social ecology is concerned with the relationships which exist between people who share a common habitat or local territory, and which are directly related to the character of the territory itself; it is a study of social structure in relation to the social environment.' (Morris 1958: 1)

The term ecology was originally borrowed from the field of biology, where attention had been drawn to 'the fact that different kinds of plants tended to grow together and, like human communities, had a temporal beginning, experienced changes, and finally entered into a decline being gradually superseded by other plants' (Morris 1958: 2). It was this application of ecology to the human situation (an idea originating in the United States of America) that appealed to the founding fathers of sociology in the nineteenth century.

Over the years, social investigators had drawn attention to the fact that although, in theory, crime might be common to all classes (and, as I have shown in Chapter 2, a good deal of it might also be hidden) the more serious and more frequent delinquencies seem to occur in the lower socio-economic groups. What were the reasons for this? Were people in these groups less moral? Did they have less opportunity for legitimate outlets and pursuits, or was there something contagious about crime which spread through these classes more easily than through the higher socio-economic groupings? These were some of the questions which interested sociologically minded criminologists in the early twentieth century. Some of their investigations were carried out in an attempt to explain increases in criminality in terms of it being learned from friends and associates. One of the principal exponents of this view was the American criminologist Edwin Sutherland, perhaps now best remembered for his theory of 'differential association'. Briefly and somewhat over-simply stated, this means that if an individual is exposed to more criminal than non-criminal influences in his immediate environment, the chances of his breaking the law are thereby greatly increased (Sutherland 1966). Sutherland suggested that moreover there might be a tendency for persons exposed to criminal influences to share the same culture, interests, and beliefs, in which case certain forms of antisocial or delinquent behaviour might be condoned and people might even feel required to conform to them. (See in this connection the discussion in Chapter 2 of failure to report crimes to the police.) It was this view that led some workers to formulate the idea of criminal territories or areas (often referred to as 'zones' in the earlier literature) and subsequently the delinquent 'sub-culture'; it was held that such beliefs might be more prevalent in these areas than in the wider community. (For a concise survey of the development of ecological approaches, see Mays 1970: Chapter 4.)

Between and during the two world wars, American social investigators such as Shaw and McKay (1942) sought to demonstrate that there was a general lack of social cohesion and a degree of social disorganization in the slum areas, accompanied by a general breakdown of social controls, which resulted in people having fewer social ties. These assumptions find confirmation in some more recent studies. For example, in relation to suicidal behaviour, McCulloch and Philip (1972) found that social problems were clustered in specific run-down areas of the city they studied; in a later investigation more specifically focused on criminal behaviour they found the same phenomena (Brown, McCulloch, and Hiscox 1972). Further confirmation of some of these findings is to be found in a more recent study in Australia by Vinson and Homel (1975).

Thrasher, who wrote what is often regarded as the classic description of gang life (Thrasher 1923), suggested that delinquency was a natural outcome of such run-down environments. Some confirmation of his views can be found in a number of English studies. Mays (1954 and 1959) has described very vividly the sub-cultural neighbourhoods of Liverpool; he claimed that he was the first person to use the term 'delinquent sub-culture'. Spinley (1953) also described working-class life very graphically, as did Kerr (1958). Harriet Wilson published a study of fifty-two problem-type families referred for child neglect in a Welsh town (Wilson 1962). Since that time Wilson has published a number of other important studies which have examined class factors in relation to child-rearing practices and family discipline. (See, for example, Wilson 1975 and 1980).

Earlier studies by Bagot (1941), Burt (1944), and Mannheim (1948) followed on the American tradition of trying to examine the relationship between such factors as unemployment, social class, and crime. In the conditions described by nearly all these writers, adolescents in particular are easily drawn to the excitements, attractions, and status satisfactions of the streets. However, Baldwin (1975), reviewing some twenty British areal studies of crime which had been carried out in recent years, found that the relationship between area and delinquency might not be quite as close as earlier investigators had thought; more recently, a study by Dunstan and Roberts (1980) lends further support to Baldwin's findings. We can now turn to examine briefly the phenomenon of the gang.

## The phenomenon of the gang

Thrasher's work has already been mentioned and when it was published in 1923 his book was certainly a significant contribution to understanding youthful delinquency. During the post-war years, and especially in the middle to late 1950s, various workers were re-examining youthful delinquency, particularly the gang, in relation to lower-class standards of behaviour and attitudes to morality. Miller (1958) maintained that gang delinquency was just one variant of lower-class behaviour and as such could not be studied in its own right with much benefit. Miller stressed the importance of role conflicts in his studies of delinquent youth and saw the gang members' behaviour in terms of how the adolescent male dealt with his male role conflicts. This aspect had also been discussed by Cohen (1955) and later by Cloward and Ohlin (1961). Their work represented a somewhat more sophisticated view of gang behaviour.

In brief, they considered much delinquency to be a form of collective solution adopted by young lower-class males to the frustrations caused by lack of opportunities for advancement and status in the social system. Many people would find support for this view in the behaviour of some young people today at a time of high unemployment. It seems likely that the rioting and associated behaviour that we have witnessed in the last year or two would seem to be explicable, at least in part, in such terms. (For a good example of this see the study of Liverpool 'gang' life by Parker 1974.) Much of Cloward and Ohlin's theorizing relies quite heavily upon the concept of *anomie*, originally developed by the great sociologist Durkheim in relation to the phenomenon of suicide. Durkheim (1970) suggested that in communities where standards and restraints were weakening, a condition of 'normlessness' would occur and that this could account for increases in crime and other forms of social deviance. Merton (1957) elaborated upon Durkheim's concept of *anomie*, suggesting that if culturally prescribed goals were unattainable (as in the case of many working and lower-class young people), then there would be a discrepancy between what was held out to be ideal and what was attainable. Merton suggested further that this discrepancy could result in frustration and subsequent rebelliousness in the form of deviant and delinquent behaviour. (For a more complete discussion of this complex issue see Phillipson 1971.)

Returning to the concept and culture of the gang more specifically, we should note that Cloward and Ohlin attempted to re-examine the phenomenon of the gang as advanced by earlier writers (Cloward and Ohlin 1961). They were especially interested in posing such questions as why it was that gangs arose, how did gangs recruit their numbers, why and how did they take to different ways of violating the law, and how did these ways persist and change? Cloward and Ohlin isolated three general types of delinquent gangs:

(1) The primarily criminal gang, chiefly devoted to illegal practices, whose members often found their way into the ranks of the professional criminals. (One wonders if there are not some parallels here with Fagin's gang of boy pickpockets.)
(2) The conflict gang, whose members are involved primarily in acts of violence as a means of establishing their status.
(3) The retreatist gang, whose members belong to a subculture which supports the use of drugs.

Cohen (1955) put forward an earlier explanation that lower-class boys were not well equipped to compete in the educational system: they were not trained, as were many middle-class children, to forgo immediate gratification, neither were they as competent as some of their middle-class contemporaries in the use of language. This could result in a tendency to 'act out' their problems rather than talk them through with parents or other authority figures.

Most of the research quoted so far has concerned itself with the American scene and as such has been criticized as not being applicable directly to the British situation. One American critic, Yablonsky (1967), has even questioned whether the cohesiveness of the gang as described by Thrasher (1923) ever existed, and Downes (1966), in his study of gangs in the East End of London, showed that it was not easy to extrapolate from the American to the British scene. Having studied the records of over a hundred remand-home boys in London, Scott (1956) concluded that there were three kinds of adolescent groups: (1) adolescent street groups; (2) structured gangs (which accounted for only about 12 per cent of his sample); (3) loosely diffused groups. Similarly Downes found that in London's East End the main pattern was the street-corner group of four or five, with a few individuals on the boundary. Although such groups persisted over time, and almost invariably possessed a dominant personality, all the other characteristics of the delinquent gang were absent.

More recent research tends to emphasize the great diversity of behaviour and attitudes that may be observed in so-called delinquent groups. Much delinquent behaviour is age-related, and the degree to which age levels are distributed and integrated in any neighbourhood will affect groupings and subsequent behaviour. This was a notable feature of Patrick's study of young people in Glasgow (Patrick 1973). South of the border, Parker (1974) studied, through the device of observer-participation, the life and behaviour of a group of youngsters in one of Liverpool's depressed inner-city areas. He examined the atmosphere and meaning of the adolescent's world, their sometimes extensive delinquent careers, and their attitudes towards authority, particularly the police. Drawing upon his own participant observation and the boys' own accounts Parker suggests that these adolescents' delinquent behaviour is almost inevitable within the constraints and pressures of their social environments. It is important to stress here that such delinquent behaviour is *almost* inevitable. Sociological approaches to crime causation cannot explain why all youngsters from such environments do not become delinquent. It is here that explanations accounting for individual differences must be examined; some of these are dealt with in the next two chapters.

The evidence is somewhat limited as to the types of crime committed by young offenders in groups. There appears to be quite a diversity of behaviour, including a mixture of theft and aggressive conduct, but not necessarily offences including serious violence. In an attempt to define the patterns of behaviour in sixteen Chicago gangs, Short and Strodtbeck (1965) suggested five different groupings:

(1) Conflict activities. Group fighting. Assault.
(2) Stable 'corner boy' activities. Mainly social activities, individual and team sports and gambling.
(3) A stable sex pattern, with intercourse. Use of alcohol.
(4) A retreatist pattern, with homosexuality, drug use.
(5) An authority protest, including car theft, running away from home, and truancy.

In none of these groupings did the investigators find that theft for gain was a dominant activity. These findings are not unlike those of Scott in his London Remand Home Survey (Scott 1956) and Downes in his London East End study (Downes 1966).

## Crime and class

The global statement that crime is more common in the lower social classes is too much of a generalization. There may well be more persistent crime among the lower social classes, but crime of all kinds is present in all grades of our society and much of it, as we have seen, is hidden. As we saw in Chapter 2, the higher social classes may well be afforded a degree of protection from exposure and conviction, particularly in relation to 'white-collar crimes' such as taxation offences.

If you are a public figure in the community, it may be that your position will afford you some immunity from prosecution. Certainly the image you present to the police may well determine whether or not you are prosecuted. If you are stopped by the police for speeding but are middle-aged, well dressed, polite, and driving a respectable-looking car, the chances are that you will merely receive a verbal informal caution, or at worst an official one. If, however, you are in your late teens or early twenties, are driving a motor cycle or somewhat ramshackle car, wearing long hair, dirty jeans, and are somewhat 'lippy' when stopped for speeding, the chances are that you may well be 'booked' for an offence. Thus your position in the pecking order of society, your appearance and demeanour, may well determine the extent to which you swell the crime figures. (See also Baldwin and McConville 1977.) In an increasingly multiracial society, it is sad that there seems to be some evidence that if you are young and black (particularly West Indian), you may well figure more predominantly in the attentions of the police than your white brother. It would be stupid to deny that there are inequalities and a degree of prejudice; it is as well that sociological writers and others point these out to us lest we see all criminal behaviour as stemming from individual 'pathological' causes.

Many years ago Mannheim (1965) suggested that there was a lack of precise information on the distribution of crime amongst the various social classes. Much of the evidence is conflicting. In an interesting study carried out in the London Juvenile Courts, Little and Ntsekhe (1959) found a much less marked excess of offenders in the lower social classes than had some earlier investigators. Palmai, Storey, and Briscoe (1967) found that young offenders in London were derived fairly evenly from all social classes, and that the type of offence committed did not vary much from class to class. McDonald (1969) found (by use of a questionnaire) that admitted delinquency was higher amongst working-class boys and that their offences were also more persistent. It is generally agreed, however, that a good deal more work needs to be done before any firm general statements can be made about the distribution of crime in the various social classes. Victimization studies (to which reference was made in Chapter 2) tend to support the view that crime *is* more likely to be committed by the working class and by racial minorities. (For a useful study in this area see Hindelang 1978.)

## The social environment of the school

Intelligence, education, and their relationships to delinquency are examined in subsequent chapters. At this point, however, it is perhaps important to state that the school provides an environment which can work for good or evil in the genesis of a delinquent career. The work of Hargreaves (1967), Sugarman (1967), Clegg and Megson (1968), and Phillipson (1971) shows the extent to which a school can influence a delinquent career. Hargreaves has argued that the school is one of the most important places in which adolescents from lower-class backgrounds may fail to obtain status. If placed in a low stream, the adolescent may fail to accept values regarded as legitimate by his teachers and thereby become the object of invidious comparison with others. He may then become increasingly negative towards teachers, school, and what the school stands for. He may subsequently drift into association with delinquent groups, often in order to obtain a status and involvement he does not achieve in the school. More dramatically, Power, Benn, and Morris (1972) showed that some schools, in comparison with others in the same area, appeared to be breeding grounds for delinquency. They demonstrated that the delinquency rates for first offenders ranged from less than 1 per cent in the best of the low-delinquency schools to nearly 8 per cent in those showing high delinquency. The difference in the rates, which remained remarkably consistent over the years, was explicable neither by the type of family from which the boys came, nor by the neighbourhood from which they were drawn. The authors acknowledged that their research was based upon one area, but suggested that, if their results were supported by similar research elsewhere, then future plans for the prevention of delinquency must include the school to a greater extent than in the past. The work of Power and his colleagues has been subjected to some criticism. For example, Baldwin suggests that 'it is by no means clear that the Tower Hamlets research has been successful in separating out the delinquency-producing potential of the school from the sources of delinquent behaviour in the relevant ecological areas to the extent that the authors claim' (Baldwin 1972: 401). Power and a co-worker, Sirey, have offered some statistical refutation of Baldwin's criticism; they maintain that the 'observations from [these] data on school delinquency rates, showing a wide range and by now remarkable consistency over a decade, should be the basis for further study' (Power and Sirey 1972: 403). For a more recent example of the alienation generated amongst (particularly working class) youngsters, readers should consult Willis (1977).

## Recent and current sociological approaches to the crime problem

From about the middle of the 1960s onwards, there has been quite a significant shift of emphasis amongst sociologists studying crime and its ramifications. Some of the younger sociologists felt acute dissatisfaction with the more traditional approaches to criminology, in particular those approaches which saw crime as an individual's pathological response to his difficulties. Admittedly, as we have already seen, many criminologists in the past had looked closely at social factors, but the 'new wave' criminologists were becoming increasingly concerned with the *processes* through which people became delinquent and the manner in which they were labelled as such. Most people are agreed, at least in theory, that once a person has become labelled as a deviant individual the label is likely to stick. Nowhere is this more apparent than in the labelling and stigmatizing of the mentally ill. (See, for example, Goffman 1963 and Scheff 1974).

The American sociologist, Matza (1964 and 1967), made a significant contribution to our understanding of the labelling process and its significance in the genesis of a delinquent or deviant career. In his view, the processes by which a person became deviant made little sense if we did not try to comprehend the inner world of the subject as he himself gave meaning to the life events he encountered. In other words, Matza suggested that we needed to move away from the notion that events merely happened to people, and that we needed to understand more fully the 'attention' that the deviant gave to his own situation, to others, and to his own world view. Matza also described three processes by which people might become delinquent or deviant; these have had an important bearing upon later sociological thinking in this country as well as in the United States. These three processes were affinity, affiliation, and signification. By affinity he meant that under bad or poor environmental circumstances, there would be a strong likelihood of a person becoming delinquent or deviant. Affiliation was the process by which a person might become converted or strongly attracted to conduct which was new for him, but already established for others in the particular social system. This obviously has similarities with the theory of differential association already referred to. By signification, Matza meant the processes by which significant or social controls set up by the community acted in various ways to identify a person as deviant and reinforced his deviancy. This reinforcement, or deviancy amplification as it is called by some, has important implications for the treatment of offenders. Once labelled and enmeshed in the system of treatment and control it then becomes very difficult for the person to rid himself of the label. As those who have worked with long-term mental patients well know, labels tend to be repeated in their case records and to stick, even though changes in attitudes or behaviour may have occurred recently.

Of the three processes described by Matza, that of signification is probably the most important from our point of view. As has already been suggested, once labelled as a delinquent, a person may either find it very difficult to break away from the label given to him by society, or alternatively he may even wish to cling to that particular label, as it may provide him with an identity that he cannot legitimately acquire by other means. It then becomes important for him to retain and maintain it. However, if he wishes to break away from his label, he may well find that society makes it very difficult for him to do so and, as has already been suggested, this is certainly a common experience of both mental patients and offenders. A discharged prisoner may feel quite justifiably that at the end of his sentence he has paid the price demanded of him by the community. This is not necessarily the way society or the law enforcement agencies will see it; he may well remain in their eyes a person likely to offend or act deviantly again. Their behaviour may well constantly remind him of this. Some support for Matza's theoretical position may be found in empirical research studies of offenders and others by Ericson (1977), Farrington (1977), Velarde (1978), Bennett (1979), and Leger (1981).

Before leaving the theme of labelling, we may usefully note one or two of the more positive aspects. The labelling process is evident even in biblical antiquity. In the Book of Genesis we find that 'Adam gave names to all cattle, and the fowl of the air, and to every beast in the field'. As Levy points out:

> 'Labelling does facilitate human transactions, at times perhaps excessively. Labelling also serves as a safety belt or a lifeline. Consider, for example, the diabetic without an instruction tag to guide a bystander or a paramedic in an emergency, the religious Catholic who is wounded on the battlefield and values the sacraments, the individual with the rare blood type, the patient acknowledged to be suicidal, or the person described as "in crisis".'          (Levy 1981: 333)

Levy acknowledges that some of these labels 'are stigmatizing in nature . . . and . . . a degree of privacy is lost in the applied designations . . . there are indeed risks and sacrifices in labelling, but short of some obvious excess and abuses, labelling is hardly always all bad' (Levy 1981: 333).

We should remember, however, that the label can and does serve to control. Contemporary sociological commentators ask not about the *ubiquity* of labelling, but rather, *whose* interests are being served as it censures the less powerful in particular instances. A useful illustration may be found in the apparent moral panic over mugging and its amplification by the media (Hall *et al.* 1978).

We shall have need to refer to the hazards of labelling again in Chapter 11, but may conclude this part of our discussion with a quotation from Schur:

> 'It is a central tenet of the labelling perspective that neither acts nor individuals are "deviant" in the sense of immutable, "objective" reality without reference to processes of social definition . . . this relativism may be viewed as a major strength of labelling theory.'          (Schur 1971: 112)

Rock (1974) and Manning (1975) have suggested that 'theory' was too grandiose a word to apply and that labelling theory was a stance based on somewhat flimsy evidence. Some support for these rather negative conclusions may be found in some empirical work undertaken by Farrington, Osborn, and West (1978).

In this country, these and allied perspectives on crime and deviance were pursued in a series of meetings mounted under the aegis of what came to be known as the National Deviancy Conference, and we saw the emergence of what has come to be known as radical British criminology. Webb, quoting NDC 1980: viii, suggests 'that there is substantial agreement amongst commentators . . . that radical British criminology emerged as an alternative to . . . the arid criminological conferences of the Institute of Criminology at Cambridge' (Webb 1981: 149). Laudable though this response may have been, it is also true to say that much of the earlier work in 'radical' criminology was characterized by political posturing, and in some instances rhetoric and dogma replaced an objective analysis of events. This tendency to over-politicize has been pointed out in a useful paper by Schichor (1980).

My colleague David Webb has pointed to a strange lacuna in the history of the 'new' or radical criminology. In the paper already referred to and entitled *A Forgotten Radical: Denis Chapman and the New Criminology in Britain*, he points to the curious neglect of the early 'radical' Liverpool criminologist, Denis Chapman. In his book *Sociology and the Stereotype of the Criminal* (1968), Chapman offered a sustained criticism of 'establishment' criminology, and he was ahead of his time in many ways. As Webb suggests:

> 'It adopted an uncompromising stand about the ideological underpinnings of a criminology which was more concerned to reform criminals than to understand crime, and it attempted to describe what were said to be the close links between class interests and judicial control exerted over the less powerful . . . its critical thrust put(s) it well to the "left" of what then, in the late 1960s, stood as radical British criminology.'                                        (Webb 1981: 148)

Webb suggests that in his early work Chapman antedated much of what emerged later as 'new wave' deviancy theory and that those who espoused this later approach never acknow-

ledged Chapman as one of its progenitors. Chapman's neglected work is significant because he pointed out the inadequacy
of the kind of questions posed by more orthodox criminology
and the manner in which criminal justice was weighted against
working-class deviants.

When we examine the history of sociological perspectives in
British criminology during the last fifteen years we can discern
certain periods characterized by such phrases as 'subjectivist',
'interactionist', 'radical', and 'new deviancy'. Although some of
these phases represented a good deal of strident dogma and
rhetoric rather than patient data collection that could then be
used to establish a sound theoretical perspective, a good deal of
value has emerged overall, especially from the less polemically
minded workers in this field. For they have reminded us forcibly
of the need to see or, to use a sociological term, 'appreciate' the
importance of action and interaction and to avoid seeing criminal conduct as purely individualized pathological behaviour.
Perhaps, most importantly, they have emphasized the need to
attach importance to the links between the law *maker* and the
law *breaker*.

## Conclusion

In this book I avoid the word 'cause' in relation to criminal
behaviour. The word cause is in many senses too precise an
expression to use in the current state of criminological knowledge; explanation is a more appropriate term. Espousal of the
word cause rests too heavily on a medical model of understanding. That such a model should have been developed and gained
acceptance is not altogether surprising, if we remember that
much of the early interest in social and allied problems was
taken by men and women with medical training; this was at a
time when science was making its early attempts to challenge
the environment and to seek explanations of both events and
behaviour. This is not to suggest that certain physical, emotional, and mental states have no influence on predisposing a person
to crime; I shall examine some of these in the following two
chapters. But, for the majority of offenders, we are probably
better advised to be aware of and examine the *processes* by which
people become deviant or criminal. As Matza (1964 and 1967)

has suggested, this attention to process makes us more aware of the ways in which people view themselves and their relationships with significant others in their environment. By way of conclusion we should again ask ourselves, what can sociological approaches contribute to our understanding of criminal behaviour? As indicated at the beginning of this chapter, sociology is concerned with asking questions about the nature and structure of society, with environmental pressures and with aspects of group behaviour. This might usefully be called the macroscopic approach and is highly relevant, although it is still unable to tell us why only *certain* individuals commit crime. For this we have to see what help the disciplines of psychology and psychiatry can afford us: this latter approach might usefully be called the microscopic.

Finally, sociological studies alert us to the social, political, and economic pressures that abound and the ways in which they impinge upon individuals. Such studies provide us with material which indicates that we may need quite drastic changes in the social structure and environment if we are to try to eliminate or control criminal behaviour. In doing so, we raise uncomfortable ethical questions about justice, about the fundamental nature of our society, about welfare, and about the distribution of wealth.

## References

Bagot, J. (1941) *Juvenile Delinquency*. London: Cape.

Baldwin, J. (1972) Delinquent Schools in Tower Hamlets. (I) A Critique. *British Journal of Criminology* **12**: 399–401.

—— (1975) British Areal Studies of Crime: An Assessment. *British Journal of Criminology* **15**: 211–27.

Baldwin, J. and McConville, M. (1977) *Negotiated Justice: Pressures on Defendants to Plead Guilty*. London: Martin Robertson.

Bennett, T. (1979) The Social Distribution of Criminal Labels. *British Journal of Criminology* **19**: 134–45.

Brown, M.J., McCulloch, J.W., and Hiscox, J. (1972) Area Criminal Offences and their Associated Social Variables. *British Journal of Criminology* **12**: 250–68.

Burt, C. (1944) *The Young Delinquent* (fourth edition). London: University of London Press.

Carson, W.G. and Wiles, P. (eds) (1971) *Crime and Delinquency in Britain*. London: Martin Robertson.

Chapman, D. (1968) *Sociology and the Stereotype of the Criminal*. London: Tavistock Publications.

Clegg, A. and Megson, B. (1968) *Children in Distress*. Harmondsworth: Penguin Books.

Cloward, R.A. and Ohlin, L.B. (1961) *Delinquency and Opportunity*. London: Routledge and Kegan Paul.

Cohen, A.K. (1955) *Delinquent Boys: The Culture of the Gang*. Illinois: The Free Press.

Downes, D.M. (1966) *The Delinquent Solution*. London: Routledge and Kegan Paul.

Dunstan, J.A.F. and Roberts, S.F. (1980) Ecology, Delinquency and Socio-Economic Status. *British Journal of Criminology* **20**: 329–43.

Durkheim, E. (1970) *Suicide*. London: Routledge and Kegan Paul. (First published 1897.)

Engels, F. (1953) *Crime and the Condition of the Working Class*. Reprinted from *The Condition of the Working Class in England*. Marx, K. and Engels, F. In W.G. Carson and P. Wiles (eds) *Crime and Delinquency in Britain* (1971: 13–19). London: Martin Robertson.

Ericson, R.V. (1977) Distance and Reaction to Criminality. *British Journal of Criminology* **17**: 1–15.

Farrington, D.P. (1977) The Effects of Public Labelling. *British Journal of Criminology* **17**: 112–25.

Farrington, D.P., Osborn, S.G., and West, D.J. (1978) The Persistence of Labelling Effects. *British Journal of Criminology* **18**: 277–86.

Goffman, E. (1963) *Stigma: Notes on the Management of Spoiled Identity*. New Jersey: Prentice Hall.

Hall, S., Critcher, C., Jefferson, T., Clarke, J., and Roberts, B. (1978) *Policing the Crisis*. London: Macmillan.

Hargreaves, D. (1967) *Social Relations in a Secondary School*. London: Routledge and Kegan Paul.

Hindelang, M.J. (1978) Race and Involvement in Common Law Personal Crimes. *American Sociological Review* **43**: 93–109.

Kerr, M. (1958) *The People of Ship Street*. London: Routledge and Kegan Paul.

Leger, R.G. (1981) Labelling and Its Consequences in a Closed Social System. *British Journal of Criminology* **21**: 109–22.

Levy, C.S. (1981) Labelling: The Social Worker's Responsibility. *Social Casework* **62**: 332–42.

Little, W.R. and Ntsekhe, V.R. (1959) Social Class Background of Young Offenders from London. *British Journal of Delinquency* **X**: 130–35.

Mannheim, H. (1948) *Juvenile Delinquency in an English Middle Town*. London: Kegan Paul, Trench, Trubner.

—— (1965) *Comparative Criminology*. London: Routledge and Kegan Paul.

Manning, P.K. (1975) Deviance and Dogma. *British Journal of Criminology* **15**: 1–20.

Matza, D. (1964) *Delinquency and Drift*. New York: John Wiley.

—— (1967) *Becoming Deviant*. New Jersey: Prentice Hall.

Mays, J.B. (1954) *Growing Up in the City*. Liverpool: Liverpool University Press.

—— (1959) *On the Threshold of Delinquency*. Liverpool: Liverpool University Press.

—— (1970) *Crime and Its Treatment*. London: Longman.

McCulloch, J.W. and Philip, A. (1972) *Suicidal Behaviour* (Chapter 4). Oxford: Pergamon.

McDonald, L. (1969) *Social Class and Delinquency*. London: Faber and Faber.

Merton, R.K. (1957) *Social Theory and Social Structure* (revised edition). Illinois: The Free Press.

Miller, W.B. (1958) Lower Class Culture as a Generating Milieu of Gang Delinquency. *Journal of Social Issues* **14**: 5–19.

Morris, T. (1958) *The Criminal Area*. London: Routledge and Kegan Paul.

National Deviancy Conference (1980) *Permissiveness and Control: The Fate of the Sixties Legislation*. London: Macmillan.

Palmai, G., Storey, P.B., and Briscoe, O. (1967) Social Class and the Young Offender. *British Journal of Psychiatry* **113**: 1073–82.

Parker, H.J. (1974) *View from the Boys. A Sociology of Down-town Adolescents*. London: David and Charles.

Patrick, J. (1973) *A Glasgow Group Observed*. London: Eyre Methuen.

Phillipson, M. (1971) *Sociological Aspects of Crime and Delinquency*. London: Routledge and Kegan Paul.

—— (1971) *Juvenile Delinquency in the School*. In W.G. Carson and P. Wiles (eds). *Crime and Delinquency in Britain*. London: Martin Robertson.

Power, M.J. and Sirey, E.C. (1972) Delinquent Schools in Tower Hamlets. (II) A Commentary. *British Journal of Criminology* **12**: 402–3.

Power, M.J., Benn, R.T., and Morris, J.N. (1972) Neighbourhood, School and Juveniles before the Courts. *British Journal of Criminology* **12**: 111–32.

Rock, P. (1974) The Sociology of Deviancy and Conceptions of Moral Order. *British Journal of Criminology* **14**: 139–149.

Scheff, T.J. (1974) The Labelling Theory of Mental Illness. *American Sociological Review* **39**: 444–52.

Schichor, D. (1980) The New Criminology: Some Critical Issues. *British Journal of Criminology* **20**: 1–19.

Schur, E. (1971) *Labelling Deviant Behaviour: Its Sociological Implications*. New York: Harper and Row. (Quoted in Levy 1981.)

Scott, P.D. (1956) Gangs and Delinquent Groups in London. *British Journal of Delinquency* **VII**: 8–21.

Shaw, C. and McKay, H. (1942) *Juvenile Delinquency in Urban Areas*. Chicago: University of Chicago Press.

Short, J.F. and Strodtbeck, F.L. (1965) *Group Process and Gang Delinquency*. Chicago: University of Chicago Press.

Spinley, B. (1953) *The Deprived and the Privileged*. London: Routledge and Kegan Paul.

Sugarman, B. (1967) Involvement in Youth Culture, Academic Achievement and Conformity in School. *British Journal of Sociology* **18**: 151–64.

Sutherland, E. (1966) *Principles of Criminology* (sixth edition). Edited D. Cressey. New York: Lippincott and Co.

Thrasher, F.W. (1923) *The Gang*. Chicago: Chicago University Press.

Tobias, J.J. (1972) *Crime and Industrial Society in the Nineteenth Century*. Harmondsworth: Penguin Books.

—— (1974) A Statistical Study of a Nineteenth-Century Criminal Area. *British Journal of Criminology* **14**: 221–35.

Velarde, J. (1978) Do Delinquents Really Drift? *British Journal of Criminology* **18**: 23–39.

Vinson, T. and Homel, R. (1975) Crime and Disadvantage. *British Journal of Criminology* **15**: 21–31.

Webb, D. (1981) A Forgotten Radical. *British Journal of Criminology* **21**: 148–58.

Willis, P.E. (1977) *Learning to Labour: How Working Class Kids Get Working Class Jobs*. Farnborough: Saxon House.

Wilson, H. (1962) *Delinquency and Child Neglect*. London: Allen and Unwin.

—— (1975) Juvenile Delinquency, Parental Criminality and Social Handicap. *British Journal of Criminology* **15**: 241–50.

—— (1980) Parental Supervision: A Neglected Aspect of Delinquency. *British Journal of Criminology* **20**: 203–35.

Woodroofe, K. (1966) *From Charity to Social Work*. London: Routledge and Kegan Paul.

Yablonsky, L. (1967) *The Violent Gang*. Harmondsworth: Penguin Books.

FURTHER READING

*Useful accounts of trends in sociological approaches to crime may be found in:*

Baldwin, J. and Bottoms, A.E. (1975) *The Urban Criminal*. London: Tavistock Publications.

Downes, D. and Rock, P. (1979) *Deviant Interpretations: Problems in Criminological Theory*. Oxford: Martin Robertson.

Rock, P. and McIntosh, M. (1974) *Deviance and Social Control*. London: Tavistock Publications.

Taylor, L., Walton, P., and Young, J. (1973) *The New Criminology*. London: Routledge and Kegan Paul.

—— (eds) (1975) *Critical Criminology*. London: Routledge and Kegan Paul.

# CHAPTER FOUR

# *Constitutional and physical explanations*

> For there are mystically in our faces certain
> characters which carry in them the motto of our
> souls.
>
> SIR THOMAS BROWNE

In Chapter 3 I examined some of the pressures and attitudes in society which might have some bearing on the phenomena of crime. I also suggested that it was necessary to study certain more individual factors that might determine the extent to which a person might be predisposed or driven towards criminal behaviour. This chapter is concerned with some of these more personal factors, mainly those derived from constitutional and physical elements and attributes.

## A criminal man?

Many people might argue that the 'criminal' is likely to be small of skull, low of forehead, and generally unprepossessing in appearance. Perhaps this is understandable, as literature provides us with numerous illustrations that support the tendency to link evil with certain physical characteristics. 'Yond Cassius has a lean and hungry look – he thinks too much, such men are dangerous', says Caesar of his feared enemy. George Cruickshank's illustrations for Dickens' *Oliver Twist* depict both Fagin and Bill Sykes as being of evil presence and bearing. It is not altogether surprising then that, in the nineteenth century, a number of people attempted to link crime with certain physical characteristics. It should also be remembered that this interest occurred at a time when attention was being paid increasingly to the need to preserve the good stock in the population, and to control the spread of the bad. Much of this thinking had probably emanated from post-Darwinian theorizing about evolution, and from the increasing interest in eugenics led by such workers as Francis Galton. Some of the concern with physical characteristics and their relationship to criminal behaviour arose from the work of phrenologists[1] such as Francis Gall, whose principal influence was to lead others to look at criminal populations. One of his disciples was the French prison doctor Lauvergne. He suggested that 'assassins' (criminals) presented 'a peculiar face stamped by a seal of brutish and impassible instinct' (quoted in East 1949: 72). Against this, however, the eugenicist Galton argued quite convincingly that the facial characteristics of criminals did not really distinguish them from others:

'I have made numerous composites [portraits] of various groups of convicts, which are interesting negatively rather than positively. They produce faces of a mean description with no villainy written on them. The individual faces are villainous enough, but they are villainous in different ways, and when they are combined, the individual peculiarities disappear, and the common humanity of a low type is all that is left.'
(Quoted in East 1949: 73)

Support for the view that vicious and criminal characteristics might be inherited had come from one or two now famous studies of degenerate families (such as the study of the Jukes family in the USA, in which, out of 1200 family members, no less than 140 were found to be criminals). It was all too easy to conclude from such studies that criminal behaviour was inherited from one generation to the next in much the same way as were certain other qualities and characteristics: as I showed in Chapter 3, interest in environmental factors was only in its infancy at this time.

One of the most notable criminologists to work within a phrenological framework was Lombroso, a psychiatrist. He had been struck initially by the anatomical similarities between the

---

[1] Phrenology is the study of the external cranium as indicator of emotional and mental faculties. It does not find much favour today.

skulls of criminals and those of savage and primitive man. Subsequently, he studied some thousands of criminals, suggesting that criminality carried certain stigma, such as a retreating forehead, a small skull, voluminous ears, and certain internal cerebral deficiencies (Lombroso 1918). Although a succession of later workers, including the English prison doctor Goring (1913), were to disprove Lombroso's theories, it should be remembered that his work was important in that it stressed the need for the careful collection of data about *individual* criminals at a time when the prevailing tendency was to think of people collectively.

It is quite likely that before 1913, when the Mental Deficiency Act provided that the mentally defective be cared for as a special group, our prisons contained a number of people whose appearance and demeanour might have accounted for the prevailing belief that criminality, lack of intelligence, and personal appearance were not only closely associated, but were also evidence of a throwback to more primitive man. It seems likely that even today, though perhaps to a lesser extent, such stereotypes persist. In a recent paper (which summarizes a good deal of their earlier work) Bull and Green (1980) have demonstrated that the general public and the police seem to share the same stereotypic notions about which face fits which particular sort of crime. Bull and Green ask some interesting questions in relation to both public and police attitudes and expectations. For example, do these have some effect upon eye-witness testimony, or upon the activities of the police, or both? Is it possible that some people come to indulge in certain criminal acts because that is what society tells them it expects of them? These questions about expectations have very interesting links with similar questions posed by sociologists, to which I referred in Chapter 3. They demonstrate yet again the inherent danger in trying to make too rigid a demarcation between social, physical, and psychological factors.

## Chromosomes and criminality

A brief word of explanation of normal chromosomal disposition may be useful by way of introduction. Normal human cells contain forty-six chromosomes; these are arranged in twenty-three pairs of different shapes and sizes. The chromosomes may be seen and classified under a high-power microscope once they have been suitably prepared for examination in a laboratory. Different chromosomes carry different genes. One pair of chromosomes called X and Y determines sex. In the female they consist of a matched pair XX and in the male a pair XY. The normal patterning may become altered in a variety of ways. This can result in an extra X or extra Y chromosome or in some other variant, as for example in Down's syndrome (Mongolism) and some other forms of mental subnormality (retardation).

In recent years, considerable interest has been shown in men having been found to carry an extra Y chromosome (West 1969, Forssman 1970, Scott 1975, Pitcher 1975, Kahn *et al.* 1976). It has been suggested that such men, when found in special hospitals (such as Broadmoor, Rampton, or Moss Side) or in prisons, are frequently taller than average, come from *essentially non-delinquent backgrounds*, and may occasionally have records of violence. To date, very few large-scale studies have been undertaken to estimate the presence of such anomalies in normal populations. Until this is done and the evidence is available, there is little to suggest that we have found a clear genetic causal factor in criminality. Over twenty-five years ago, a leading geneticist, Penrose, stated that 'criminality is not a suitable trait for [genetic] studies except where it is associated with a clearly defined pathological condition . . . it is certain that the disposition to crime is not a single gene effect' (Penrose 1955: 15). However, it may be that as the science of cytology advances and our laboratory techniques become more sophisticated, we *may* find evidence that would lead us to suggest a closer link between chromosomal abnormalities and crime than can be discerned at the present time. So far, the criminal courts have not been quick to accept evidence of chromosomal abnormalities as providing evidence for exculpation from criminal responsibility, though Hall Williams (1969) quotes one or two interesting and isolated instances.

## Nature v. nurture

Behavioural and other scientists have always been keenly interested in trying to assess the relative importance to be attached to nature (heredity and constitution) on the one hand and to nurture (environment) on the other. This interest has been particularly marked in relation to the development of intelligence and to the cause of psychiatric disorders, but rather less so in trying to explain the development of criminality. One way of trying to compare the relative importance of such influences is to examine the phenomenon of twins. (For a useful survey of general twin studies, see Mittler 1971.) Two types of twins are described in the literature; dizygotic or fraternal twins who are non-identical, and monozygotic or uni-ovular twins who are identical. The first major twin study in relation to crime was carried out by Lange (1930). He examined thirty pairs of adult male criminal twins (13 of whom were identical and 17 fraternal). In the identical group he found that 77 per cent were criminal but in the fraternal group only 12 per cent. Lange's work has been criticized understandably on account of small sample size, although subsequent work by Rosanoff, Rosanoff, and Handy (1934) tended to confirm his results. Their work has also been criticized on similar grounds. More wide-ranging studies have been carried out by Christiansen (1968 and 1977), and some of these are still in progress. In one of his early surveys Christiansen (1968) studied 6000 pairs of twins in the Danish islands, all born between 1880 and 1910. His preliminary results tended to show that there was a higher degree of more serious crime amongst identical than amongst non-identical twins. However, in a later piece of research, Dalgard and Kringlen (1976) cast some doubts on the validity of many earlier twin studies, suggesting that many of the variables studied were difficult to control statistically and that some of the cytological and other laboratory techniques used were not wholly reliable. Christiansen himself modestly suggests that

'No study carried out up to now can be said to have provided conclusive evidence of the dominance of genetic over environmental factors in the genesis of criminality. Given the nature of the genetic and environmental facts, it is still an appropriate *a priori* hypothesis that *heredity and environment always interact in a dynamic fashion to bring about and shape criminal behaviour*, and that both the mutual interaction and the mutual strength of the two factors form a continuous dimension for all persons and situations.'

(Christiansen 1977: 88; italics in original)

The geneticist Shields conducted an interesting comparative study of identical twins, *some reared apart and some together*. Although his study was not specifically concerned with delinquency, the evidence he produced showed that there was a marked genetic factor underlying certain measurable traits of personality, some of which might be associated with crime (Shields 1962). There is also the danger of assuming that environmental factors remain constant for identical twins, whereas parents may adopt a different attitude towards each and thus treat them differently, a fact which was borne out very clearly in Whelan's detailed study of one pair of identical twins (Whelan 1951).

Despite the number of more carefully researched studies that have appeared in recent years, the most that can be said on this issue at the present time is that twin studies are inconclusive as indicators of the importance of nature over nurture in the genesis of criminality. It is conceivable, however, that a *predisposition* to crime may be transmitted genetically. Hutchings and Mednick (1973) demonstrated that the delinquency of adopted sons in Denmark bore a closer relationship to the criminality of their *biological* fathers than to that of their *adoptive* fathers.

## Physique and crime

Sheldon (1949) suggested that there were links between certain kinds of body-build, personality, and criminal behaviour. According to his system, which was developed from the work of earlier investigators, people can be divided into three main physical types (he did suggest others, but for brevity only three are included here).

(a)  Endomorphs: Such people are often given to food, drink, company, and sleep.
(b)  Ectomorphs: These show a liking for books and privacy, and show a youthfully intent manner.
(c)  Mesomorphs: These tend to be more aggressive in personality, more muscular, and less sensitive to pain.

It is of considerable interest to note that mesomorphs tend also to be more highly represented amongst criminals than do the other two groupings. This is evidenced by the extensive research carried out by the Gluecks (1956) in America, and also by the work of Gibbens (1963) in this country. There may well be, however, a simple explanation for this; if a boy is muscular, more may be expected of him by way of outgoing, robust behaviour, with the result that he may find himself in situations of delinquent temptation. Moreover, by his size, he may be more conspicuous, and therefore spotted more easily and thus apprehended. A more recent study by McCandless, Parsons, and Roberts (1972) found no firm association between either convicted or self-reported offending and physique in a group of 177 males aged 15–17. We must conclude then that studies of physique in relation to delinquency do not get us very far – we can probably learn more from a consideration of *physical illness and disability* and their relationships to crime.

## Physical illness and crime

### ORGANIC PSYCHIATRIC ILLNESS

Psychiatric illness of a non-organic type will not be considered here. I give some consideration to it and to its relationship to criminal behaviour in Chapters 5 and 9. There are, however, certain organic diseases that have psychiatric implications and bring about behavioural changes. One of these is Huntington's Chorea, a directly inherited and rare disease that produces a progressive deterioration of mental and emotional functioning in addition to very serious physical disability. Occasionally people suffering from it have been known to have shown criminal behaviour.

Various types of senile and pre-senile dementia, which may reduce inhibition in the individual, and GPI (General Paralysis of the Insane), caused by syphilitic infection, occasionally lead to an appearance in court. More rarely, a person may be suffering from a brain tumour, trauma, or lesion which may lead to criminal behaviour. Epilepsy is another important organic condition that has interested workers in the delinquency field, as it is felt that it could have some relationship to crime, particularly crimes of violence. Much of the evidence (e.g. De Haas 1963) indicates that there is no positive link between these two phenomena, and that background conditions are mainly responsible for the behavioural disturbances observed in epileptics. However, in more recent studies, Gunn and his colleague made two significant discoveries: first that a larger number of epileptic males are received into custody than would be expected by chance, and second that in one particular form of epilepsy (idiopathic, i.e. without known cause such as injury or brain damage) the offender was likely to have received previous convictions for violence (Gunn and Bonn 1971, Gunn 1974, and Gunn 1977). Gunn (1974) puts forward four very important points in attempting to explain the large number of epileptics in prison. They are worth summarizing here for they demonstrate yet again the close relationships between physical, psychological, and social factors in explaining criminal behaviour.

'A. Brain dysfunction is responsible for both the ictal phenomena and the antisocial behaviour.
B. The epilepsy generates social and psychological problems (e.g. rejection, feelings of inferiority) which in their turn lead to antisocial reactions.
C. Harmful social factors such as overcrowding, parental neglect and the like lead to an excess prevalence of both epilepsy and antisocial behaviour.
D. Environmental factors, such as parental rejection, subcultural norms etc. lead to behaviour disturbances which not only produce conflict with the law but also accident and illness proneness (because of self neglect and recklessness). Such accidents and illnesses in their turn produce an excess prevalence of epilepsy.'

(Gunn 1974: 514)

There is also evidence that there is a higher proportion of epileptics among some murderers than among the general population, and that aggressive psychopaths are often found to have abnormal brain rhythms as recorded by the electro-encephalogram (EEG) (Hill and Pond 1952). Stafford Clark, Pond, and Lovett-Doust (1951), who made a study of psychopaths in prison, concluded that EEG abnormalities seemed to be most common in aggressive psychopaths, less common in the inadequate psychopath, less common still in the ordinary prisoner, and least common amongst non-offenders. It is apparent from most of the studies that have been carried out in connection with abnormal brain rhythms that they are most likely to be found in relation to certain types of offenders (mainly aggressive psychopaths), and it may be that if such disturbances (whether accompanied by epileptic phenomena or not) can be detected, there will be the possibility of providing medication in certain cases. This may help to control outbursts of impulsive aggressive or violent behaviour.

## ORGANIC PHYSICAL ILLNESS

There are certain other physical diseases which may produce changes in behaviour, without necessarily bringing about lasting impairment of personal functions or permanent changes in attitudes. Very occasionally, a late middle-aged or elderly man may appear before the courts on a charge of indecent exposure; subsequent physical examination may reveal that he has been suffering from an enlargement of the prostate gland. Much more rarely a person can be found to have been suffering from the long-term effects of taking some toxic compound, or from a metabolic upset such as evidenced in diabetes or thyroid disorders. In addition, extreme fatigue may of course induce irritability and a resultant tendency to behave impulsively.

## STRESS, ILLNESS, AND INJURY DURING PREGNANCY

Some studies have suggested that there may be an association between pre-natal or birth injury and delinquency in later life. Stott (1963) found some evidence of a congenital defect in juvenile behaviour disturbances and in delinquency proneness. He suggested that stress or anxiety in the mother in pregnancy might result in mental retardation or maladjustment in the child. His work followed on that of Drillien (1963) in the UK and Pasamanick, Rogers, and Lilienfeld in the USA (1956). Drillien found that, particularly in cases of premature births, the child could be neurally impaired and thus be more likely to succumb to environmental stress. Neurally impaired children are often unforthcoming in their social relationships, are easily frustrated, and show a very low stress tolerance, all of which could well set up hostile responses in their parents, such as 'he was always difficult', 'always a strange child', 'we could never understand him'. As Stott said, 'The neurally impaired child tends to create an unfavourable human environment for himself', and thus a vicious circle is all too easily started (Stott 1963: 10). These studies obviously throw up very important areas for further exploration, but the hypotheses presented by them require to be validated on larger groups in the general population before any firm conclusions can be drawn. (See also Herbert 1974: Chapter 2.)

## Endocrine disturbances and crime

It has for long been recognized that there are certain periods of life in which people may be particularly vulnerable because of the glandular and other changes that are taking place in their bodies. One thinks immediately of the turmoils of adolescence, and to a lesser extent the menopause, which can make women particularly vulnerable, though the evidence collected by Epps (1962) as part of a study of female shoplifters seems to indicate that this is not quite as important as had previously been thought to be the case. More recent work suggests that the female shoplifter is of a typically mixed variety of physical and mental symptoms (Gibbens, Palmer, and Prince 1971). The menstrual cycle has for long been considered important in relation to stress reactions in women (Frank 1931). In some studies, a high percentage of women were found to be menstruating at the time of their offence (Dalton 1961, D'Orbán 1971). In a recent study, which examined *crimes of violence* committed by a consecutive sample of fifty women remanded to prison, D'Orbán and Dalton (1980) found that 44 per cent of their sample committed their offence during the *paramenstrum*. In contrast, there was a significant lack of offences during the *ovulatory* and *pre-ovulatory phases*. On the basis of these findings the authors concluded that considerations for treatment should take into account behavioural changes rather than subjective symptoms. Changes in hormone balance after the birth of a child may be particularly important. The law recognizes this possibility in the special offence of infanticide for women who, in certain legally defined circumstances, kill their newborn child within a year of its birth. The special problems of the female offender are considered further in Chapter 10.

## Physical handicaps and crime

The fact that most of us take for granted a measure of good health and a reasonably personable appearance may explain why the absence of these qualities is not often considered as being of much importance in relation to criminal behaviour. School teachers will be very familiar with the child who seems inattentive, disobedient, and generally unco-operative, who in addition frequently seems to be suffering from a running nose or discharging ears, and who on physical examination by the school doctor is shown to have inflamed tonsils or an ear infection. A child who labours under such handicaps is hardly likely to give of his best, and may drift into delinquent or other antisocial ways as a means of drawing attention to his or her plight.

Defects, such as deafness, poor vision, squints, and so on, may certainly give rise to feelings of inferiority. According to Maberly, 'physical handicaps cause a far greater sense of inferiority in children than is commonly recognized . . . efforts to compensate or to overcome social ostracism may give rise to delinquent behaviour' (Maberly 1950: 126). Physical handicap, especially if it develops at critical growth periods in a child's life, may be important for the child not necessarily because of the illness itself, but through its effects upon parent-child and other relationships. An obvious example would be the over-protectiveness that might ensue on the part of the parents, especially if they had developed guilt feelings about their part in the cause of the child's disability. The handicapped child might even be singled out for special treatment at the expense of other brothers and sisters, which might result in him drawing upon himself a good deal of antagonism and hostility from them.

> 'Children who have had more than their fair share of physical illness in early life tend to be timid and fearful. But once a child starts to be over-dependent or is perceived as being so by his mother, he becomes a stimulus to the mother and

influences her behaviour to him . . . this can lead to a circular build-up of tension.'                                    (Scott 1962: 64)

Important though physical handicaps may be, however, we should not fall into the error of thinking that if we dealt with them by more adequate medical services the delinquency rate would necessarily decrease. When Eilenberg (1961) made a comparison of the health of samples of delinquent children in London for the years 1930 and 1955, the children seen in 1955 were markedly better in health, nutrition, and stature than those seen in 1930, even though we know that the rate of delinquency had increased considerably by 1955. Yet despite this general comparative improvement in health, Eilenberg found that when he compared the 1955 sample of remand-home boys with a non-delinquent control group, there was among the delinquents an increased percentage of minor physical disorders such as skin complaints, eye troubles, ear, nose, and throat problems, and so on. He suggested three areas deserving of further study.

(1) The problem of inadequate communication between the child and his environment because of disease, deafness, speech defects, and so on.
(2) The relationship of chronic states of infection to subsequent lowered resistance to psychological and other stresses in the child's life.
(3) The neglect of minor physical conditions being symptomatic of chronic parental inadequacies.

More positively, Ogden (1959), a Borstal medical officer, showed that cosmetic surgery (for facial scars, squints, and nasal deformities) could bring about improvements in attitudes which resulted in a lessening of criminal conduct. It should also be noted here that there is some experimental evidence to suggest that delinquents are more clumsy at performing certain skills requiring manual dexterity than are non-delinquents – a further area in which delinquents may well under-achieve (West 1967: 137–39).

## Conclusion

In conclusion the most important points in this chapter may be summarized as follows:

(1) The theory of a 'criminal man' has not been proven valid.
(2) Chromosomal studies have not fulfilled their early promise, though refinements in cytological techniques may yet supply some further clues worth following.
(3) As far as crime is concerned, research on nature versus nurture as undertaken in twin studies has not as yet produced any conclusive results.
(4) The relationship between physical disease, handicap, and crime is equivocal.

Careful studies in all of the above areas emphasize the need to examine individual cases cautiously, in order that we may try and assess the relative importance of inborn and associated characteristics in relation to environmental and particularly family pressures. In other words, we seek to discern the stress situations which will affect particularly vulnerable individuals.

This is a particularly important point for probation and police officers, magistrates, and judges to bear in mind when trying to assess the attitudes and motivations of people who appear before them in court. A sudden onset of odd or apparently inexplicable behaviour, on the part of a defendant of mature years who has no previous record of antisocial behaviour, should cause sentencers and those who advise them to reflect. It may well be advisable to ask for full psychiatric and physical reports. These and related matters are considered further in Chapter 5.

## References

Bull, R.H.C. and Green, J. (1980) The Relationship Between Physical Appearance and Criminality. *Medicine, Science and the Law* **20**: 79–83.
Christiansen, K.O. (1968) Threshold Tolerance in Various Population Groups. In A.V.S. De Rueck and R. Porter (eds) *The Mentally Abnormal Offender*. London: J. and A. Churchill. (For CIBA Foundation)

68    *Criminal Behaviour*

—— (1977) A Review of Studies of Criminality Among Twins. In S.A. Mednick and K.O. Christiansen (eds) *Biosocial Bases of Criminal Behaviour*. New York: Gardner Press.

Dalgard, S. and Kringlen, E. (1976) A Norwegian Twin Study of Criminality. *British Journal of Criminology* 16: 213–32.

Dalton, K. (1961) Menstruation and Crime. *British Medical Journal* 2: 1752–753.

De Haas, L. (1963) Epilepsy and Criminality. *British Journal of Criminology* 3: 248–56.

D'Orbán, P.T. (1971) Social and Psychiatric Aspects of Female Crime. *Medicine, Science and the Law* 11: 104–15.

D'Orbán, P.T. and Dalton, J. (1980) Violent Crime and the Menstrual Cycle. *Psychological Medicine* 10: 353–59.

Drillien, C.M. (1963) *The Growth and Development of the Prematurely Born Infant*. Edinburgh: Livingstone.

East, Sir Norwood (1949) *Society and the Criminal*. London: HMSO.

Eilenberg, M.D. (1961) Remand Home Boys. *British Journal of Criminology* 2: 111–31.

Epps, P. (1962) In T.C.N. Gibbens and J. Prince *Shoplifting*. London: Institute for the Study and Treatment of Delinquency.

Forssman, H. (1970) The Mental Implications of Sex Chromosome Abberrations. *British Journal of Psychiatry* 117: 353–63.

Frank, R.T. (1931) The Hormonal Causes of Premenstrual Tension. *Archives of Neurology and Psychiatry* 26: 1053–57.

Gibbens, T.C.N. (1963) *Psychiatric Studies of Borstal Lads*. Oxford: Oxford University Press.

Gibbens, T.C.N., Palmer, A.C., and Prince, J. (1971) Mental Health Aspects of Shoplifting. *British Medical Journal* 3: 612–15.

Glueck, S. and Glueck, E. (1956) *Physique and Delinquency*. New York: Harper.

Goring, C. (1913) *The English Convict*. London: HMSO.

Gunn, J. (1974) Social Factors and Epileptics in Prison. *British Journal of Psychiatry* 124: 509–17.

—— (1977) *Epileptics in Prison*. London: Academic Press.

Gunn, J. and Bonn, J. (1971) Criminality and Violence in Epileptic Prisoners. *British Journal of Psychiatry* 118: 337–43.

Hall Williams, J.E. (1969) *Chromosome Abnormalities and Legal*

*Accountability*. In D.J. West (ed.) *Criminological Implications of Chromosome Abnormalities*. Cambridge: Institute of Criminology.

Herbert, M. (1974) *Emotional Problems of Development in Children*. London: Academic Press.

Hill, D. and Pond, D.A. (1952) Reflections on a Hundred Capital Cases Submitted to Electroencephalography. *Journal of Mental Science* **98**: 23–43.

Hutchings, B. and Mednick, S.A. (1973) *Major Issues in Juvenile Delinquency*. In World Health Organisation Symposium. Copenhagen: WHO Regional Office.

Kahn, J., Reed, F.S., Bates, M., Coates, T., and Everitt, B. (1976) A Survey of Y Chromosome Variants and Personality. *British Journal of Criminology* **16**: 233–44.

Lange, J. (1930) *Crime as Destiny*. (English Translation.) New York: Beni.

Lombroso, C. (1918) *Crime: Its Causes and Remedies*. Boston: Little Brown.

Maberly, A. (1950) Delinquency in Handicapped Children. *British Journal of Delinquency* **I**: 125–28.

McCandless, B.R., Parsons, W.S., and Roberts, A. (1972) Perceived Opportunity Delinquency, Race and Body Build Among Delinquent Youth. *Journal of Consulting Clinical Psychology* **38**: 281.

Mittler, P. (1971) *The Study of Twins*. Harmondsworth: Penguin Books.

Ogden, D.A. (1959) The Use of Surgical Rehabilitation in Young Delinquents. *British Medical Journal* **2**: 432.

Pasamanick, B., Rogers, M.E., and Lilienfeld, A.M. (1956) Pregnancy Experience and the Development of Behaviour Disorders in Children. *American Journal of Psychiatry* **112**: 613–18.

Penrose, L.S. (1955) Genetics and the Criminal. *British Journal of Delinquency* **VI**: 15–25.

Pitcher, D.R. (1975) The XYY Syndrome. In T. Silverstone and B. Barraclough (eds) *Contemporary Psychiatry*. Ashford: Headley Brothers.

Rosanoff, A.J., Rosanoff, I.A., and Handy, L.M. (1934) Criminality and Delinquency in Twins. *Journal of Criminal Law and Criminology* **24**: 923–34.

Scott, P.D. (1962) The Prevention of Crime. *Royal Society of Health Conference Paper.* 29/62.

—— (1975) Medical Aspects of Delinquency. In T. Silverstone and B. Barraclough (eds) *Contemporary Psychiatry.* Ashford: Headley Brothers.

Sheldon, W.H. (1949) *Varieties of Delinquent Youth.* New York: Harper.

Shields, J. (1962) *Monozygotic Twins Brought Up Apart and Together.* Cambridge: Cambridge University Press.

Stafford Clark, D., Pond, D., and Lovett-Doust, J.W. (1951) The Psychopath in Prison. *British Journal of Delinquency* **II**: 117–29.

Stott, D.H. (1963) New Possibilities in the Aetiology of Delinquency. *International Annals of Criminology* **2**: 1–11.

West, D.J. (1967) *The Young Offender.* Harmondsworth: Penguin Books.

—— (ed.) (1969) *Criminological Implications of Chromosome Abnormalities.* Cambridge: Institute of Criminology.

Whelan, L. (1951) Aggressive Psychopathy in One of Uniovular Twins. *British Journal of Delinquency* **II**: 130–43.

FURTHER READING

Gunn, J., Robertson, G., Dell, S., and Way, C. (1978) *Psychiatric Aspects of Imprisonment.* London: Academic Press.

Mark, V.H. and Ervin, F.R. (1970) *Violence and the Brain.* Maryland: Harper and Row.

Mednick, S.A. and Christiansen, K.O. (1977) *Biosocial Bases of Criminal Behaviour.* New York: Gardner Press.

Penfield, W. (1975) *The Mystery of the Mind. A Critical Study of Consciousness and the Human Brain.* Princeton, New Jersey: Princeton University Press.

Powell, G.E. (1979) *Brain and Personality.* Farnborough: Saxon House.

Scott, D.F. (1978) *About Epilepsy* (third edition). London: Duckworth.

# CHAPTER FIVE

# Psychiatric and psychological explanations

> The fathers have eaten a sour grape and the children's teeth are set on edge.
>
> JEREMIAH: 31:29

## Mental disorder and crime

The relationship between mental disorder and crime is at best equivocal and can only be touched upon briefly in this book. Those interested in pursuing this fascinating subject further should refer to my earlier work, *Offenders, Deviants, or Patients?* (particularly Chapter 3). I consider the procedures for dealing with the mentally abnormal offender in hospital, in the penal system, and in the community in Chapter 9 of the present work.

There are a number of difficulties for those who wish to study the relationship between mental disorder and crime. In the first place, there are problems in defining crime, and, as I pointed out in Chapter 2, crimes 'come and go' on the statute book. Second, only in very rare instances can we find a direct causal link between any given psychiatric disorder and crime; more often than not we may merely find some suspected association. As I shall show in Chapter 9, this gives rise to problems in determining exculpation from criminal responsibility. Third, there is by no means agreement about what constitutes mental disorder or its causes. The following is a very simplified outline classification of mental disorder and it would probably find acceptance by the majority of workers in the mental health field (*See Table 5(1)*).

Table 5(1)    *Outline classification of mental disorders*

| | |
|---|---|
| the functional psychoses | the affective disorders (manic depressive illnesses) schizophrenic illnesses |
| the neuroses (psycho-neuroses) | anxiety states mild depression hysteria obsessional states |
| mental disorder as a result of infection, disease, metabolic disturbance, and trauma | (including epilepsy) |
| mental disorder due to the ageing process | (for example, the pre-senile and senile dementias) |
| abnormalities of personality and psycho-sexual disorders | (including psychopathic personality disorders and sexual deviation (variation)) |
| alcohol and other drug addictions and abuse | |
| mental subnormality, (deficiency, handicap, retardation) | (including chromosomal abnormalities) |

(Modified from Prins 1980: 54.)

*Table 5(1)* requires some comment. The *functional psychoses* (see below also) are generally regarded as a group of severe mental illnesses for which no clear organic basis can be discerned at present. The *neuroses* (or *psycho-neuroses* as some describe them) are less severe but no less disabling for the sufferer. Mental disorder as a result of *infection, disease, metabolic disturbance*, and *trauma* and mental disorders due to the *ageing process* will not be dealt with here, as the most important criminological implications of these have already been dealt with, albeit briefly, in Chapter 4. This affords yet another example of the hazards in trying to make neat classifications of illnesses. *Abnormalities of personality* include *psychopathic personality disorder* and this will be the subject of later comment. Many people would rightly not regard psycho-sexual disorders, which may include male and female homosexuality, as mental disorders at all. However, *sexual deviation* (variation) may lead people to break the law and for this reason sexual *offenders* are discussed as a separate group in Chapter 10. The same reservations must be applied to alcohol and other drug addiction and abuse. But, as such addiction and abuse can lead to law-breaking, such law-breakers are also considered in Chapter 10. *Chromosomal abnormalities* have already been dealt with in Chapter 4.

Although formal psychiatric disorder is found very rarely even in the highly selected populations of remand institutions and prisons (Scott 1969, Prins 1980: 45–7), persons convicted of certain serious crimes such as murder, other serious personal violence, and arson are found occasionally to be suffering from one or other of the more serious psychiatric disorders such as schizophrenic illness, affective disorder (manic depressive illness), or severe personality disorder (psychopathy). In view of this, and in line with my comments at the end of Chapter 4 about the need to pay careful attention to the individual case, it is appropriate to make a few comments on each of the major disorders and their possible relationship to criminality.

### SCHIZOPHRENIC ILLNESSES

These may involve serious disturbances of personality, mood, and behaviour. The sufferer may become hallucinated, and thinking and ideation may be so disturbed that speech and writing become quite incomprehensible. The person's emotional balance may be seriously disturbed, he may lack insight into his condition, and occasionally he may act violently towards persons or property whilst under the influence of his delusions or hallucinations. Such persons may in rare instances commit such offences as murder, other serious personal assault, or arson. It is as well to stress that these occurrences are *rare* and it is unfortunate that sufferers from schizophrenia, and by implication their families, are sometimes saddled with the additional label of 'bad' as well as 'mad'.

### AFFECTIVE DISORDERS (MANIC DEPRESSIVE ILLNESSES)

This group of illnesses is characterized by severe changes in mood (hence the term affective), with resultant disturbances in thought and behaviour. In mania or hypomania, the person shows grandiose ideas and becomes elated and excited far beyond that which would be in keeping with his circumstances. He is quite without insight into his condition, will brook no interference with his grandiose plans, and thus may behave thoughtlessly and impulsively with no heed for the consequences of his actions. Because of this, he may well engage in antisocial acts and come to the attention of the courts. In severe depression (which varies considerably in form and in intensity) he may well feel that his own life and the lives of those near to him are no longer worth living. In extreme cases, as West has shown (1965), murder followed by suicide may result.

## PSYCHOPATHIC PERSONALITY DISORDER

This is probably best regarded as a serious personality deviation which is not in most cases the result of any other formal psychiatric or organic illness. Psychiatrists and others are divided as to whether it really constitutes an illness at all. Its position on a continuum of personality disorder can best be seen from an examination of *Figure 5(1)*.

In *Figure 5(1)* I have used the terms personality and behaviour disorder synonymously, but some authorities prefer to reserve the term behaviour disorder for use only in childhood conditions. It will also be noted that I have suggested in my classification that there may be some forms of psychopathy

*Figure 5(1)*    Continuum of personality disorder

| 1 minor behaviour disorder | 2 more serious personality (character) disorder, unusual and affectionless personalities | 3 'pseudo-psychopathy' (due to established brain damage, temporal lobe disease, infections etc., e.g. encephalitis) | 4 'essential' psychopathy |
|---|---|---|---|

(Reproduced from Prins 1980: 143.)

(Category 3) in which organic and other physical factors *may* play an important part in the cause of the disorder. A vast amount of research has been carried out into the causation and classification of psychopathic disorder, and this cannot be reviewed here. Suffice it to say that some authorities regard 'essential' psychopathy as a true mental illness (e.g. Cleckley 1976); other workers have investigated neuro-physiological aspects of causation (Hare and Schalling 1978), whilst sociologists tend to see psychopathic behaviour as stemming from deficient role-taking capacity (Gough 1956). The law in this country (that is in England and Wales) defines psychopathy as 'a persistent disorder or disability of mind (whether or not including subnormality of intelligence) which results in abnormally aggressive or serious irresponsible conduct on the part of the patient and requires or is susceptible to treatment' (Mental Health Act 1959, Sec. 4(4)). Unfortunately, there has been a tendency amongst penal and other workers to use the term psychopathic as a kind of 'dustbin' label, through which it is possible to disclaim responsibility for trying to manage offenders or patients who are merely unresponsive, irresponsible, unlikeable, or difficult. Once again we are reminded here of the dangers of labelling to which I referred in Chapter 3. It is felt by not a few people that it *is* possible to define quite clear criteria for those persons suffering from 'true' or 'essential' psychopathy and that the term can usefully be applied if these criteria are satisfied. (See Prins 1980 (Chapter 5) for a discussion of this issue.)

THE NEUROSES (PSYCHO-NEUROSES)

The neuroses in their classical forms do not figure largely in penal populations. Occasionally, men or women suffering from mild depression may resort to such offences as shoplifting, either because they have become confused through the effects of the illness or in order perhaps to draw attention to their distress. Much more rarely, hysterical amnesia may be claimed in relation to the commission of an offence in order to seek exculpation from criminal responsibility, as occurred in the well-known Podola case in 1959[1]. It is well established that it is

[1] R. v. Podola [1959] 3 All E.R. (418).

very difficult to determine with any degree of accuracy the causes of an amnesic state. Some such states may be due to the kind of neurotic condition just described, others may be due to malingering, while others still may be due to organic disorders or injury affecting the functions of the brain. Some anxiety states accompanied by depression may lead to a buildup of tension which is sometimes then discharged through criminal activity (see Prins 1980: 71).

*Mental subnormality and crime.* This is dealt with under *Intelligence and crime* below.

## Clinical approaches to criminal behaviour

Over the years psychiatrists and psychologists have made many significant contributions to the study of crime. As far as the courts are concerned the psychiatrist's important function is to screen offenders so that any formal mental illness may be detected and an assessment made of its relevance to the case and to its disposal. It is the psychiatrist's task to appraise as objectively as he can all aspects of the defendant's life history and pattern, taking into account any concurrent investigations carried out by his colleagues (particularly those of the psychologist and social worker). In recent years psychologists have been engaged in forensic psychiatry much more frequently and are now increasingly becoming recognized as professional experts and witnesses in their own right (Haward 1981). Social workers, notably probation officers, have always played a very significant role in assessing the background and motivation of the offender, and a more detailed discussion of this and other aspects of their work will be found in Chapter 11. There is always the danger of course that too much reliance will be placed upon the 'expert's' opinion, particularly the psychiatrist. We should note that, once having excluded formal psychiatric illness, his opinion may be no more well informed than anyone else's. It is unfortunate that in recent years there has been a tendency to 'medicalize' social problems; this again can lead to unrealistic expectations of psychiatrists and other medical men and women. Kahn (1971) has suggested that there is still a great deal of public ambivalence towards psychiatry and psychiatrists. The psychiatrist may well find that he is expected to have an answer to every human problem, but at the same time his claim may be challenged even while his help is being requested. Psychiatric opinion is in fact asked for in very few cases that come before the courts. In my own research I found it to be asked for in less than 2 per cent of cases (Prins 1975 and 1976). This was in line with the findings of other investigators such as Sparks (1966). One of my more interesting discoveries was that nearly all the magistrates (in answer to a questionnaire administered anonymously) saw the need for psychiatric opinion in relation to the offender's crime and his conduct in court, while the probation officers in my sample (in answer to a similar questionnaire) saw the investigation of family and personal background as being of more importance. There are interesting implications here because of the differing perspectives of psychiatrists, magistrates, and probation officers and how they view the needs of offenders. The evidence I obtained suggested that there was a need for better communication and consultation between all three groups if offenders were to be dealt with more effectively.

Much of this chapter is concerned with what might usefully be described as the clinical approach to criminology in contrast to the wider approach of sociologists. Both are important and, as I have already shown, both are complementary. In an important paper (West 1980), West, an academic forensic psychiatrist, sees clinical criminology as being concerned with the offender as an individual, with his peculiarities, with his personal motivation, and with his idiosyncratic relationships with penal and other social institutions. He acknowledges the criticisms made by some of the radical sociologists, but suggests that focus on the individual does not necessarily lessen the need for, or detract from, political sensitivity. West sees the task of clinicians working in the penal field as one of helping to distinguish more accurately between the individual who is a social nuisance and the individual who is a social menace. Within this broad distinction he suggests it is then possible to identify further sub-groups who may respond to a variety of treatment measures. He would include as examples of such groupings the desperate parents at risk of battering their child, the clinically depressed (as distinct from the merely miserable) shoplifter, the husband who has an uncontrollable urge to expose himself when his wife upsets him, and the addicts who have to steal to pay for their intoxicants. West's comments provide a useful corrective for the somewhat prevalent tendency to explain all criminal behaviour as a response to pressures and inequalities in the political and social system. Such a view emphasizes once again the need for a multi-disciplinary approach to the problem of criminal behaviour. This need for a multi-disciplinary approach can be exemplified usefully in our consideration of the relationship between intelligence and crime.

## Intelligence and crime

Since the turn of the century, psychologists and psychiatrists have been particularly concerned with the relationship between level of intelligence and crime. As I showed in Chapter 4, there was once a tendency to associate moral turpitude with certain physical and other characteristics of so-called degeneracy. Following the introduction of special provisions for the subnormal (or mentally defective, as they were then called), such people were less frequently found in penal establishments. Today those classified as subnormal figure to a very small extent in criminal and penal populations. Most studies have shown that the average intelligence of offenders as a group is not much below that of the general population. In a comprehensive study and review of the subject, Woodward (1955) concluded that offenders were not more than eight points below the general average (i.e., IQ of about 100); but even this eight-point depression may be partly explained by the fact that these were the offenders who were caught and therefore subjected to study. Intelligence, at least that measured by intelligence tests, seems to be of less importance in relation to criminality than does the offender's capacity to communicate his thoughts and feelings. Many offenders seem to do badly on tests of verbal facility, and rather better on non-verbal tests. Those who work with delinquents are only too familiar with the inarticulate offender, who because of serious difficulty in verbal communication may act out his problems instead. We know also from sociological studies that low-class status and lack of educational and other opportunities may be more important than lack of innate intellectual ability, at least for those who are of near average intelligence or marginally below it. Some confirmation of this view can be found in a study by Gibson and West (1970), who found that on tests of verbal and non-verbal intelligence boys convicted before the age of fourteen were not only of lower IQ, but came from the community's most impoverished and socially deprived families. For those adjudged to be well below average intelligence (the mentally subnormal or mentally handicapped) rather different considerations apply. I now consider this group briefly.

## MENTAL SUBNORMALITY (DEFICIENCY, HANDICAP, RETARDATION) AND CRIME

The terms subnormality, deficiency, handicap, and retardation are frequently used synonymously. In recent years, however, the term mental retardation seems to be preferred to others, though the term mental handicap is preferred by the DHSS and the term subnormality is used in the Mental Health Act 1959. The layman often, but understandably, confuses mental illness with mental retardation; the two conditions are entirely separate though they may coexist in some individuals. In general and over-simplified terms it can be said that the mentally ill individual starts life with normal intellectual and mental endowments, but for various reasons becomes ill and then deviates from commonly accepted standards of normality and mental health. The subnormal person has never had the endowment of intellectual normality, or has lost it in infancy or in later life. This point is demonstrated very clearly in the use of the old descriptive term for subnormality – *amentia* – meaning literally 'lack of mind'. In the Mental Health Act 1959, mental subnormality is defined as 'a state of arrested or incomplete development of mind . . . which includes subnormality of intelligence and is of a nature and degree which requires or is susceptible to medical treatment or other special care or training' (Mental Health Act 1959, Section 4:3). The Act also distinguishes between subnormality and severe subnormality. Mental subnormality (of which there are some 300 known *possible* causes) cannot be assessed purely in terms of intellectual capacity. Though such capacity is important, it is imperative to have regard equally for the social situation and functioning of the individual, in particular family and kindred supports or lack of them. Clinically it is usual to distinguish between four categories of subnormality: *mild*; *moderate*; *severe*; and *profound*.

From a criminological and penological point of view we are most likely to be concerned with people showing mild or moderate degrees of subnormality. I suggest nine ways in which such persons may come within the purview of the criminal law and the penal system.

(1) The degree of subnormality may be severe enough to prevent the individual concerned from understanding that his act was legally wrong. (See also Chapter 9.)

(2) Mild or moderately subnormal offenders may be caught out more easily in their criminal acts.

(3) Such offenders may be very easily used by others in delinquent escapades, wittingly or unwittingly. (See for example Weber 1953.)

(4) Subnormality may be associated with an organic disorder that makes the person particularly impulsive and unpredictable.

(5) A number of subnormal individuals have quite understandable problems in making their often harmless intentions understood. Thus a friendly social overture may be misinterpreted by an uninformed or unsympathetic recipient as an attempted assault. The initial overture may therefore be rebuffed. This may lead to surprise and anger on the part of the subnormal person who may then retaliate aggressively.

(6) A few subnormal individuals suffer from types of disorder that make them subject to unpredictable explosive outbursts.

(7) Moderately subnormal persons may be easily goaded into uncharacteristic acts of violence; a colleague and I have described such a case elsewhere (McCulloch and Prins 1978: 171-72).

(8) The attitudes to legitimate expressions of sexuality of some mentally subnormal persons may be naive, primitive, or unrestrained. This may account in part for what appears to be a high proportion of sexual offences in the backgrounds of compulsorily detained mentally subnormal patients. Shapiro (1969) gives a figure as high as 35 per cent and Tutt

(1971) found that out of a sample of forty-four known delinquents admitted to the psychopathic unit of a subnormality hospital, 15.91 per cent had been convicted of a sex offence prior to admission. These figures are significantly higher than the figures for sex offenders in the general population (something in the order of 3 per cent).

(9) Mentally subnormal individuals may be particularly vulnerable to changes in their social environments that would not have the same impact upon their more well-endowed brethren. A moderately subnormal individual may manage perfectly well as long as he[2] has the support of parents or other relatives. Should this be disrupted by death or for any other reason, he may be particularly vulnerable to social pressures and stresses. He may then indulge in crime as a means of trying to resolve them.

THE BRIGHT DELINQUENT

Far less attention has been paid to the problems of the bright or gifted delinquent, though most of those who work with offenders are only too familiar with the difficulties of handling the very bright delinquent or the apparently highly intelligent and verbally facile 'con-man'. It has been suggested that bright delinquents may be more emotionally disturbed than delinquents of average or below average intelligence. In a study of 318 adolescent girl offenders, Cowie, Cowie, and Slater (1968) found that those girls with 'abnormal personalities' were of highest intelligence, those with psychiatric symptoms were of intermediate intelligence, and those with no psychiatric abnormality were of lowest intelligence. In a survey of boy delinquents, Gath, Tennent, and Pidduck (1970) examined fifty boys of superior intelligence (IQ score of 115 or above) detained in a London remand home and compared them with a control series of fifty boys of average intelligence matched for age, etc. The two groups were found to be largely similar in their social and

---

[2] Here, as elsewhere in this book, the term 'he' is used generically. This is meant as no mark of disrespect to female readers, but in my view is preferable to using the somewhat clumsy expression he/she. In any event, the majority of offenders are male, though as I shall show in Chapter 10 women may appear to be catching up with their male counterparts.

criminological characteristics, but not only was there a greater severity of psychiatric disorder found in the boys of higher intelligence, it also appeared that the offences committed by those boys were largely psychologically determined. (Gath, Tennent, and Pidduck's findings were much in line with an earlier study by Simmons (1956 and 1962), who reported on a group of highly intelligent boys detained in an approved school.) However, a three-year follow-up study by Tennent and Gath (1975) of the remand home sample reported upon above indicated that there were no significant differences between the two groups in recidivism, number or type of offence, or the way in which the offences committed in the follow-up period were dealt with. They concluded that high intelligence made no difference to prognosis, at least over a three-year follow-up period. In the light of the paucity of hard evidence on this question, we are forced to conclude that the relationship between high intelligence and crime is somewhat equivocal. However, a highly intelligent offender, young or old, may well be considered something of a threat to control or status by penal workers; because of this they may respond inappropriately to the offender's needs so that opportunities for trying to change attitudes may be missed.

## Deprivation of parental care and criminality

In Chapter 3 I referred to a number of studies that examined the wider social and neighbourhood environment and their association with crime. Such environments are of course made up of families in their various forms. The remainder of this chapter is devoted to a consideration of certain aspects of family life that may have a bearing upon the genesis of criminal behaviour, particularly in the young. In most western societies, there is an almost universal assumption that children need the continuing loving care of both their parents in order to fulfil themselves. Moreover, as Hawthorne has pointed out, 'one's family of origin is still, by definition, the one institutional affiliation one cannot choose; and it is moreover an affiliation which is almost certainly more difficult to renounce in later life than any other' (Hawthorne 1971: 876). However, the need for close parent–child relationships must to some extent be culturally determined as, in other so-called primitive societies, parenthood is shared quite successfully within the wider family network. Even in cultures nearer to our own, for example in the kibbutzim of Israel, children are said to be reared reasonably successfully in conditions of collective care. Because of the emphasis placed on the need for continuing loving care expressed in our culture, any events or circumstances which tend to disrupt this are seen as inimical to later satisfactory personal adjustment and development. However, it is perhaps as well to note that in a study by Douglas and Bromfield (1958) it was shown that one in three of a sample of 5380 children had been separated from their mothers for at least a week before the age of four and a half. Hawthorne (1971) suggests that about 10 per cent of people in Britain have been brought up in the absence of one or both natural parents at some time in childhood. We should also note that the family as a social institution has itself been subjected to much critical comment in recent years.

During the last fifty years or so a number of workers have concentrated on various aspects of deprivation of parental (particularly maternal) care. Quite early on in this century, paediatricians had pointed to the harmful effects of prolonged hospitalization on small children; in more recent years the work of the Robertsons has been most influential in this particular sphere (Robertson and Robertson 1967–72). During and since the Second World War a good deal of attention has been drawn to the plight of orphaned children and also to those deprived of a normal home life through such events as evacuation. Because of these earlier studies and the interest they aroused, a number of others were inspired which investigated such diverse phenomena as the possible relationship between childhood deprivations and delinquency, mental illness, and suicidal behaviour. In a comprehensive survey, Munro (1969) concluded that, in relation to psychiatric disorders, the association between deprivation in childhood and later disorder in adult life was by no means clear. This is partly because, until recently, little attempt has been made to distinguish sufficiently clearly between deprivation and separation and the varying degrees of severity of both these experiences.

VARIATIONS OF DEPRIVATION

Deprivation may vary both in intensity and in duration. Total lack of contact with other human beings coupled with sensory deprivation of other kinds has been shown to produce, under experimental conditions, phenomena akin to serious (though transient) mental disorder. History provides examples of children (such as Itard's Wild Boy of Aveyron) abandoned by their parents, reared subsequently by wild creatures, becoming themselves like animals quite unable to speak or to communicate in any human fashion. And there are on record other instances in which children have been locked away in rooms or cellars, sometimes for years, to emerge grossly retarded, both emotionally and intellectually. Subsequent attempts to socialize such children were only minimally successful. They are obviously gross examples, but their meaning is clear, namely, the vital importance of close personal communication and contact with others for the development of personality. Some confirmation of these views may be found in the results of various experiments investigating the attachment behaviour of young monkeys. The best known of these are the experiments conducted by Harlow (1958) and Harlow and Harlow (1965) with rhesus monkeys. Removed from their mothers at birth, these baby monkeys were provided with the choice of two varieties of model mothers, one that they could cling to and the other offering food from a bottle. In all cases the preferred model was the one more comfortable to cling to, rather than the one which provided food; moreover, Harlow also showed that young monkeys deprived of these clinging experiences developed serious disturbances in adult life, notably in the sphere of sexual behaviour.

Returning to the human species, we know that parents may be physically present, but not in spirit. A child does not have to be separated physically for it to be deprived. For example, there are many fathers, as Andry (1960) has shown, who may be present physically but absent emotionally, that is to say not involved in the upbringing of their children. This may be particularly serious in the case of sons. The reverse of this kind of situation can also be true: a parent may be dead, but his spirit kept alive successfully. In other cases, however, the departed parent may be for ever present, like some incubus from which the family never succeed in escaping. More recent evidence suggests that the death of a boy's father can be important in making him vulnerable to delinquency (Virkkunen 1976).

## DEPRIVATION AND DELINQUENCY

Interest in the connection between parental deprivation and delinquency received impetus from the pioneer work of John Bowlby. On the basis of research carried out on a small and highly selected group of young offenders in the late 1940s, Bowlby concluded that there was a strong case for believing that prolonged separation of a child from his mother or mother substitute at some time during the first five years of life was a predominant cause of the development of a delinquent character (Bowlby 1946 and 1951). Bowlby never made the more extravagant claims for his results that some of his critics have suggested he did. (See for example Wootton 1959 and Ainsworth 1962.) In his original 1946 study Bowlby stated that:

> 'we must remember that the cases studied in this investigation are not a typical sample of Court cases. They are a highly selected sample, referred to a Child Guidance Clinic because they were specially difficult or because the child was obviously not emotionally normal.' (Bowlby 1946: 53)

Bowlby has continued with his researches into parent–child relationships and in recent years has produced some rich clinical material concerning these, notably the development of the concept of attachment and loss. Not only do his researches have important implications for all human relationships, in addition they add considerably to our understanding of the problem of delinquency and other disorders. (See Bowlby 1979 for an up-to-date statement and summary of his thinking.) The importance of Bowlby's earlier work lay in the fact that it highlighted the needs of children receiving long-term care in large impersonal institutions. It is probably fair to say that his researches have had a greatly beneficial influence on child-care practice in this country. Subsequent researches have stressed the importance of a number of other inter-related factors in the child's experience of separation and/or deprivation. Some of these may be summarized as follows:

(1) The age of the child is of considerable importance. It is possible that children under the age of three years are the most vulnerable to separation experiences; some workers would put the beginning of this vulnerability period at six months. If separation occurs at such a tender age it is considered that a serious degree of deprivation may result.

(2) The nature of the relationship between the child and his parents before separation takes place is crucial. In general, the more secure the relationship has been, the less harmful will be the separation experience.

(3) If there has also been adequate preparation for the separation experience, then the harmful effects may be minimized.

(4) The qualities of the parent substitutes are crucial. If these are good, then lasting damage is less likely. The most harmful effects seem to have occurred when children have been separated from their parents because of a pre-existing stressful home environment, and when the children have subsequently been placed in institutions lacking in qualities of close personal care.

A number of workers have re-examined Bowlby's original hypothesis concerning criminality in some detail. Lewis (1954) studied 500 children received into a children's reception centre between 1947 and 1950. She considered that the evidence from her study was not sufficiently strong to support Bowlby's original hypothesis, and concluded that parental neglect (an important form of deprivation) was possibly of greater significance than the act or length of separation itself. And Naess (1959 and 1962) went so far as to suggest that mother-child separation as such was a minor causal factor in crime, but might be seen as part of the picture of an unstable family life. A study made by Little (1965) on a group of borstal boys who had suffered parental loss or separation sought to show whether or not they had a greater likelihood of reconviction; his results showed mainly a negative relationship. Grygier, Chesley, and Tuters (1970) carried out a further comprehensive study of the whole field. They stressed the importance of looking at both parents and their relationships with the child instead of examining the mother/child or father/child relationship separately. In an Australian study, Koller and Castanos (1970) examined two prison populations, one consisting of male prisoners with short-term sentences for less serious crimes, another consisting of male recidivists whose crimes were more serious, and a third group, drawn from the general population, serving as a control group. Their findings were of interest in that they tended to sum up and confirm much of the evidence already available in this field. Long-term prisoners, they discovered, had experienced parental loss in excess of their short-term fellows, but in fact both groups for one reason or another had experienced loss of both parents and were subsequently cared for in institutions.

The lessons to be learned from all these studies are fairly clear. First of all, family stress should be dealt with by methods of social intervention as early as possible so that the crisis of complete family breakdown is avoided. Secondly, if separation has to take place, it should be carefully prepared for if at all possible. Third, those families in which it has taken place should be helped back to normal functioning as soon as possible, and fourth, where long-term or total separation is inevitable, ways should be found of making the substitute care as personal as possible. Happily, the institutions and child-care services that were in existence at the time of Bowlby's early work have improved greatly, but even today there are deficiencies in these services, which give us no right at all to remain complacent (see Rutter 1972).

## Parental attitudes and crime

So far I have examined a number of specific factors and situations which may help to promote crime and delinquency, stressing the importance of the relationship between the growing child and his parents or parent substitutes. Psycho-analysts, for example Friedlander (1949), have pointed out that the infant develops a conscience (in Freudian terms the super-ego) by internalizing the demands of his parents, demands which he eventually comes to terms with, and which help him develop his own standards of right and wrong. It is thought by psycho-analysts that too strict an upbringing, with too rigid an enforcement of standards, may at a later stage result in a breakdown of control of one kind or another. Unfortunately, however, such a breakdown once it occurs is difficult to treat, as much of the development takes place at an unconscious level and is only made available for exploration through the special techniques of psycho-analytical psychotherapy (such as dream interpretation, free association of the patient's thoughts, and so on). I shall show later in this book that very few offenders respond to such classical psycho-analytical methods of treatment.

Other researchers have suggested that we do not need to look very deeply into the unconscious for those influences which may produce or be conducive to delinquency. Sears, Maccoby, and Levin (1957) suggested that mothers who used love-orientated methods of discipline rather than material or physical techniques produced relatively more children with high conscience formation. The Gluecks (1962), in summarizing their well-known long-term studies of delinquents, concluded quite positively that maternal love is a strong antidote to crime, and that paternal love, unless coupled with maternal neglect, tended to prevent it (see also Robins 1966). Scott (1954), on the basis of lengthy clinical experience of delinquents, suggested that too strict or too lax a form of discipline was probably less harmful than discipline which was inconsistent and which blew 'hot and cold'. He also suggested that even the most innocent maternal affection, if not complemented by paternal affection, might predispose to crime, particularly in adolescence.

Perhaps the most searching attempt in this country to understand the significance of family and personal factors in relation to youthful crime has been the long-term studies carried out by West and his colleague (West 1969, West and Farrington 1973, and West and Farrington 1977). This research (the Cambridge Study of Delinquent Development) set out to follow the lives of some 400 males born in the years 1951–54. The sample was drawn from a working-class area of London. At the start of the survey the boys attended six adjacent state primary schools, being between the ages of eight and nine. These boys had been followed up for some fourteen years and at the time of presentation of the last report were all past their twenty-first birthdays (West and Farrington 1977). This latest report 'shows the extent to which young adult delinquents differ from their social peers in personal circumstances, attitudes, and behaviour'

(West and Farrington 1977: 1). They found that delinquency in
the youths was related closely to convictions of their parents and
siblings. They also demonstrate how antisocial conduct may
well consist of a cluster of behaviours, such as gambling,
drinking, smoking, sexual promiscuity, driving offences, drug
use, and violence. The study also showed that the

> 'youths who acquire criminal convictions as young adults
> [or] display the greater variety of deviancy behaviour at age
> eighteen to nineteen tended to be badly behaved in their
> primary schools and to come from families with a constella-
> tion of adverse features such as poverty, large numbers of
> children, and poor parental supervision.'
>
> (West and Farrington 1977: 2)

(It is of interest to compare this finding with those of Power
and his colleagues – see Chapter 3.)

Perhaps more importantly in the context of the arguments
being put forward in this chapter, West and Farrington concluded that their

> 'findings harmonize most readily with those criminological
> theories that attribute importance to individual tempera-
> ment and individual social learning. They do not negate, but
> they do not lend much support to, those theoretical models
> which neglect individual character and circumstances in
> favour of exclusive concentration upon the interplay of social
> forces.'
>
> (West and Farrington 1977: 159)

This seems a convenient point to make brief reference to the
question of social learning and delinquent behaviour. I deal
with it briefly here as I shall return to it in Chapter 11 when I
discuss the management of offenders. For many years, there has
been a considerable degree of interest in the manner in which
socialization occurs (Danziger 1971) and the extent to which
bad habits of various kinds may be learned. Whereas psycho-
analysts postulate that behaviour is more often than not the
product of forces operating at an unconscious level, learning
theorists and behavioural psychologists suggest that most forms
of behaviour may be seen as conscious and learned responses to
external stimuli. (See for example Trasler 1962 and 1979.)
Eysenck (1977) has undertaken a number of research studies

into the application of theories of personality and learning to criminality. His views on the genesis of criminality may be summarized rather baldly and over-simply as follows. First, a propensity to crime, he suggests, is universal, but is held in check by a given individual's conscience. (Studies of the dark or hidden area of crime – see Chapter 2 – would tend to support this view of crime's universality.) Second, this conscience is essentially a generalized set of conditioned responses built up during childhood and adolescence. Third, such a conscience might be expected to be under-developed, either because of failure of social and family conditions to provide the proper means of developing it, or, through innate (inborn) weakness of the person concerned in the development of conditioned responses. (See the earlier reference to psychopathic personality disorder.) Eysenck claims, on the basis of empirical research studies, that extraverted people (i.e., those who are more outgoing, sociable, and concerned more with action than with feeling) tend to condition less well than introverted ones. (Introverts are said to be cautious, reflective, and introspective.) Eysenck suggests on the basis of this evidence that extraverts are thus more likely to behave in an antisocial fashion. From other empirical evidence he also suggests that a number of delinquents also exhibit high degrees of neuroticism and anxiety as measured on specially constructed tests.

Much of Eysenck's work is theoretically attractive and has useful practical implications. However, some have been critical of it for not defining accurately enough what is meant by the terms 'criminal', 'delinquent', 'law-breaker', 'moral imbecile', and 'psychopath', because he uses such terms with a great deal of inter-changeability. A further criticism that might be made of his views is that they tend to over-emphasize fixed reactions to given stimuli and thus omit the importance of the finer and more subtle responses that individuals make to stressful situations. In an interesting paper Woodmansey (1971) suggests an approach which seems to bring together the apparently conflicting views of the psycho-analysts and the learning theorists. He considers that the essence of many delinquents' condition is that of hostility to other people. If for any length of time a child or young person has to endure the real or imagined hostility of adults, he may come to believe that others are against him and turn delinquent. Woodmansey's approach has very important implications for treatment, as many delinquents do in fact appear to be very hostile towards those who seek to control or help them. I shall refer to this matter again in Chapter 11.

## Conclusions

I conclude by emphasizing once again that the subject matter of Chapters 3, 4, and 5 should be read as part of a whole, since the material they contain overlaps and the classification I have adopted is somewhat arbitrary. West sums up the need for a multi-disciplinary perspective very usefully.

'The most glaring division occurs between those who regard juvenile misbehaviour as a sign of personal maladjustment, and those who see it as a normal and natural response to contemporary social circumstances. The former theorists tend to look for defect either in the individual delinquent himself (as in the theory that much restlessness and misconduct results from sub-clinical brain damage) or in the individual home (as in the theory that inadequate maternal care in the earliest formative years leads to permanent distortion of character). The social theorists, on the other hand, point to extraneous influences, such as the burgeoning of the penal bureaucracy with its urge to apply labels, controls and statistics to naughty boys, or the effect of increased leisure in affording time for mischief, or the special opportunities and temptations to steal in a newly affluent, money-mad society. *The truth cannot lie in one or other, but rather in various combinations and interactions of both personal and social influences* [my italics], but the question of the relative importance of these contributory elements provides scope for controversy, and hence for investigation.'                                    (West 1969: 1)

## References

Ainsworth, M.D.S. (1962) The Effects of Maternal Deprivation: A Review of Findings and Controversy in the Context of Research Strategy. In *WHO Public Health Papers* No. 14. Geneva: World Health Organisation.

Andry, R.G. (1960) *Delinquency and Parental Pathology*. London: Methuen.

Bowlby, J. (1946) *Forty-Four Juvenile Thieves: Their Characters and Home-Life*. London: Baillière, Tindall and Cox.

—— (1951) *Maternal Care and Mental Health*. Monograph Series No. 2. Geneva: World Health Organisation.

—— (1979) *The Making and Breaking of Affectional Bonds*. London: Tavistock Publications.

Cleckley, H. (1976) *The Mask of Sanity* (fifth edition). St Louis: The C.V. Mosby Co.

Cowie, J., Cowie, V., and Slater, E. (1968) *Delinquency in Girls*. London: Heinemann.

Danziger, K. (1971) *Socialization*. Harmondsworth: Penguin Books.

Douglas, J.M.B. and Bromfield, J.M. (1958) *Children Under Five*. London: Allen and Unwin.

Eysenck, H.J. (1977) *Crime and Personality* (revised edition). St Albans: Paladin.

Friedlander, K. (1949) *The Psychoanalytical Approach to Juvenile Delinquency*. London: Routledge and Kegan Paul.

Gath, D., Tennent, G., and Pidduck, R. (1970) Psychiatric and Social Characteristics of Bright Delinquents. *British Journal of Psychiatry* **116**: 151–60.

Gibson, H.B. and West, D.J. (1970) Social and Intellectual Handicaps as Precursors of Early Delinquency. *British Journal of Criminology* **10**: 212–32.

Glueck, S. and Glueck, E. (1962) *Family Environment and Delinquency*. London: Routledge and Kegan Paul.

Gough, H.G. (1956) A Sociological Study of Psychopathy. In A.M. Rose (ed.) *Mental Health and Mental Disorder*. London: Routledge and Kegan Paul.

Grygier, T., Chesley, J., and Tuters, E.W. (1970) Parental Deprivation: A Study of Delinquent Children. *British Journal of Criminology* **9**: 209–53.

Hare, R.D. and Schalling, D. (1978) *Psychopathic Behaviour: Approaches to Research*. London: John Wiley.

Harlow, H.F. (1958) The Nature of Love. *American Psychologist* **13**: 673–85.

Harlow, H.F. and Harlow, M.R. (1965) The Affectional Systems. In A.M. Schrier, H.F. Harlow, and F. Stollnitz (eds)

*Behaviour of Non-Human Primates* (Volume 2). New York and London: Academic Press.

Haward, L.R.C. (1981) *Forensic Psychology*. London: Batsford Academic and Educational Ltd.

Hawthorne, G. (1971) A Sociological Portrait: Family Background. *New Society* 4.11.71: 876–79.

Kahn, J.H. (1971) Uses and Abuses of Child Psychiatry: Problems of Diagnosis and Treatment of Psychiatric Disorders. *British Journal of Medical Psychology* **44**: 229–38.

Koller, K.M. and Castanos, J.M. (1970) Family Background in Prison Groups: A Comparative Study of Parental Deprivation. *British Journal of Psychiatry* **117**: 371–80.

Lewis, H. (1954) *Deprived Children*. Oxford: Oxford University Press.

Little, A. (1965) Parental Deprivation, Separation and Crime: A Test on Adolescent Recidivists. *British Journal of Criminology* **5**: 419–30.

McCulloch, J.W. and Prins, H.A. (1978) *Signs of Stress: The Social Problems of Psychiatric Illness*. London: Woburn Press.

Munro, A. (1969) The Theoretical Importance of Parental Deprivation in the Aetiology of Psychiatric Illness: A Critical Review. *Journal of Applied Social Studies* **1**: 81–92.

Naess, S. (1959) Mother Child Separation and Delinquency. *British Journal of Delinquency* **X**: 22–35.

—— (1962) Mother Separation and Delinquency: Further Evidence. *British Journal of Criminology* **2**: 361–73.

Prins, H.A. (1975) Psychiatric Services and the Magistrates' and Juvenile Courts. *British Journal of Criminology* **15**: 315–32.

—— (1976) Remands for Psychiatric Reports. *Medicine, Science and the Law* **16**: 129–38.

—— (1980) *Offenders, Deviants, or Patients? An Introduction to the Study of Socio-Forensic Problems*. London: Tavistock Publications.

Robertson, J. and Robertson, J. (1967–72) *Young Children in Brief Separation*. (Film Series) London: Tavistock Institute of Human Relations.

Robins, L. (1966) *Deviant Children Grown Up: A Sociological and Psychiatric Study of Sociopathic Personality*. Baltimore: The Williams and Wilkins Co.

Rutter, M. (1972) *Maternal Deprivation Reassessed*. Harmondsworth: Penguin Books.

Scott, P.D. (1954) In N. East (ed.) *The Roots of Crime*. London: Butterworths.

—— (1969) Crime and Delinquency. *British Medical Journal* **1**: 424–26.

Sears, R.R., Maccoby, E.E., and Levin, H. (1957) *Patterns of Child Rearing*. Evanston: Row Paterson and Co.

Shapiro, A. (1969) Delinquent and Disturbed Behaviour Within the Field of Mental Deficiency. In A.V.S. De Rueck and R. Porter (eds) *The Mentally Abnormal Offender*. London: J. and A. Churchill (for CIBA Foundation).

Simmons, M.M. (1956) Intelligent Delinquents. *Times Educational Supplement* March 2.

—— (1962) Symposium on Highly Intelligent Children. *Times Educational Supplement* January 26.

Sparks, R.F. (1966) The Decision to Remand for Mental Examination. *British Journal of Criminology* **6**: 6–26.

Tennent, G. and Gath, D. (1975) Bright Delinquents: A Three Year Follow-up Study. *British Journal of Criminology* **15**: 386–90.

Trasler, G. (1962) *The Explanation of Criminality*. London: Routledge and Kegan Paul.

—— (1979) Delinquency, Recidivism and Desistance. *British Journal of Criminology* **19**: 314–32.

Tutt, N. (1971) The Subnormal Offender. *British Journal of Mental Subnormality* **17**: 42–7.

Virkkunen, M. (1976) Parental Deprivation and Recidivism in Juvenile Delinquents. *British Journal of Criminology* **16**: 378–84.

Weber, H. (1953) The 'Borderline Defective' Delinquent. *British Journal of Delinquency* **3**: 173–84.

West, D.J. (1965) *Murder Followed by Suicide*. London: Heinemann.

—— (1969) *Present Conduct and Future Delinquency*. London: Heinemann Educational Books.

—— (1980) The Clinical Approach to Criminology. *Psychological Medicine* **10**: 619–32.

West, D.J. and Farrington, D.P. (1973) *Who Becomes Delinquent?* London: Heinemann Educational Books.

—— (1977) *The Delinquent Way of Life*. London: Heinemann Educational Books.

Woodmansey, A.C. (1971) Understanding Delinquency. *British Journal of Criminology* **11**: 155–66.

Woodward, M. (1955) The Role of Low Intelligence in Delinquency. *British Journal of Delinquency* **VI**: 281–303.

Wootton, B. (1959) *Social Science and Social Pathology*. London: Allen and Unwin.

FURTHER READING

*Current thinking and progress in psychiatry is well reviewed in:*

Clare, A. (1980) *Psychiatry in Dissent. Controversial Issues in Thought and Practice* (second edition). London: Tavistock Publications.

Wing, J.K. (1978) *Reasoning about Madness*. Oxford: Oxford University Press.

*Those wishing to seek a more basic introduction to psychiatry should consult:*

Fish, F.J. (1978) *An Outline of Psychiatry for Students and Practitioners* (third edition) (edited by Max Hamilton). Bristol: John Wright.

Rees, W.L. (1976) *A Short Text-book of Psychiatry* (second edition). London: Hodder and Stoughton.

*On mental subnormality see:*

Ward-Heaton, W.A. (1977) *Left Behind: A Study of Mental Handicap*. Plymouth: Macdonald and Evans.

*On Psychiatry and Crime more generally see:*

Guze, S.B. (1976) *Criminality and Psychiatric Disorders*. Oxford: Oxford University Press.

Macdonald, J.M. (1969) *Psychiatry and the Criminal* (second edition). Illinois: Charles Thomas.

Trick, K.L.K. and Tennent, T.G. (1981) *Forensic Psychiatry: An Introductory Text*. London: Pitman.

*For a psychological approach to criminality see:*
Feldman, M.P. (1977) *Criminal Behaviour: A Psychological Analysis.* London: Wiley.

*Useful Journals*
In addition to the journals cited in the references to Chapters 4 and 5, the following frequently carry articles dealing with the matters discussed in these two chapters:
*British Journal of Medical Psychology, International Journal of Law and Psychiatry, International Journal of Offender Therapy and Comparative Criminology, Howard Journal of Penology and Crime Prevention, Journal of Child Psychology and Psychiatry.*

# PART THREE
# Methods of Disposal

**Introductory note to Part Three**

This book's division into four parts is to some extent arbitrary; it is merely used as a device to clarify the presentation of the subject matter and to facilitate its assimilation. However, in adopting this somewhat artificial device there is the danger that the material may seem to fall into rather neat, water-tight compartments. Much of the material discussed in Part Three of this book will be influenced by many of the issues discussed in Parts One and Two. Because it is only possible to provide a somewhat sketchy account of some aspects of the functioning of the courts and the judicial and penal systems, readers may lose sight of the fact that the operation of such systems is influenced by many of the attitudes and prejudices referred to in Parts One and Two. This has become such an important area of concern in recent years that a new specialist subject area has been developed to encompass it, namely the discipline of the sociology of law. Because it would be tedious to repeat the need to maintain these links in the text that follows, readers are alerted to its importance here.

# CHAPTER SIX

## *The court system and the sentencing process*

Vengeance is mine saith the Lord. This means
that it is not the Lord Chief Justice's.
GEORGE BERNARD SHAW

In this chapter, I consider briefly the manner in which cases
come before the criminal courts and the procedures adopted for
dealing with them. (Penalties for adult offenders are dealt with
in Chapter 7.) The machinery of justice is a very complex
subject and those wishing to examine it in more depth should
consult Jackson's comprehensive work *The Machinery of Justice in
England* (1977).

In theory, anyone can launch a criminal prosecution, but this
rarely happens in practice. Indeed, there are very many situations in which prosecutions can only be launched with the
approval of the Attorney-General, the Director of Public Prosecutions, or, in cases such as criminal libel, a judge. In practice
almost all prosecutions are carried out by the police on behalf of
the public. There are, however, certain other instances in which
specially designated officials may also conduct prosecutions,
officers of the NSPCC, for example, who may prosecute neglect-
ful parents, or officials of central government departments such
as the DHSS, Customs and Excise, Inland Revenue, or the
Local Authorities. In recent years considerable dissatisfaction
has been expressed with the system whereby the police act as
prosecutors. Many people think that it is unsatisfactory that the
authority responsible for investigating a case – namely the
police – should also be responsible for its prosecution. In the
light of this feeling and other evidence, the *Royal Commission on*

*Criminal Procedure* (1981) recommended that a statutory local prosecuting service should be established for all police force areas in England and Wales. This would be in line with the system that obtains in Scotland, where police and prosecution powers are split and prosecution lies in the hands of a separate official – the Procurator Fiscal.

We must now turn to some further aspects of crime classification, already referred to in Chapters 1 and 2. I noted in that earlier discussion that the somewhat anachronistic distinction between felonies and misdemeanours had been abandoned and replaced (through the Criminal Law Act 1967) by a new distinction, namely that of *arrestable* and *non-arrestable* offences. In the case of *arrestable* offences, police constables and (in theory) members of the public have certain powers of arrest and search without a warrant. Arrestable offences are also those for which the sentence is fixed by law (for example, murder) or for which a person, not previously convicted, may in most cases be sentenced to imprisonment for five years or more. We should also note that under the terms of the Theft Act 1968 an offence may be declared by statute to be arrestable, although the maximum period is less than five years. In the case of *non-arrestable* offences, a warrant for arrest is required. In order to obtain a warrant, an 'information', as it is called, has to be sworn on oath before a magistrate. To obtain a summons (which is the more usual way of bringing an accused person before a court) an 'information' must still be made out ('laid') although it does not have to be on oath.

From the point of view of court and sentencing procedures and the different penalties available to courts, a further threefold classification of offences must now be mentioned; this was given effect in the Criminal Law Act 1977 (Section 14). This classification consists of: (a) *offences triable summarily only*; (b) *offences triable only on indictment*; (c) *offences triable either way*.

In general, *offences triable summarily only* consist of the less serious crimes, which can only be dealt with in the Magistrates' Courts. However, this class also includes some offences that were previously triable summarily *or* on indictment; the reason for the introduction of this new facility was to ease some of the heavy workload of the Crown Court.

*Offences triable only on indictment* include all the most serious offences against the person, such as murder and serious sexual attacks, certain very serious theft, forgery, manslaughter offences, and certain other offences in which the complex nature of the circumstances of the case makes it unsuitable for summary trial. In such cases the magistrates sit as 'examining justices' and, if they find a case to answer by the accused, they must commit to the Crown Court.

*Offences triable either way* (in the past sometimes known as 'hybrid' offences) consist of certain offences in which the defendant may exercise a right to be tried at the Crown Court if he so wishes. In the case of offences triable either way, it is for the court to decide upon the most suitable form of trial, having regard to the circumstances of the case and after having heard the views of the accused and the prosecution. If the court decides that summary trial of the case is the more suitable, it must inform the accused of his right to jury trial and only proceed to summary trial if the accused consents. Under this new classification Magistrates' Courts are also empowered to deal with certain other cases, such as bigamy and sexual intercourse with a girl under sixteen, which were formerly triable only on indictment.

## The Magistrates' Courts

About 98 per cent of all criminal cases begin and end in the Magistrates' Courts. These courts (of whom some 1000 or more may be in session on any given day) also deal with a substantial amount of *civil* business, for example, matrimonial and affiliation cases, consent to marry, and rate arrears. The magistracy was first established as a local institution by the Justices of the Peace Act 1361, and various further enactments have extended and modified its functions over the past 600 years. Under the provisions of the Justices of the Peace Act 1949, the responsibility for the administration of the magistracy and for training was given over to local Magistrates' Courts Committees, national oversight being vested in the Lord Chancellor's Department. Some people take the view that this essentially local service should be more firmly controlled by a central organization which would be responsible not only for the organization of Magistrates' Courts throughout the country, but also for the appointment of Magistrates' Clerks and other court officers. Most Magistrates' Courts are presided over by at least two (and preferably three) magistrates.[1]

Lay (i.e. non-legally qualified) magistrates, of whom there are over 20,000 in this country, are appointed by the Lord Chancellor on the recommendation of local committees whose constitution is customarily kept secret, though their workings are now becoming more open to inspection and comment. The general aim is to appoint persons who are representative of the various sections and interests of the local community. Some areas now solicit candidature for magisterial office through press advertisements. The English system of lay magistracy has much to commend it. Not only is it a way of involving members of the local community in the administration of justice, but it appears to be moderately efficient and it is also cheap. Its greatest disadvantage is that it makes considerable demands upon the time of ordinary citizens. Because of this the pool of suitable people tends to be a small one, usually more heavily weighted with people from the upper classes. Baldwin has carried out a number of studies into the social composition and training of the magistracy (Baldwin 1974, 1975, and 1976). In his study of their social composition he discovered that some 35.7 per cent of his sample were women, which was a proportion higher than the 30 per cent noted by Hood (1972). Baldwin found that the age of recruitment was coming down but that it was still high. Not one in the sample of 255 he studied was under thirty on appointment and fewer than one in six were under forty. He also found that the professional and managerial groups still tended to be over-represented in appointments. There seemed to be a marked lack of working-class representation on the bench, though there had been some increase in the appointment of salaried workers. Baldwin concluded that 'It is no surprise to find that the magistracy is not representative in any real sense of the wider community, although it is disturbing to find that patterns of selection in the recent past have not succeeded in affecting this situation' (Baldwin 1976: 14).

It is understandable therefore that many working-class offenders and those from ethnic minority groups may feel, because of

[1] Some of the larger cities have full-time stipendiary magistrates who are legally qualified. Currently there are about fifty of them.

this implicit distancing, that their problems and points of view are not understood. Socio-legal commentators such as Dell (1970) and Carlen (1976 a and b) suggest that defendants find it frustrating that 'at the very times when they are both subject to and object of its rules, a fog of mystification permeates the court' (Carlen 1976 (a): 54). Earlier studies of the perceptions of children and their parents of the procedures in the juvenile courts are given confirmation by these more recent conclusions (Younghusband 1957, Scott 1959, and Voelcker 1960). In the courts presided over by lay magistrates, the Magistrates' Clerk is a key figure; he is responsible for guiding the lay justices on questions of law and practice, but not on questions of guilt or innocence.

## Juvenile Courts

The Juvenile Court is of much more recent origin. It was introduced by statute in 1908, though there had been some experimental Juvenile Courts before then (Cavanagh 1967). The rules governing their procedure have been modified by various enactments over the years. They differ from Magistrates' Courts in that members of the public are not allowed to be present unless directly involved in the case, there are restrictions on the publication of the names of those appearing before the court, and the procedure is less formal than in the Magistrates' Courts. The Juvenile Courts may be said to have a threefold jurisdiction. First, they deal with criminal matters, that is, the hearing and determination of criminal offences committed by children and young persons. Second, they hear non-criminal matters, that is, cases in which offences have been committed against children and young persons or in which they have been alleged to be in need of care, protection, or control. Third, they deal with applications for the adoption of children (such cases may also be dealt with in the County Court and in the High Court). Juvenile Court magistrates outside the metropolitan area of London are selected from amongst the ordinary benches of magistrates, more usually because of their special experience of or interest in the needs of children. In London they are nominated by the Lord Chancellor. In the last ten years or so, the procedures for bringing children and young persons before the courts, and the measures available for dealing with them, have undergone substantial changes (see Chapter 8).

## Courts of higher jurisdiction

The higher courts have their origins in the Middle Ages. Before the Courts Act 1971, they were known as Quarter Sessions and Assizes. Now known as the Crown Court, it deals with all the more serious cases.[2] The Crown Court also deals with cases on appeal from the Magistrates' Courts and with persons sent for sentence from these courts. For administrative purposes, the Crown Court is divided into six circuits and the judges of the Crown Court consist of: (a) High Court Judges (the red-robed judges), who hear the most serious cases such as murder, and other serious offences against the person and against property; (b) Circuit Judges; (c) Recorders. The two latter categories deal with the less serious cases. The Crown Court sits in three 'tiers', each tier dealing with a different type of criminal business. The ancient offices of Clerk of Assize and Clerk of the Peace have been replaced by a group of permanent administrators.

Appeals from the Crown Court are generally heard in the Court of Appeal (Criminal Division). In a case involving a point of law of general public importance, appeal can be made to the House of Lords. More exceptionally, the Sovereign may exercise the Prerogative of Mercy acting upon the advice of the Home Secretary. It is important to note that in this country, unlike some others, there is no Ministry of Justice as such, but rather a division between the judiciary and the executive, with the latter controlling and implementing the penal system. On the one hand, the office of Lord Chancellor is a political appointment, a new appointment being made with every change of government, whereas on the other hand the Judges hold non-political and permanent appointments. Although there may appear from time to time to be some confusion as to the respective functions of the Lord Chancellor and that of the Home Secretary as Minister responsible for penal measures, every effort is made to ensure that political influence has no part to play in the way that justice is administered.

[2] The use of the singular noun is strictly correct. The Courts Act 1971 established a single Crown Court which would sit in three tiers in various parts of the country.

## Relationships between the lower and higher courts

We have already seen that about 98 per cent of criminal business begins and ends in the Magistrates' Courts, the remaining two per cent being passed on from there to the higher courts – apart from very exceptional instances of a direct committal of a defendant for trial on the presentation of a private 'Bill of Indictment'. Until the passing of the Criminal Law Act 1977, it was also possible for a person to be committed for trial on a coroner's warrant.

Committal proceedings from the Magistrates' Court to the Crown Court are of two kinds: committal for trial and committal for sentence. The former is used either when the accused may only be tried by the higher court, or when he has elected to be tried there. As already noted, in either of these events the magistrates will sit as 'examining justices', and may only commit for trial if they find that the prosecution has made out a *prima facie* case that should be enquired into at the higher court. In practice, magistrates seem almost invariably to find that such a case has been made out.

In cases of committal for sentence the procedure is rather different. A Magistrates' Court may send for sentence an offender convicted by them of an indictable offence but for whom they feel their powers of punishment are insufficient. In practice, they commit the offender to the most convenient sitting of the Crown Court for sentence. The higher court is not bound by law to pass a heavier sentence, and in some cases may in fact deal more leniently with the defendant than the magistrates had been minded to do.

The relationships between the various criminal courts are illustrated in greatly simplified form in *Figure 6(1)*.

## The sentencing process

In the past, sentencing was a comparatively simple exercise. 'The primary objective was to fix a sentence proportionate to the offender's culpability, and the procedure has been loosely described as the "tariff system"' (Streatfeild Report 1961: 257). However, over the years, as we saw in Chapters 4 and 5, regard has increased for the offender as a person and account has been

*Figure 6(1)*    The system of criminal courts (greatly simplified)

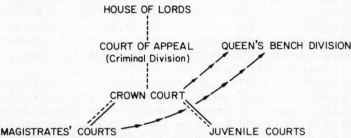

THE SOVEREIGN
(Prerogative of Mercy)*

HOUSE OF LORDS

COURT OF APPEAL          QUEEN'S BENCH DIVISION
(Criminal Division)

CROWN COURT

MAGISTRATES' COURTS                    JUVENILE COURTS

\* Not strictly part of the court system or sentencing process, but inserted here
for completeness.

*Notes to Figure 6(1)*

(a)  Broken line = Channel of Appeal.
(b)  Unbroken line = Committal for trial or for sentence.
(c)  Arrowed line = appeal by way of 'case stated' on a point of law.
(d)  For the sake of simplicity the figure does not include Coroners' Courts or
     Courts Martial. The office of coroner is a very ancient one and coroners
     have wide powers. Their functions however are largely inquisitorial in
     nature. Courts Martial may deal with criminal offences committed by
     members of the Armed Forces and offences against service order and
     discipline. There is also a Courts Martial Appeal Court which has powers
     generally similar to those of the Court of Appeal (Criminal Division).
(e)  Forms of address: High Court and other circuit judges are addressed as 'My
     Lord'; recorders generally as 'Sir'; magistrates as 'Your worship(s)', or 'Sir'
     or 'Madam'.

taken increasingly of situational stresses which might have an
important bearing upon his criminality. Sentencing has therefore become a much more complicated task, with the courts now
seeking a wide range of information about offenders that will
help them in the difficult task of reconciling the conflicting aims
of retribution, reformation (rehabilitation), and deterrence.

### FACTORS WHICH MAY INFLUENCE THE COURT IN
### DETERMINING SENTENCE

There are a wide range of factors which will influence courts in
their sentencing decisions. Sentencers may feel that they should

make some attempt to pass comparable sentences for like offences, such as, for example, two different kinds of infringement of the motoring regulations, so that some kind of average sentence is passed. It is obvious, however, that this will not always be possible. In cases of violence, for example, the courts in determining sentences will need to bear in mind the actual harm done to the victim and the nature of his relationship with the offender, particularly where it is thought there may have been a degree of provocation. Age is another important factor – in general, special consideration is given to very young and to elderly offenders – as is the defendant's way of life and criminal history and, less frequently, his mental state. (The latter is the subject of special consideration in Chapter 9.) The offender's attitude to his crime, as shown before and during the court hearing, often plays a significant part in influencing the court's decision, as does the attitude of the victim (for example the wife who enters a plea for mercy for the husband who has violently assaulted her in a fit of jealous rage).

The attitudes of sentencers are less open to public scrutiny, but it is a well-known fact that some may have 'blind spots' and biases concerning certain types of offence, so that their sentences may tend to err either on the side of too great leniency or of severity. And finally of course there is the public interest, which may demand exemplary punishment transcending the interests and welfare of the individual offender, as for instance with the lengthy sentences handed out in the famous Notting Hill 'race riot' case some years ago. However, there is no conclusive evidence that exemplary punishments necessarily deter others. Reasons other than the imposition of condign punishment may influence the outcome. For example, a few years ago there was a spate of telephone-kiosk vandalism in Birmingham. When some of the accused were brought to trial and sentenced, the Recorder passed very heavy sentences. Within a short time it was reported that the vandalism had ceased and it was automatically assumed that this could be explained by the heavy penalties handed down. In point of fact, further investigation revealed that the Post Office authorities had installed new equipment that was very hard to vandalize, and it seemed just as likely that this had brought about the reduction of these offences.

Judges will sometimes consider that a severe sentence is

required in a case not necessarily involving questions of public order and safety. Some years ago, a good deal of interest was aroused by the passing of a sentence of three years' imprisonment on a young woman who stole another's baby. When the case was heard in the Court of Appeal, the Lord Chief Justice, the late Lord Widgery, said:

> 'If one sought to measure the punishment by the anguish which she (the defendant) caused to the child's parents one could not say that three years was excessive . . . if one sought to measure the sentence by the public mischief caused – 200 Police Officers searching through 2500 houses – again one would say that three years is not too much.'
>
> (*The Guardian*, 4 December 1971)

The Lord Chief Justice admitted that he and his colleagues had found it a very sad and distressing case (the court had evidence before it which indicated that the defendant had been the subject of very considerable emotional upset when she took the child) and that they had been 'much moved by what had been said on [her] behalf'. Accordingly, they felt able to reduce the sentence of three years to twenty-one months. A leading article, commenting on the case, took the view that '[this] prison sentence nevertheless remains a measure of retribution . . . in the view of the Appeal Court, society may exact vengeance on the wrong-doer by punishment' (*The Guardian*, 4 December 1971). The article concluded that 'retribution unaccompanied by constructive purpose is sadly out of key with current thinking in penology'. This admittedly fairly exceptional case illustrates very clearly the constraints and influences upon sentencers when they have to reconcile the conflicting aims of punishment. I now consider some of the ways in which they may be aided in this difficult task.

INFORMATION FOR SENTENCERS

In 1961, a Departmental Committee (under the chairmanship of Mr Justice Streatfeild) produced a report on the 'Business of the Criminal Courts' (Streatfeild Report 1961). The Committee made a number of recommendations for improving the quantity and quality of information that should be made available to the higher courts, suggesting also that their recommendations could apply to the lower courts. Probation officers, they said, should be able to make social enquiries about accused persons who were to appear before the (then) Quarter Sessions or Assize Courts, even though they had not yet been convicted, provided that the accused person did not object. The Committee also recommended that such enquiries should always be made if: (a) the accused was under thirty; or (b) he had recently been in touch with the probation service; or (c) he had not been previously convicted.

These and certain other recommendations (concerning the availability of reports from the medical profession and from prison establishments) were accepted, and brought into effect in August 1963. With the implementation of the Criminal Justice Act 1967 (Section 57) they were extended to the Magistrates' Courts. The Home Secretary now has power through the provisions of the Powers of Criminal Courts Act 1973 (Section 45) to make it compulsory to ask for such reports, but to date he has chosen to rely upon exhortations through various Home Office circulars. All courts are now urged to obtain a social enquiry report in the following cases:

(1) Before a sentence of detention in a Detention Centre is passed.
(2) Before imposing a sentence of borstal training.
(3) Before imposing a sentence of imprisonment of two years or less, or a suspended sentence on an offender who has not received a previous sentence of imprisonment or borstal training.
(4) Before passing any sentence of imprisonment on a woman.
(5) In cases of men over the age of thirty who have one or more previous convictions, but who have not received a previous custodial sentence, and for whom the court has in mind a sentence of two years' imprisonment or less.
(6) In cases of women over the age of thirty who have one or more previous convictions for an offence punishable with imprisonment.

It is also urged that probation reports be asked for before a probation order is made and before an offender is committed to the Crown Court for sentence. Specific provision is made in the

Powers of Criminal Courts Act 1973 (Sections 19 and 20) that a probation officer's report *must* be obtained before a person aged under twenty-one is sentenced to imprisonment and before a person over that age is sentenced to imprisonment for the first time.

We should note in passing that in the Juvenile Court there is an obligation to obtain social enquiry reports in all except trivial cases (Children and Young Persons Act 1969).

These recommendations and instructions place a considerable burden on the probation and after-care service. In 1974, the service provided just under 220,000 social enquiries to the criminal courts in England and Wales (Home Office 1976). Some of the practical aspects concerning the presentation of such reports can best be shown by the use of two case illustrations. I shall then consider some criminological and penological implications.

### Case illustrations

*Case 1* illustrates the procedure in the higher court.

Brown, aged twenty-six, was committed for trial at the Crown Court charged with wounding with intent to do grievous bodily harm. He had not previously been convicted and was represented by counsel. The probation officer had ascertained that he was pleading not guilty to the major charge, but would, if the prosecution accepted the plea, plead guilty to a lesser charge of causing grievous bodily harm (without intent). Neither the accused nor his counsel objected to the probation officer making enquiries, and he proceeded accordingly. In the course of his enquiries, in which he interviewed both the defendant (who was on bail) and his wife, it emerged that Brown was a young married man of good background. Having drunk more than was good for him, he got into an argument with some of his mates. A fight ensued in which the defendant picked up a bottle (he said in self-defence) and attacked the victim about the head. As he was a man not used to drinking large quantities of alcohol, in a good job, and was well thought of by his employers, when his case came up before the Crown Court a plea of guilty to the lesser charge was accepted. Following a brief outline of the facts, a detective officer gave the court the defendant's 'antecedents', consisting of a statement about his employment, wages, record at work, reasons for leaving, and absence of previous convictions. The defending counsel then drew the attention of the judge to the report from the probation officer.

It should be emphasized that the social enquiry report is the property of the court, but a copy of any such report (or any other) before a Magistrates' or a higher Court must be made available to the defendant or his counsel (Powers of Criminal Courts Act 1973, Section 46). The provisions in the Juvenile Court are somewhat different (see Chapter 8).

It is for the court to decide whether or not the probation officer will be called, though the court will normally accede to such a request from defending counsel. The probation officer will, if called, be asked to comment on oath on his report, or to answer specific questions from either counsel or the judge. Since what he has to say comes after conviction and is not strictly evidence, he may also include opinion. The court may for example require further information from the probation officer as to his impressions of the defendant's capacities to avoid this kind of occurrence in future, taking into account the impression already gained from the officer's interviewing of both the defendant and his wife. The officer may or may not have made a fairly specific recommendation as to what the disposal might be, though it is entirely for the court to decide whether to accept it or not. The Streatfeild Committee (para. 346) advocated that probation officers should be able to make recommendations in their reports, and this has also been the view of the Home Office as expressed in various circulars. On the basis of all the facts before the court, including the background information provided by the probation officer, in this case the judge decided that a monetary penalty would suffice and imposed a fine of £100.00. He told the defendant that being in drink was no excuse for unlawful conduct but, as his previous record and employment history were good, a fairly stiff monetary penalty would seem to be adequate.

*Case 2* illustrates the procedure in the lower court.

Jones, aged eighteen, appeared before a Magistrates' Court and pleaded guilty to taking and driving away a motor cycle without authority. He had one previous finding of guilt (at

sixteen) for a similar offence when he was fined £10.00. The
magistrates adjourned the case for three weeks for a probation
officer's social enquiry report.[3] The report revealed that Jones
came from an outwardly respectable home but that there had
been considerable tension between father and son, which the
probation officer considered had led Jones to find unlawful
outlets for expressing his hostility towards figures in authority.
The officer considered that Jones, an intelligent young man,
had some insight into his difficulties. He also thought that a
better understanding might be achieved between father and son
if each of them had the chance of discussing their attitudes with
an independent person who could take a more objective view of
their problems. He therefore recommended that the court might
care to make a probation order. This recommendation was
accepted, and a probation order made for two years. (See
Chapter 7 for a discussion of probation.)

## PROBATION OFFICERS AND THE IMPLEMENTATION OF THE TARIFF

It will be apparent from these two case illustrations that
probation officers in their social enquiry reports very often have
to walk a 'tightrope' between the conflicting demands of ideologies of justice on the one hand and welfare on the other. Some
research findings indicate that the *personal characteristics* of those
making reports are as influential in determining the contents as
the nature of the available information. In other words, a
considerable degree of slanting may occur (Hood and Sparks
1970: 160–70). Bean (1975) goes as far as to suggest that social
enquiry reports should be abandoned. He has also suggested,
somewhat cynically, that the offender 'ought to choose his
pre-sentence official with the same care that he should choose
his judge and magistrate' (Bean 1976: 112).

My colleague, Pauline Hardiker, has carried out what is
probably the most comprehensive study yet of the ideologies

---

[3] A court has the power to remand a convicted offender for a period of up to four
weeks for social and/or medical (psychiatric) reports *if on bail*, and for *three weeks*
if in custody (Criminal Justice Act 1967, Section 30). It is of course open to the
court to ask for a further remand if additional information is required or the
investigations are incomplete.

espoused by probation officers in compiling and presenting social enquiry reports (Hardiker 1977, Hardiker 1979, and Hardiker and Webb 1978). She found, on the basis of a detailed study of some thousand cases, that a number of those who had criticized the probation service had taken too simplistic a view of the problem (e.g. Bean 1975 and 1976, and Perry 1974). She suggests that social enquiry reports reflect the increasing importance of experts in the courts and that, in essence, the probation officer is concerned with the operation of the tariff in reverse. She says, 'Probation officers have to consider a form of *tariff* in which punishment is set against offence, as well as the individual's social or psychological *needs*' (Hardiker 1979: 118; italics in original). The magistrate or judge through the medium of the social enquiry report is thus helped to define the position of an offender on a continuum of social need. Hardiker found (as had Ford 1972) that probation officers played a number of roles in preparing and presenting their court reports. In 80 per cent of Hardiker's cases they considered that they were merely advising sentencers, whereas in the remaining 20 per cent they saw themselves as either 'leaving a case to classical justice or influencing the court towards a social work decision respectively' (Hardiker 1979: 124). Hardiker concludes that the probation officer's position in advising the court is a very complex one and because of this complexity it is a situation that can easily lead to ill-informed and simplistic criticism (see above).

> 'Probation officers straddle judicial and welfare systems and their social enquiry reports often encapsulate this dual aspect of their role. . . . Their credibility is at stake if they exaggerate their roles either as servant of the court or as social worker. Even if they end up playing a classical justice role, at least the offender has been given some consideration at the social enquiry stage. When they actively attempt to manipulate the sentencers towards making a social work decision, there will always be boundaries to their influence, given their structural location in the courts.'
>
> (Hardiker 1979: 132–33)

I now go on to consider some broader aspects of sentencing practice.

## Broader aspects of sentencing practice

Reference has already been made to the difficulty in examining the attitudes of sentencers. Bottomley surveyed a great deal of the research that had been carried out in this area and suggested that 'the most fundamental influences upon sentencing behaviour are the penal philosophies and attitudes of individual magistrates' (Bottomley 1973: 169 and Bottomley 1979). (For an earlier survey of sentencing research, see Hood and Sparks 1970: Chapter 5.) Spreading the net rather more widely to cover community influences, Hood (1962) examined the use of prison sentences for property offenders and found that the magistrates in the more middle-class and 'community-conscious' towns tended to be more severe in their sentencing practice than were the magistrates in towns with a wider social mix. It is interesting to note here that studies in the exercise of police discretion and enforcement, both in America (Wilson 1968) and in this country (Cain 1973), confirm the importance of such community expectations and attitudes. In a later study concerned with the sentencing of motoring offenders, Hood (1972) concluded that the wide disparities in the way cases were dealt with could be explained by the manner in which the magistrates learned their trade and were influenced by local practices. In view of such disparities, we may well ask: 'How might sentencing practice be improved?' Hood and Sparks (1970) once proposed a model that would direct much-needed attention to the complicated links between sentencers, the aims of penal measures, information about the crime, the offender, and the choice of sentence. Such a model has many attractions and has considerable implications for penal practice, philosophy, and research.

More modest measures have included the provision of guidebooks for sentencers, such as the government's small handbook *The Sentence of the Court* (HMSO 1978). This contains information for sentencers about the main disposals available and the known effectiveness of some of them. In some of the higher courts, judges have been provided at their own request with feedback information on the results of the sentences they have imposed. In recent years, both judges and magistrates have been encouraged to visit the various institutions to which they commit offenders so that they may gain first-hand knowledge not only of the resources available but of their limitations. Such visits are customarily part of the training programmes arranged for newly appointed magistrates.

A number of voluntary organizations, such as the Magistrates' Association, The National Association for the Care and Resettlement of Offenders, The Institute for the Study and Treatment of Delinquency, and The Howard League for Penal Reform, have all done valuable work by organizing conferences for sentencers and other workers in the penal field so that information and views may be shared. In recent years, the Lord Chief Justice, in consultation with the Lord Chancellor, has instituted rather more formal sentencing conferences for judges, recorders, and others concerned with the implications of penal practice for the higher courts. However, despite all these excellent arrangements, it is true to say that the training of most sentencers is still somewhat sadly lacking in the type of material covered in this book, particularly that covered in Parts One and Two.

## Conclusions

Even though the task of sentencing has only been touched upon in this chapter, it should be apparent that sentencers have a tremendously difficult task in taking into account the numerous variables that are important in the sentencing process and in trying to reconcile the often conflicting aims of punishment. In recent years some progress has been made, both in the availability of more detailed information on the backgrounds of offenders, and in the extent to which opportunity has been sought for bringing together all those involved in the sentencing process. It is inevitable that, as more information becomes available, more questions need to be asked, and thus the task of sentencing becomes more complicated and more anxiety-provoking for those who have to carry it out. Research in this emotive area is notoriously difficult to put into effect, partly because of the understandable sensitivity of both lay magistrates and professional sentencers to public scrutiny. Some improvements might occur if sentencers were required to give reasons for their decisions more frequently so that their rationale could be subjected to scrutiny and discussion. Bottomley, writing about justice more generally, makes a statement that is most applicable to the matters I have been discussing in this chapter.

> 'Justice should be seen as the outcome of a three-way process, involving the community, the defendant and the public agents of law and order – not a private arrangement between them and the defendant alone . . . effective means of accountability should be established at every possible stage, so that the community knows and approves of what is being done in its name. The defendant must be kept fully informed of what is happening to him and given meaningful opportunities to participate effectively in the process. Reasons for decisions should be given and the procedures for appealing against decisions should be accessible and fair.'
>
> (Bottomley 1979: 121)

In Chapters 7 and 8 I discuss the measures available for dealing with adult and young offenders in more detail.

## References

Baldwin, J. (1974) Magistrates and their Training. *Justice of the Peace* **138**: 715–17.

—— (1975) The Compulsory Training of the Magistracy. *Criminal Law Review* **November**: 634–43.

—— (1976) The Social Composition of the Magistracy. *British Journal of Criminology* **16**: 171–74.

Bean, P. (1975) Social Enquiry Reports – A Recommendation for Disposal. *Justice of the Peace* Part I, 11 October: 568–69, and Part II, 18 October: 585–87.

—— (1976) *Rehabilitation and Deviance*. London: Routledge and Kegan Paul.

Bottomley, A.K. (1973) *Decisions in the Penal Process*. London: Martin Robertson.

—— (1979) *Criminology in Focus: Past Trends and Future Prospects*. Oxford: Martin Robertson.

Cain, M. (1973) *Society and the Policeman's Role*. London: Routledge and Kegan Paul.

Carlen, P. (1976a) The Staging of Magistrates' Justice. *British Journal of Criminology* **16**: 48–55.

—— (1976b) *Magistrates' Justice*. London: Martin Robertson.

Cavanagh, W.E. (1967) *Juvenile Courts and the Law*. Harmondsworth: Penguin Books.

Dell, S. (1970) *Silent in Court*. London: Bell.

Ford, P. (1972) *Advising Sentencers: A Study of Recommendations Made by Probation Officers*. Oxford: Blackwell.

*Guardian, The* (1971) *4 December*.

Hardiker, P. (1977) Social Work Ideologies in the Probation Service. *British Journal of Social Work* **7**: 131–54.

—— (1979) The Role of Probation Officers in Sentencing. In H. Parker (ed.) *Social Work and the Courts*. London: Edward Arnold.

Hardiker, P. and Webb, D. (1978) Explaining Deviant Behaviour: The Social Context of 'Action' and 'Infraction' Accounts in the Probation Service. *Sociology* **12**: 1–17.

HMSO (1978) *The Sentence of the Court: A Handbook for Courts on the Treatment of Offenders* (third edition). London: HMSO.

Home Office (1976) *The Annual Probation and After Care Statistics*. London: HMSO.

Hood, R.G. (1962) *Sentencing in Magistrates' Courts*. London: Stevens.

—— (1972) *Sentencing the Motoring Offender*. London: Heinemann.

Hood, R. and Sparks, R. (1970) *Key Issues in Criminology*. Weidenfeld and Nicolson: London.

Jackson, R.M. (1977) *The Machinery of Justice in England* (seventh edition). Cambridge: Cambridge University Press.

Perry, F.G. (1974) *Information for the Courts: A New Look at Social Enquiry Reports*. Cambridge: Institute of Criminology.

Royal Commission on Criminal Procedure (1981) *The Balance of Criminal Justice. Summary of the Report*. London: HMSO.

Scott, P.D. (1959) Juvenile Courts: The Juvenile's Point of View. *British Journal of Delinquency* **IX**: 200–10.

Streatfeild Report (1961) *Report of the Inter-Departmental Committee on the Business of the Criminal Courts*. Cmnd. 1289. London: HMSO.

Voelcker, P.M.W. (1960) Juvenile Courts: The Parents' Point of View. *British Journal of Criminology* **1**: 154–66.

Wilson, J.Q. (1968) *Varieties of Police Behaviour*. Cambridge, Mass: Harvard University Press.

Younghusband, E. (1957) The Juvenile Court and the Child. *British Journal of Delinquency* **VII**: 181–95.

FURTHER READING

*On sentencing:*

Thomas, D.A. (1979) *Principles of Sentencing* (second edition). London: Heinemann.
*and, more generally,*
Walker, N. (1969) *Sentencing in a Rational Society*. London: Allen Lane.
—— (1980) *Punishment, Danger and Stigma: The Morality of Criminal Justice*. Oxford: Basil Blackwell.

*On the criminal law:*

*The major text on the substantive law of crime is:*

Smith, J.C. and Hogan, B. (1977) *Criminal Law* (fourth edition). London: Butterworths.

*On psychology and the criminal process:*

*Those interested in examining the extent to which psychological factors influence the perceptions of witnesses, and the reliability of confessions, should consult:*

Bostock-Loyd, S.M.A. (1981) *Psychology in Legal Contexts: Applications and Limitations*. London: Macmillan.

# CHAPTER SEVEN

# Penal measures for adults (aged seventeen and over)

'A punishment may not be an act of violence, of one, or of many against a private member of society, it should be public, immediate and necessary; the least possible in the case given; proportioned to the crime, and determined by the laws.'

CESARE BECCARIA

## A note on legal punishment

I made reference in Chapter 6 to some of the conflicting aims of punishment that sentencers needed to reconcile in order to try and determine a just and appropriate penalty. The literature on legal punishment is vast and it would be foolhardy to attempt to review even a fraction of it here; readers wishing to pursue the topic further are invited to refer to the suggested further reading listed at the end of this chapter. However, before going on to describe and discuss some of the measures available for dealing with adult offenders, it is necessary to say something about punishment in so far as it determines the aims of a penal system, for these aims are to a greater or a lesser extent reflected in the penal measures available at any given point in time. Rawls provides a useful definition of legal punishment:

'A person is said to suffer punishment whenever he is legally deprived of some of the normal rights of a citizen on the ground that he has violated a rule of law, the violation having been established by trial according to the due process of law, provided that the deprivation is carried out by the recognised legal authorities of the state, that the rule of law clearly

specifies both the offence and the attached penalty, that the
courts construe statutes strictly, and that the statute was on
the books prior to the time of the offence.'

(Rawls 1969: 107–8)

It will be seen that this definition contains a number of the
ingredients of the statement by Beccaria which introduces this
chapter, a statement written in the eighteenth century.

In some respects, a strictly legal view of punishment is
comparatively easy to state, but the moral implications and the
variously stated aims of punishment are much less easily dealt
with. One might suggest that one of the essential ingredients of
legal punishment is that it is the authorized reaction of a
community of people against one of its members. In other
words, legality has been established to prevent private acts of
vengeance; punishment is taken out of the private sector and
becomes a matter of public concern. The element of vengeance
is most important. It has been commented upon by many
writers, especially psycho-analysts, who consider that it is
probably based on irrational feelings and beliefs having their
origins in the unconscious. It does appear that we tend to desire
severe punishments for those in whom we see mirrored our own
worst feelings and fears – feelings and fears we need to keep
heavily repressed. As Oscar Wilde once said, it is 'the rage of
Caliban on seeing his own face reflected in the glass'.

It is an unfortunate fact that the relations and friends of
victims frequently thirst to enjoy the discomfort of the evil-doer;
this can often be seen, for example, in the attitudes of parents
towards someone who has indecently assaulted their child, or in
community attitudes towards the hitherto unsuspected neigh-
bour who has embezzled the street's Christmas Club funds.
Such offenders may be safer for a time in custody than exposed
to the possible uncontrolled vengeance of the public at large. It
is worth noting, however, that as a community we have for far
too long tended to ignore the claims and feelings of victims; only
in recent years have those working with offenders taken a more
positive interest in their victims. In some cases, value has
accrued from bringing together victim and offender where this
has seemed appropriate and been possible. It is very easy for
those working with offenders to become over-identified with

them and to forget the victim's feelings and point of view. In an interesting study Maguire (1980) has demonstrated just how emotionally damaging the experience of burglary can be to a victim. (See also Wright 1977.) As I shall show later, recent innovations in penal treatment, such as the use of Community Service Orders, have reflected this need to involve the offender in more direct forms of reparation for his wrongdoing.

## Aims of the penal system

For centuries there has been wide-ranging debate concerning various theories of punishment and their implications for the penal system. A simple way of stating these theories is to make a threefold classification: (a) *rehabilitation (reformation)*; (b) *incapacitation (disablement)*; (c) *deterrence*. A slightly more detailed classification shows the following more explicit aims of punishment:

(1) *In the interests of society:*
- (i) *deterrence* (of the offender and of others).
- (ii) *retribution* (which may come near to the danger of vengeance referred to earlier).
- (iii) protection of the public and the maintenance of law and order.
(2) *In the interests of both society and the individual: reform (rehabilitation)* of the individual.

Admittedly, this is also a far too 'neat' and arbitrary classification, since many of the aims will inevitably overlap. Implicitly, legal punishment in the present context may be seen both as a means for the individual to expiate his guilt (which may or may not lead to his reform) and as the vicarious means through which society satisfies its urge to punish. This summary statement is true to a degree, but does inevitably over-simplify very complex ethical and legal problems. Walker (1966, 1969, and 1980) has written extensively on the aims of a penal system and has attempted to provide a classification that points the way for more rational and humane penal measures. The following is an outline of his classification, in modified form.

(1) *The protection of offenders and suspected offenders from unofficial retaliation* (i.e., protection from vengeance).

(2) *Reductivism*   This aims to reduce the frequency of the types of behaviour prohibited by the criminal law. A reductivist will approve of measures of social prophylaxis, if they can be shown to reduce opportunities for crime, and will accept measures that will promote general and individual deterrence.

(3) *Humanitarianism*   The intention here is for the penal system to cause the minimum of suffering (whether to offenders or to others) in its attempts to achieve its aims. Humanitarianism, as Walker and others have pointed out, has its origins in the thinking of both Beccaria and Bentham (who termed it frugality of punishment).

(4) *Retributivism*   The aim here is for the penal system to ensure that offenders atone by suffering for their misdeeds. An ardent retributivist would hold the belief that the enforcement of atonement is a proper aim of the penal system. In days gone by, sentences such as being placed in the pillory (a punishment in its own right) led the offender to suffer additional public retaliation by virtue of his being exposed to public insult and assault. However, the retributivist would probably also accept that certain punishments were too inhuman to be regarded as just atonement no matter what the crime. Walker also suggests a further aim in the form of a retributivist compromise, namely that a penal system should be so constructed that atonement for offences does not lead to the imposition of excessive unofficial retaliation, inhuman suffering, or increase the incidence of offences. Paradoxically, a truly consistent retributivist would probably argue that homosexual offenders should be sent to prison even though it can be said that such sentences are likely to encourage rather than reduce homosexual conduct. The retributivist aim also implies that there should be consistency in sentencing, with little need for the attention to individuals and their differing circumstances outlined in Chapter 6. It requires, too, that the sentence should be related to the amount of harm caused by the offence.

(5) *Limited retributivism*   The aim here is to ensure that the unpleasantness of a penal measure must not exceed the limit that is appropriate to the culpability of the offence.

This is exemplified in the extent to which there are maximum penalties laid down for certain offences but the courts are left free to impose less than the maximum if they think it appropriate.

(6) *Denunciation* This is an aim which seeks to demonstrate society's abhorrence of crime. In the past, and even today, it has often been argued as an important aim in relation to the imposition of capital punishment for murder, the view being held that such a drastic penalty denounced murder as a crime particularly abhorrent to society.

Balancing these conflicting aims in relation to any one case is an extremely difficult task and in any event such aims cannot be implemented in isolation from the social, political, and economic climate obtaining at any point in time. Most people would try to achieve a balanced eclecticism which sees the reduction of unlawful conduct as the main aim of a penal system, provided that such reduction is consonant with humanitarian principles. With some of these difficulties in mind we can now turn to an examination of the measures that are available within the penal system for dealing with convicted offenders.

## Custodial measures

### BRIEF HISTORY OF IMPRISONMENT

I can only make brief reference to the history of imprisonment here. Readers wishing to pursue this most important facet of our social history should consult some of the excellent standard works on the subject – for example, Fox (1952), Howard (1960), Sparks (1971) – and the suggested further reading. Suffice it to say that the use of imprisonment as a form of *punishment* is comparatively recent in this country. In early times, imprisonment was used almost exclusively to detain suspects during investigation and trial. Prisons were essentially local in character, all manner of offenders were herded together and, as is well known, in the absence of firm control, abuses of all kinds were common. During Elizabethan times, there grew up alongside the local gaols the 'Houses of Correction', intended originally under the provisions of the Poor Law for dealing with vagrants and 'idle persons'. Gradually the two came to be run side by side and then, in the mid-sixteenth century, the systems were merged.

In the eighteenth century the public conscience was stirred to some extent through the efforts of such reformers as John Howard and Elizabeth Fry, whose work revealed the appalling conditions of filth and corruption that existed. As we have already noted, at about this time social philosophers and jurists, such as Bentham in this country and Beccaria in Europe, were calling attention to the ethical aspects and purposes of punishment. The time was ripe for change, and mainly through the work of these reformers improvements were brought about. However, they were still not adequate, largely because there was no machinery for adequate central control and enforcement of standards. Transportation to the United States (in lieu of other punishments) had been introduced in the eighteenth century, and later, after the War of Independence, prisoners were sent to Australia. By the time transportation ended in 1867, the Australian system had provided some very progressive and enlightened penal regimes which were to influence considerably penal practice in this country. Inspectors of prisons had been appointed in 1835, but it was not until 1877 that the prisons became 'nationalized' and placed under the direct control of central government. In 1895, the Gladstone Committee was set up to enquire into complaints against prison administration, largely because the Chairman of the Prison Commission, Edmund du Cane, had so rigidly and severely enforced the system that 'for death itself, the system had substituted a living death' (Fox 1952: 51).

In a very forward-looking report, the Committee called for much more flexibility in the treatment of prisoners, for more training and rehabilitation, with the result that a new Act of 1898 placed more power in the hands of the Prison Commission. We might well ask why events took the turn they did at this particular time. One of the answers is probably to be found in the general trend I have already described as the 'individualization' of the treatment of both offenders and those who were classed as social deviants. There were a number of different reasons for this. The pioneer work of Freud had persuaded some people that the causes of human behaviour were anything but obvious. To Freud and his followers, man was not nearly so consciously responsible for his actions as had previously been supposed. No doubt also the seeds for a change in beliefs about the natural dignity of *'homo sapiens'* had been sown by Darwin some years earlier. Less frequently were the poor and the unemployed being regarded as merely feckless – reasons were now being sought for their behaviour. As I showed in Chapters 4 and 5, interest in the causes of mental illness and mental deficiency was also growing, and generally speaking, men and women were being regarded increasingly as individuals in their own right. The legislation passed at the turn of the century bears witness to these changes: for example, the Prevention of Crime Act of 1908 introduced both the borstal system, for the treatment of young offenders, and preventive detention, for those for whom other penal measures seemed to be largely ineffective. A further effort to individualize treatment was made in the Probation of Offenders Act of 1907, which instituted the probation system on a statutory basis, and, as already noted, in 1908 the Children Act made provision for Juvenile Courts, thus officially separating juvenile and adult offenders.

In the 1920s, penal, and particularly prison, policy was much influenced by humane and forward-looking men such as the late Sir Alexander Paterson; he felt strongly that offenders should be sent to prison *as* a punishment and not *for* punishment. Then, in the years immediately preceding the Second World War, developments in the behavioural sciences also had their effect.[1] Just before the war broke out a Criminal Justice Bill had been introduced by the late Lord Templewood, but its passage was postponed by the war until 1947. When implemented eventually as the Criminal Justice Act of 1948, it made a number of major changes in the penal system.

Among the more important were:

(1) The extension of the powers of the courts to keep people out of prison, in particular young persons and the mentally disordered.

(2) The introduction of refinements (which had to be abandoned later because they did not fulfil their early promise of

---

[1] Between the two World Wars and in the 1950s there were a number of enquiries into prison conditions and prison officers' pay and conditions of service. (See report of the May Committee (HO, 1979a: 16–18).)

success) in methods of dealing with persistent offenders – namely the systems of preventive detention and corrective training.

(3) The abolition of corporal punishment, except for offences committed by prisoners against prison staff.

By the late 1950s there was mounting pressure to re-examine some of the measures introduced by the 1948 Act, with the result that the 1961 Criminal Justice Act almost totally abolished sentences of imprisonment on young persons under twenty-one. Then, with the implementation of the Criminal Justice Acts of 1967 and 1972, further flexibility of treatment was made possible by the introduction of parole, the suspended sentence, and other measures.

A brief and simplified historical summary of developments in the English penal system is given in *Table 7(1)*.

RECENT DEVELOPMENTS

It is probably fair to say that only in recent years have we become so acutely security-conscious that this preoccupation has visibly seemed to cut across treatment considerations. It was not until 1966, with the dramatic escape of George Blake (who, it must be remembered in this context, was a political prisoner), that the problem began to cause concern, and the late Earl Mountbatten of Burma was commissioned to undertake an enquiry into the whole question of escapes and prison security (Home Office 1966). His remit was subsequently broadened to include the escape of such persons as Frank Mitchell, the 'Mad Axeman', from Dartmoor, who it could be said posed a different kind of security problem – although not a threat to national security: Mitchell had been a dangerously aggressive criminal with a long record of violent conduct. Earl Mountbatten concluded that new measures should be introduced in all prisons aimed at improving security, and that these should include guard dogs and closed-circuit television. He did, however, recognize that the escape problem was exacerbated by overcrowding in the prisons and also by the increasing need to pass longer sentences on some of the more dangerous criminals – as, for example, in cases of murder and the sentences of thirty years passed on some of the 'Great Train Robbers'.

Table 7(1)  *Brief historical summary of developments in the English penal system*

| | |
|---|---|
| *pre-Saxon and Saxon times* | Imprisonment not used specifically as a punishment. Penal measures mainly those of death, banishment, or mutilation. |
| *Middle Ages* | Introduction of some state control over justice. Development of higher and lower courts. Prison began to be used as a method of penal treatment. |
| *Elizabethan period* | Provisions of the Poor Law applied to offenders as well as to the 'idle' and 'vagrant'. |
| *eighteenth century* | Development of interest in prison conditions. Work of John Howard. Use of transportation. The problem of punishment considered increasingly by philosophers. |
| *nineteenth century (first part)* | Further work of prison reformers. Some control vested in central government. Payment of gaolers, etc. |
| *nineteenth century (second part)* | Major prison-building programme. Many of these prisons in existence today. Control of prisons finally vested in central government. |
| *early twentieth century* | Increasing flexibility and individualization of treatment. |
| *mid and late twentieth century* | Restrictions on imprisonment for certain classes of offender. Increase in use of control under 'open' conditions. The dilemma of rehabilitation in conditions of captivity still unresolved . Prison riots, staffing problems. The report of the May Committee. |

In view of these and other developments, the Home Secretary remitted the problem of the 'regime for long-term prisoners detained in maximum security' to the Advisory Council on the Penal System. A report prepared by a sub-committee under the chairmanship of Professor (Sir Leon) Radzinowicz made a number of recommendations (Home Office 1968). One of them was that long-term high-security-risk prisoners should be detained in three or four long-term 'dispersal' prisons, each equipped with the means to enforce maximum security. On the question whether prison officers should be armed, the subcommittee was divided. One of its members, the late Dr Peter Scott, argued very cogently that arming prison staffs would be counter-productive, and that there was a need to subdivide the high-risk group more carefully.

The early 1970s witnessed not only a continuing rise in the prison population (*see Table 7(2)*), but in addition chronic overcrowding, decaying buildings, poor conditions for both staff and inmates, and deteriorating industrial relations. All these factors no doubt contributed to a number of demonstrations and 'riots' that took place during this time.[2] In 1978 matters came to a head following a long period of unsatisfactory industrial relations. The Home Secretary appointed a Committee of Inquiry under the chairmanship of Mr Justice (Sir John) May to examine the state of the Prison Services in the United Kingdom (i.e. England, Wales, Scotland, and Northern Ireland). He also urged the Committee to report quickly; it is to its credit that it was able to produce a report of some 300 pages eleven months later (Home Office, Scottish Office, and Northern Ireland Office 1979a). The Committee was asked to make particular enquiry into the use of resources, conditions of staff, structure and management of services, industrial relations, and pay and allowances for all staff. The report has been the subject of a good deal of criticism by some commentators (see for

[2] It is as well to note here that 'riots' and 'mutiny' were not new to the prison scene in this country. There was considerable unrest in the 1930s – the famous 'mutiny' at Dartmoor in 1932 being but one example. Critics of penal reformers, and of those who wished to introduce more humanitarian ideas into the prison system, were quick at that time, as now, to suggest that harsher regimes were required and that prison should not become a 'soft' measure. Happily, such views have not on the whole moved the prison department to abandon the introduction of more progressive regimes.

example Rutherford 1980) but, if one acknowledges the size of the task and the pressure on the Committee to report quickly, this criticism seems largely unjustified.

The Committee recognized that there was unlikely to be a time in the foreseeable future when there would not be a need for society to support a substantial prison population, but it did reiterate concerns that had been expressed for some time, namely that there were far too many socially inadequate and mentally disordered offenders in prison. The Committee considered that there was a need to restate modern objectives, less in terms of treatment and training and more in terms of 'positive custody'. These would incorporate greater opportunities for more satisfying and productive work regimes, greater use of education, and perhaps most importantly, in view of the background that led up to the report, 'penal establishments [would] be consistently characterised by an openness of approach and mind not only to the staff but to all public requirements as well as to the interests of the inmates' (p. 278). The Committee also recommended that existing prison establishments needed updating, and in doing so made some excoriating observations about some of the older establishments. Alongside this updating would be the continuance and expansion of existing plans for building new establishments. It also made specific recommendations for an overhaul of overtime rates for uniformed staff and for the introduction of new pay and superannuation scales for all staff. The Prison Officers' Association, despite having hoped for a larger pay award than that recommended by the Committee, accepted it. With this very brief summary of recent events we can now turn to some consideration of the *prison system today*.

## THE PRISON SYSTEM TODAY

In this section, prisons, borstal institutions, and detention centres are discussed together since all come within the control of the Prison Department of the Home Office. In addition, both borstals and detention centres may receive offenders under the age of seventeen. For convenience and to save repetition, the classification both of prisoners and of institutions is considered in the section dealing with prisons. More *detailed* consideration of detention centres and borstals is afforded later in the chapter. As can be seen from *Table 7(2)*, the most significant factor influencing the prison system today has been the steady growth in the prison population.

Table 7(2)    *Daily average number of men and women in prison custody 1913–79*

| | |
|---|---|
| 1913 | 18,155 |
| 1938 | 11,086 |
| 1948 | 19,765 |
| 1958 | 25,379 |
| 1964 | 28,800 |
| 1968 | 32,461 |
| 1972 | 38,328 |
| 1979 | 42,220 |

* In November 1979, the figure had climbed to 43,036; at the end of July 1981, it stood at 45,044 (Parliamentary all-party Penal Affairs Group 1981).

(Sources: Home Office 1969: 14 and Home Office 1980a: 4)

It will be seen from *Table 7(2)* that since 1948 the daily average prison population has more than doubled. We also know that the number of remand prisoners (i.e. those unconvicted or unsentenced) has increased 'more than fourfold: this is partly the result of increases in reception, but also partly due to the increased average time these prisoners are held on remand' (May Committee 1979a: 31).

It would be a mistake to assume, however, that *all* our prisons are overcrowded; the greatest pressure is upon the local and remand prisons. To my personal knowledge there are prisons that are far from being used to their capacity, largely because of staffing and associated problems. It is a matter for regret that in some establishments inflexible attitudes about pay and conditions have prevented use being made of accommodation so that pressures in institutions elsewhere could be relieved (see Pease 1981). The numbers of staff employed within the prison service and the consequential cost have also increased dramatically in recent years. Whereas in 1950 there were about 5500 persons employed at a cost of £6 million, the number employed today stands at some 22,500 at a cost of some £285 million (Home Office 1980a: 5 and 8). The make-up of the prison population for the year 1979 is set out in *Table 7(3)*.

Table 7(3)   *Prison population in 1979*

|  | average | |
| --- | --- | --- |
|  | *males* | *females* |
| *prison (including remand centres)* | | |
| (1) awaiting trial or sentence | 5823* | 309* |
| (2) sentenced (adults) | 24,750 | 815 |
| (3) sentenced (young prisoners) | 2558 | 101 |
| (4) non-criminal prisoners | 478 | 19 |
| *borstal* | 5250 | 214 |
| *senior detention centre* | 1265 | (not used for girls) |
| *junior detention centre* | 638 | (not used for girls) |
| Total: | 40,762 | 1458 |

(Source: Home Office 1980a: 4)

* In June 1981, the total stood at 7439, an all-time high (Parliamentary All-Party Penal Affairs Group 1981).

THE USE MADE OF PRISON

*Prisons are used for the following purposes:*

(1)  Safe custody of prisoners pending trial.
(2)  Safe custody of prisoners awaiting sentence, or for investigation and reports (see Chapter 6).
(3)  The detention of those sentenced for criminal offences, non-payment of debts and fines, or for contempt of court.

Inspection of the figures in *Table 7(3)* reveals a disquieting number of persons still being detained in penal establishments who are awaiting trial or sentence. We know that a large proportion of these are not subsequently awarded a custodial sentence for their offence. Until 1975, the courts were given almost unfettered discretion in their powers to permit or refuse bail. However, under the provisions of the Bail Act 1976, a general presumption in favour of bail was introduced for all defendants. Despite this provision and the provision of bail hostels (Powers of Criminal Courts Act 1973, Section 47), a significantly large inroad has still not been made into the large numbers remanded in custody before trial or sentence. This applies particularly to those offenders remanded for reports into their medical and psychiatric condition, a matter of much concern to the Butler Committee on mentally abnormal offenders. I shall refer to this matter again in Chapter 9.

## TYPES OF PRISON

Prisons may be classified in a variety of ways. The simplest is probably to divide them up as follows: local prisons; remand prisons (centres); training prisons (open or closed) (see also Home Office 1977: 22). It should be noted, however, that a number of establishments may have multiple or dual functions (for example, Wormwood Scrubs combines on one site the functions of a local prison, a training prison, and a borstal allocation centre). Training prisons may be short term, medium term, or long term, and may be either open or closed. Within this very over-simplified classification, there are a number of further complex variations. Since the local prisons are the receiving centres for almost all convicted prisoners, they could be described as the cornerstones of the system and the establishments under the most pressure because of overcrowding and poor facilities. Those prisoners for whom training is considered appropriate will be sent to prisons that can fulfil this task. Allocation has to take into account security risks; those prisoners presenting the highest security risks or handling difficulties will most likely be allocated to one of the 'dispersal' prisons referred to earlier. Other factors to be considered will be special training and welfare needs and length of sentence. Probably the most promising development in the prison system over the years has been the introduction of the 'open prison'. Many of these open prisons have been developed from disused wartime service and other camps. Considerable freedom is allowed to inmates, absconding is not common, and the open system has much to commend it for the non-potentially dangerous long-term prisoner and for the man serving a long sentence (for example, the 'lifer') who, nearing release, needs an experience approximating to conditions obtaining in the outside world. The potential of the open-prison system is discussed in a useful article by Atkinson, an experienced open-prison governor (Atkinson 1981).

## CLASSIFICATION OF PRISONERS

Prisoners, as we have already seen, may be classified in a number of ways. These can now be further briefly categorized as follows:

(1) Male
(2) Female
(3) Civil
(4) Criminal
(5) Remand
(6) Sentenced
(7) Adult
(8) Young (under twenty-one).

Obviously these categories overlap; they are only set out in this way to indicate the numerous allocation considerations that have to be taken into account. For purposes of management the additional classification into security-risk groups is probably the most important.

*Categories*
A. Those whose escape would be highly dangerous.
B. Those who need less secure conditions, but for whom escape must be made very difficult.
C. Those who cannot be trusted in open conditions, but who do not have the ability or resources to make a determined attempt at escape.
D. Those who can be trusted in open conditions (Home Office 1978: 34).

## MANAGEMENT AND STAFFING

From the information already given in this book about the complicated explanations of criminality, the conflicting aims of legal punishment, and the steady growth of the numbers of people in prison, it will be obvious that today's prison service has to cope with problems of considerable complexity. The days of the small local gaol are now a thing of the past; prison staffs now include all manner of experts, many of them accountable for their work to institutions and organizations outside the prison service. The May Committee (Home Office 1979a) was quick to recognize the communication problems involved between staff and between staff and inmates. The staff of a nineteenth-century prison might have consisted of a governor, a chaplain, and a small number of gaolers – a very small organization compared with today's complex system. In *Figure 7(1)* I have tried to present the staffing structure for a hypothetical ('model') training prison for some thousand inmates. It is unlikely that any such structure exists in exactly the form I have given it, but it will serve to illustrate the complexity of prison organization. In the notes to the figure I expand upon the responsibilities of the staff and include reference to the roles and functions of the headquarters staff of the Prison Department.

BORSTAL TRAINING

Borstal detention (as it was then called) was introduced formally in this country by the Prevention of Crime Act 1908. In the early years of its operation, it was based very largely upon public-school traditions of hard work, fair play, and service to the community. Initially it met with a fair degree of success, partly because numbers were fairly small and partly because the type of young adult ordered to be detained was possibly less sophisticated criminally than his modern counterpart. In recent years, the success rate has declined considerably. A borstal sentence is available for young persons between the ages of 15 and 21, but will not normally be imposed upon a young offender under the age of 17 unless the court considers that there is no other way of dealing with him. A borstal sentence can only be passed by the Crown Court and the average length of training is now about 9–10 months. Following discharge, an offender is placed under the statutory supervision of the probation service (see below).

The activities and regimes of borstals vary considerably and there are some institutions that specialize in the training and

*Figure 7(1)* Staffing structure and organization of a hypothetical ('model') training prison for approximately 1000 inmates

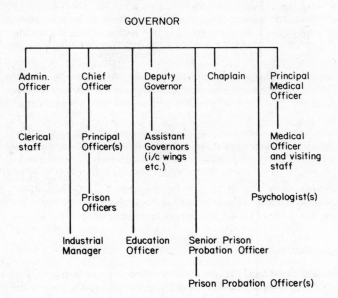

*Notes to Figure 7(1)*

(1) The governor is officially responsible for the management and functioning of the prison, though he may delegate some of these responsibilities. There are various governor grades, the most senior having control of the larger and more complex prison establishments.

(2) Until recently, assistant governors were divided into two grades; this is now no longer the case. It is proposed that a probationary grade of Assistant Governor (Training) be introduced. In borstals assistant governors are usually known as housemasters.

(3) Subordinate discipline staff such as prison officers may be responsible to their own superior officer(s), who in turn will be responsible to the governor.

(4) Some of the other professional staff (for example medical officer, chaplain, psychologist, prison probation officer) will have responsibilities and professional allegiances to their own professional senior colleagues. The prison probation officer will turn to his chief probation officer (not to the governor) for consultation concerning the social-work aspects of his duties and the way in which he should exercise these. The education officer is the organizer of educational activities within the prison. He may be employed full or

part-time. He will be employed by the local education authority but
seconded to the prison.

(5) Central control of the prison service is vested in the Prison Department of
the Home Office and within the Prison Department various subsections
deal with specific aspects of prison work (for example borstals, detention
centres, training, organization, life-sentence prisoners). For administrative
purposes, the country is divided into four regions, each under a regional
director, a deputy, and assistants. Headquarters are in London.

A complex management structure exists under the leadership of a
director-general (who is also the chairman of the Prisons Board). There is a
deputy director-general and three directors (Operations, Regimes, and
Personnel and Finance). There is also a chief inspector. The May Committee recommended a somewhat different headquarters structure, with the
Inspector of Prisons being independent of the Prisons Board. It also
recommended that the Prisons Board itself be reconstituted and that it
should include in its membership two entirely independent members who
would be representatives of the wider community (Home Office 1979a:
90–1). The headquarters staff also includes the heads of the various
professional services, such as the director of the Prison Medical Service
(who is a member of the Prisons Board), the chief psychologist, the
chaplain-general, and the chief education officer.

(6) Two other important groups must be mentioned here. They have not been
inserted in *Figure 7(1)* because they are not in the paid employ of the Prison
Department or of the other services. These are (a) *Prison visitors* and (b)
*Boards of visitors*.

*Prison visitors* are appointed by the Prison Department; they have a long
and useful history of involvement in voluntary work in prisons. The aim of
prison visiting is 'simply to give the prisoner regular contact during his
sentence with a sympathetic and sensible person unconnected with the
prison staff with whom he can talk in a free and friendly manner' (Home
Office 1977: 45). In 1979, there were just under 600 of these voluntary
workers (Home Office 1980a: 51).

The Home Secretary is required to appoint a *Board of visitors* for every
Prison Department establishment. The membership, which is voluntary
and unpaid, must include a proportion of magistrates. From time to time
the work the Boards do has been criticized for not being sufficiently vigilant
and for erring too much on the side of the 'establishment', particularly in
cases of dispute between inmates and staff over prison disciplinary matters.
The May Committee saw the Boards as 'agents of local accountability and
control over the good management of institutions. They should, therefore, be
well informed and acute but friendly watchdogs of the public interest'
(Home Office 1979a: 104). The Committee recommended that, in addition
to their adjudicatory and inspectorial functions, Boards of visitors should in
future not only be obliged to concern themselves with the welfare of prison
inmates, but also with the welfare of *prison staff and their families* (my italics).
The Committee also made a further important recommendation, namely
that Boards of visitors should be encouraged to do more to involve their
prison, staff, and inmates in the local community. These recommendations,
if implemented, will make many demands on existing Board members, not

least in the duality of functions implicit in the proposals. However, if they are able to rise to the occasion, a most valuable opportunity will be presented for making prisons more open, more accountable for their activities, and more involved in their local communities. In this way, the harmful secrecy that hangs over so much that goes on, and which merely feeds rumour and fantasy, might be avoided. (Those wishing to pursue the subject of the roles and functions of Boards of visitors should consult the Jellicoe Report 1975.)

treatment of the more highly disturbed offender, as at Feltham in Middlesex and Glen Parva in Leicestershire. In all borstals, the aim is not merely to provide a means of social re-education and to encourage the offender to stay clear of further crime, but also to encourage voluntary and allied work in the local community. During 1979, 6580 males were serving sentences of borstal training and some 1500 of these were under seventeen. The closed borstals were generally full in the Midlands and in the north of England, but there was some spare capacity in the open institutions in the Midlands and the south (Home Office 1980a: 23). Those wishing to read more about the regimes in borstals for both males and females should consult *Prisons and The Prisoner* (Home Office 1977: 78–88).

### DETENTION CENTRES

Detention centres were introduced by the Criminal Justice Act 1948. They were originally designed as a means of providing a 'short sharp shock' for young people between the ages of 14 and 21 who were not so sophisticated in crime that they needed a longer period of training, but who needed a lesson to remind them that society would not continue to tolerate their bad behaviour. (For their historical evolution see Choppen 1970.) There are junior centres for boys aged 14 and under 17 and senior centres for those aged 17 and under 21. A centre for girls was closed after a comparatively short time, largely as a result of the recommendations of a government committee of inquiry. This committee also suggested that efforts should be made to make the training experience in detention centres more positive and less punitive, so that within the limits of the average stay (then about three months) some real attempt could be made to inculcate good habits and behaviour (Home Office 1970b). For some years endeavours were made to put this recommendation into practice, but in the last two years the Government has reverted to a more punitive line; currently, two centres are providing a much more strict and punitive regime (*The Observer*, 16 August 1981). Much more recently, two further centres have been designated to offer similar regimes (*The Guardian*, 2 September 1981). In 1979, 6231 young men were sentenced to detention in the senior centres, and 5247 young men were received in the junior centres. The figures for 1979 showed an increase on those for preceding years and the resulting overcrowding was a matter of concern to the Prison Department (Home Office 1980a: 23–4). Over the years, research has indicated that detention centres are marginally successful with young people who have appeared before the courts on more than one occasion, but much less successful with those who have already received institutional sentences in, say, community-homes education (formerly known as approved schools). Young offenders with serious emotional or physical handicaps are not suitable for such sentences (Field 1969).

### ESTABLISHMENTS FOR YOUNG PERSONS CONVICTED OF GRAVE CRIMES

Since most of these young people will be under the age of seventeen, it is more appropriate to consider the provisions for them in Chapter 8. However, from time to time, some of these young people will need to be accommodated in Prison Department establishments.

### FUTURE DEVELOPMENTS IN PROVISION FOR YOUNG ADULT OFFENDERS

The Government has recently made proposals for a rationalizing of the provisions for both young adult and juvenile offenders. I shall also consider these in Chapter 8.

Before moving on to consider non-custodial measures it will be useful to summarize the custodial measures available for adult offenders. These are set out in *Table 7(4)*.

Table 7(4)    *Summary of custodial measures available*

| age group | measure |
| --- | --- |
| *17 and under 21* | Detention in a place approved by the Secretary of State (1) |
| | Detention Centre |
| | Borstal (2) |
| | Imprisonment (3) |
| | Hospital Order (4) |
| *21 and over* | Imprisonment (3) |
| | 'Extended' Imprisonment (5) |
| | Hospital Order |

*Notes to Table 7(4)*

(1)  For offenders convicted of murder when under eighteen (detention during Her Majesty's pleasure).

(2)  By Crown Court; a Magistrates' Court and a Juvenile Court can commit to the Crown Court with a view to such a sentence being passed if they consider this to be appropriate.

(3)  Only if no other means of dealing with the case is considered appropriate, in which case the court must state the reasons for committing to prison. No court may impose a sentence of imprisonment on a person *under the age of seventeen*. There are also restrictions on the court's powers to sentence to detention centre, borstal, and prison a person who has not received these penalties before and any person not legally represented (Powers of Criminal Courts Act 1973). A *Magistrates' Court* may not impose a sentence of more than six months' imprisonment for any one offence. The total consecutive sentence that may be passed for more than one offence is twelve months. Courts can of course pass *concurrent* sentences for several offences.

(4)  A hospital order is not of course strictly speaking a penal measure, but is inserted here merely for completeness. It is dealt with in Chapter 9.

(5)  A sentence of 'extended' imprisonment may only be passed by the Crown Court upon certain clearly defined offenders who persist in crime (but not necessarily serious or violent crime). The court must be satisfied that the offender is eligible for such a sentence according to clearly laid-down criteria which include a substantial record of previous convictions (Powers of Criminal Courts Act 1973). This sentence of 'extended imprisonment' (maximum ten years) replaces the old sentence of 'preventive detention' introduced by the Prevention of Crime Act 1908. It is specifically designed to protect the public from the depredations of the persistent recidivist (habitual criminal).

## Non-custodial measures

INTRODUCTION

Before describing and discussing the non-custodial measures that are available to the courts it is necessary to return briefly to my earlier reference to concern over the steady increase in the prison population. Although, as I shall show, the courts were provided with a wide range of additional non-custodial penalties through the Criminal Justice Act 1972, there has been a good deal of concern recently that more use should be made of these and that they should be further extended. In the summer of 1980, the Home Office, the DHSS, and the State Departments for Scotland and Wales produced a White Paper which contained comments and observations by a government select committee aimed at trying to reduce the pressure on the prison system (Home Office 1980b). Simultaneously there appeared a report by the Parliamentary All-Party Penal Affairs Group which made some fairly radical proposals to ensure the reduction of this pressure (Parliamentary All-Party Penal Affairs Group 1980). They made their recommendations under six headings, which are now summarized briefly.

(1) *Offenders for whom imprisonment is wrong in principle.* This group would include the mentally disordered (see also Chapter 9). Consideration should be given to the integration of the prison medical service with the NHS. Greater facilities should be made available outside the penal system for the treatment of drunkenness offenders and for those whose addiction to other drugs brings them into contact with the criminal law and the penal system. The Home Office should initiate 'as a matter of urgency a research project evaluating the relative results of (a) imprisonment (b) probation orders and (c) probation and conditional discharge combined with a rehabilitation programme, on comparable samples of drug offenders' (PAPPAG 1980: 52).

(2) *Measures aimed at further reducing the penal population without endangering the public.* There should be a substantial increase in the provisions of hostels, day centres, and specialist employment schemes for offenders. The use of community service orders should be extended. Senior attendance centres should

also be extended on a national basis and conditional discharge and binding over should be used more frequently for petty offenders. Police cautioning should be extended, fining should be used more flexibly, and prison as a means of enforcement for non-payment used only as a last resort. The offence of soliciting for prostitution should not be punishable by a prison sentence, and custodial sentences for the possession of small amounts of cannabis for personal use,[3] for sleeping rough and begging, and for indecent exposure should no longer be available. The Committee also made recommendations for the abolition of the contentious 'sus' law (i.e., 'being a suspected person loitering with intent'). This has now been implemented in part, but time alone will tell whether the new legislation provides a more effective and less punitive means of dealing with offences of loitering. The Committee also recommended that the question of those offenders awaiting deportation and the methods of such deportation should be reviewed urgently.

(3) *Untried and unsentenced prisoners.* Measures should be introduced to increase the use of, and facilities for, bail in obtaining psychiatric reports. They also recommended an urgent review of the factors affecting time spent awaiting trial or sentence.

(4) *Length of sentences.* The Committee recommended legislation aimed at limiting the length of prison sentences. Since the report, a good deal of publicity has been given to this question. The matter is a somewhat delicate one, because, as I indicated in Chapter 6, the executive (i.e., the Home Secretary) does not normally seek the means to interfere with the 'tariff' discretion exercised traditionally by the judiciary. However, there are those who consider that if sentencers (notably the judges) persist in passing longer sentences than seem merited on the facts of the case or on grounds of public safety, then this hitherto unfettered discretion should perhaps be curbed.

(5) *Additional approaches.* No court should pass a *first* custodial sentence on an offender without first considering a social enquiry report. The government should also investigate the systems for deferring a custodial sentence which are in use abroad, with a view to introducing a suitable model in this country.

(6) *Victims of crime.* Consideration should be given to extend-

---

[3] These proposals have not been accepted by the government at present. The others are still under consideration but are not likely to pass into law.

ing the scope of the Criminal Injuries Compensation Board to include compensation for financial loss or damage to property. The development of victim support groups should be encouraged.

Taken together, the recommendations of this committee indicate the recognition of a continuing need to increase the diversification of penalties, to improve resources, to bring offender and community closer together, and to 'decriminalize' some forms of behaviour which now attract penal sanctions. With this background in mind we can now turn to consider some of these non-custodial penalties in a little more detail. I begin with orders for absolute and other forms of discharge.

### ORDERS FOR ABSOLUTE AND CONDITIONAL DISCHARGE

When a court convicts an offender, but does not wish to impose any penalty, it may discharge him absolutely. Such an order is often made in cases where there has been a technical breach of the law. It must be distinguished from a finding of not guilty, with which it is frequently confused.

A court may also order the discharge of an offender *conditionally* for a period of not more than three years. If, during the currency of such an order, the person does not commit any other offence, he will hear no more about it. If, however, he does commit a further offence during the discharge period, he may be brought back before the court and tried both for the original and the new offence. Having granted absolute or conditional discharge, the court may also find it necessary to hold the defendant responsible for costs and compensation, in which case it will make an order for these. As already noted, there is a feeling that these penalties should be used more widely.

### OTHER FORMS OF DISCHARGE

In certain circumstances a court may order an offender to be 'bound over' (enter into a recognizance) to be of good behaviour and keep the peace, and to come up for judgement if required (Courts Acts 1971). In the Magistrates' Court there is also the additional power (under Acts of 1961 and 1968) to bind a person over to prevent a *future* breach of the peace.

## PROBATION

The methods used by probation officers will be considered in Chapter 11; at this stage consideration will be given to the history and organization of the service. It is part of the story of numerous attempts that have been made over the years to mitigate the harsher penalties of the law. Some examples are the fight for abolition of the so-called 'benefit of clergy' (by statute in 1827), for judicial reprieve, for the release of an offender on his own recognizance, and for provisional release on bail. The most extreme example, perhaps, of what might be called a public conscience acting in defiance of a harsh law was seen in the reluctance of juries in earlier times to return verdicts of guilty for trivial offences, knowing that if they did so the victim would be hanged.

Like many other social services now provided by statute, probation had its origins in voluntary endeavour. In 1876, the Church of England Temperance Society established police court missions; the agents of this society, subsequently known as police court missionaries, were assigned to work (in the first instance) in the London courts. Initially, their work was concerned with the reclamation of drunkards and the abuses of alcohol, but their range was soon to be extended. The Probation of First Offenders Act of 1887 had made provision for certain first offenders to be released and to come up for sentence when called upon, such offenders being supervised in a voluntary capacity by the police court missionaries. In 1907, the Probation of Offenders Act made statutory (but permissive) provision for the appointment of probation officers. In 1925 their appointment was made compulsory, and in the Criminal Justice Act of 1948 the law relating to probation was further revised. This Act also made it possible to include specific requirements in probation orders for the offender to receive treatment for psychiatric illness. From the mid-1930s onwards, various Acts of Parliament extended probation officers' activities into many other fields: matrimonial and divorce court work, social enquiry work for both lower and higher courts, after-care, and parole. In the last twenty years the Service has moved increasingly from an almost exclusive concern with direct face-to-face work with individual offenders to work on a much broader front. This involves working with groups, with the community (as, for example, in the implementation of community service orders), in homes and hostels, and in organizing and managing voluntary effort. It may now be said to be a much more outgoing service concerned with the social re-education and rehabilitation of offenders in the broadest sense. As we shall see in Chapter 11 the work requires diverse skills and attributes of a high order.

Under the provisions of the Criminal Justice Act 1972, the activities of the Probation and After-Care Service (as it is now called) were further extended into the organization of community service schemes, with the supervision of suspended sentence orders and the supervision of day training centres. (For a discussion of the impact of these developments see Haxby 1978.) In 1979 there were 5300 probation officers of all grades. In the same year the Probation Service dealt with approximately 43,000 probation orders, some 17,000 cases involving children and young persons, 5394 money-payment fine cases, and 55,545 persons discharged from various custodial and training institutions. In the same year, they made about 217,000 full-scale social enquiries for the Magistrates' and higher courts, over 21,000 enquiries concerning children's welfare (in the adoption and matrimonial courts), and handled some 8000 matrimonial cases (Home Office 1980c). The work of probation officers may be summarized as follows. (For convenience one may make a superficial division between criminal and non-criminal matters, but for obvious reasons such as distinction is an arbitrary one.) The organization of a 'model' local service is given in *Figure 7(2)*.

(1) *Criminal Cases*
   (i)   The supervision of offenders on probation and under money-payment supervision orders. (The latter work is customarily undertaken by ancillary workers in the probation service.)
   (ii)  Social work with and supervision of persons in, and discharged from, a wide range of institutions (e.g. prisons, borstals, detention centres, special hospitals, hostels, etc.). In most cases, such supervision is compulsory, but in some it is not. It also includes persons

on parole (see below). Work with the families of such offenders whilst in institutional care and subsequently.

(iii) Carrying out various social enquiries for Juvenile, Magistrates', and Crown Courts.

(iv) Organization of community service schemes.

(v) Organization of day centres.

(vi) Training and supervising volunteers and auxiliaries.

(2) *Non-Criminal Cases*

(i) Carrying out enquiries for the divorce and Magistrates' Courts concerning care and custody of children. Supervision of children as a result of orders made in the Juvenile, matrimonial, and higher courts.

(ii) Social work with matrimonial conciliation and allied cases in both lower and higher courts.

(iii) Work in adoption, guardianship, and consent-to-marry proceedings.

(iv) Various other duties and tasks under the broad heading of 'kindred social work' (e.g., arbitration in neighbours' quarrels), work with unmarried mothers, work with drug abusers, advice about difficult children (work in this last-mentioned area has diminished to some extent in recent years because much of it is now undertaken by Social Services Departments).

The Probation and After-Care Service is essentially a court social work service, though there are some who are of the opinion that it should have become part of the new Social Service Departments when they were established in 1970. Others consider that it should have even stronger links with the penal (i.e., custodial) system. It is organized at the local level by sixty-two probation committees made up of magistrates and specially co-opted members representing the court area(s) served. Overall oversight is vested in the Home Office who have powers of inspection and a degree of financial control.

*Availability of probation*

Probation may be used for any offence for which the penalty is not fixed by law, in effect for anything except murder and, theoretically, treason and some forms of piracy. The lower age limit is now seventeen, but there is no upper age limit. Offenders must consent to the making of an order, and the court is under an obligation to explain, in clear terms, its implications and the consequences of breaching it. Probation orders are now made for periods of not more than three years.[4] During this time the offender must keep certain conditions such as remaining in touch with the probation officer and so on. Although, strictly speaking, courts are enjoined not to insert conditions in orders

*Figure 7(2)*    'Model' of the organization of a large-sized probation and after-care service*

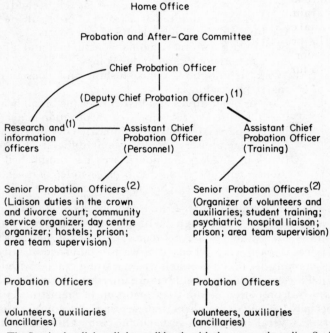

*    The Service has liaison links at all levels with the courts, the police, Social Services Departments, Education, and the Manpower Services Commission among others.
(1)  These posts are usual only in the larger areas.
(2)  These divisions of functions are for illustrative purposes only.

[4] Until May 1978, the minimum period was for one year. The Criminal Law Act 1977 now makes it possible for an order to be for not less than six months.

which cannot be enforced, from time to time unenforceable or technically illegal conditions are inserted – for example, that the offender (if an alcoholic) shall refrain from entering licensed premises. (Many years ago, I was in court when a recorder dealing with the case of a youth who had been involved in sexual offences in cinemas made it a condition of probation that 'the defendant shall not, for the period of this order, enter cinemas or other dark places'!) Clearly, such conditions are not only quite unenforceable, but go far beyond the intention of probation. Certain very useful specific conditions may be inserted, such as requirements that the offender shall reside in a hostel, attend a day training centre, or receive psychiatric treatment either in hospital or as an out-patient (see also Chapter 9).

The probation order has one feature in common with the order for conditional discharge: if the person concerned commits a further crime, he may be brought back before the court and dealt with for the offence for which he was originally placed on probation. But additionally, if he commits a breach of the order by failing to obey any of the conditions, he may be brought back before the court and either charged again with the original offence or fined and allowed to continue under the order. The probation officer, or the probationer, may ask for the order to be discharged at any time, and many orders are discharged for 'good progress'. The main duties of the probation officer are to a large extent still very much as stated in the Probation of Offenders Act of 1907, that is, to 'advise, assist and befriend' those placed under supervision. Although the techniques used in probation work today are a good deal more sophisticated than they were seventy years ago, the words 'advise, assist and befriend' still usefully epitomize the probation officer's duties towards those he supervises. It is probably not overstating the case to suggest that, in the last seventy years, the Probation Service has been an important agency of penal reform, both directly and indirectly. Before moving from the Probation Service more specifically to an examination of other measures, only some of which concern the Probation Service, reference must be made to *after-care and parole*. In the first edition of this book, these two items found their place in the part of this chapter dealing with custodial measures. It could be argued that this is still their rightful place, but, as they concern the management of offenders *in the community*, I have, somewhat arbitrarily, relocated them here.

### AFTER-CARE AND PAROLE

Although in practice the after-care of discharged prisoners has a long history in this country, it was only in fairly recent years that it became a widespread statutory duty of the Probation Service. From the middle of the 1960s, after-care became the official responsibility of the Probation and After-Care Service (the change of name to include 'after-care' reflects the importance that was attached to these duties). Probation officers, as can be seen from *Figure 7(1)*, are now seconded full-time to all prisons. They are also to be found in detention centres and in one or two borstals. Before 1966, much of the after-care service within the prisons was provided by welfare officers appointed and employed by voluntary after-care societies. I have already made reference to the duty of probation officers to encourage and assist voluntary efforts in the care and re-settlement of offenders. It is in the area of after-care especially that this effort can be used to considerable advantage; there are now not only many individual volunteers working with prisoners and their families under the guidance of the Probation Service, but also a number of highly successful groups being run for prisoners' wives and their families. It is also worth noting that volunteers have also been involved in some highly successful work with victims and their families. (See Parsloe 1979 for a general discussion of these and other duties.)

Since 1968, by virtue of the Criminal Justice Act 1967, it has been possible for prisoners serving determinate sentences to be considered for parole (i.e., release on licence after having served either one-third of their sentence or, in practice, eighteen months, whichever is longer). The implementation of the parole scheme is in the hands of the Parole Board.[5] This body (currently of some fifty men and women representative of the judiciary, psychiatry, criminology, work with offenders, and of the wider community) advises the Home Secretary on the exercise of his parole functions. All men and women are eligible to have their cases considered, first by a local review committee (whose

[5] There is a separate Parole Board for Scotland.

members include probation officers, the prison governor, members of the Board of visitors, and independent members) at the prison and then by the Parole Board. In certain cases; defined from time to time by the Home Secretary, local review committees may make a direct recommendation for parole without the case going before the Parole Board (Criminal Justice Act 1972). It seems likely that this provision will be extended to more prisoners in the near future, thus enabling earlier parole for persons serving short sentences. In considering whether or not a prisoner should be recommended to the Home Secretary for parole, account is taken of his previous record, his response to imprisonment, the nature and circumstances of his offence, his circumstances on release, and any local community or national implications. It should be noted here that the Parole Board also advises the Home Secretary on the exercise of his responsibilities concerning the release of life-sentence (indeterminate-sentence) prisoners. All persons released on parole are under the supervision of a probation officer and may be liable to be recalled to prison to serve the unexpired portion of their sentence in the event of a breach of the terms of the licence or the commission of a further offence during the parole period. In 1979, 4771 prisoners were recommended for release on parole. The recall rate has, over the years, remained fairly constant at about 9 per cent (Home Office 1980a). (For more detailed information consult the Annual Reports of the Parole Board.)

Before concluding this section, brief mention must also be made of *remission and pardon*, though of course these are not penalties.

*Remission*: Every prisoner (other than those serving a life sentence) who has been sent to prison for more than one month is eligible, subject to good conduct and industry, for release after serving two-thirds of his sentence. Remission, which is *automatically* credited at the start of the sentence, can only be lost through the commission of specific offences against prison discipline.

*Pardon*: In exceptional cases, the prerogative of a free pardon is exercised by the Home Secretary, acting on behalf of the Sovereign. Such pardons may be granted for a number of reasons, some of them technical, such as the failure of evidence to comply with legal requirements, or they may be granted on more substantial grounds, such as mistaken identity. Occasionally, a *conditional pardon* may be granted. This involves the *special*, as distinct from automatic, *remission* of part of the sentence and may be awarded for compassionate reasons. In 1978, some 92 persons were given *free pardons* and 218 persons given *special remission of sentence* (Home Office 1979b: 453).

## Further non-custodial measures

### SUSPENDED SENTENCES AND SUSPENDED SENTENCE SUPERVISION ORDERS[6]

Under the provisions of the Criminal Justice Act 1967 (Section 39) a court which passed a sentence of immediate imprisonment for a term of not more than two years could order that the sentence should not take effect unless, during a period specified in the order, the offender committed another offence punishable with imprisonment. For certain offences of imprisonment of six months or less, suspension was made mandatory and the maximum terms of suspension allowed was three years. Under the Criminal Justice Act 1972, as amended by the Powers of Criminal Courts Act 1973, the maximum period of suspension was reduced from three to two years and it was made possible for the court, where the term of suspended sentence of imprisonment was for more than six months, to place the offender under the supervision of a probation officer for a period not exceeding the term of the suspended sentence. In 1978, some 35,000 persons were awarded suspended sentences. In the same year, some 10,000 persons were dealt with for breaches of suspended sentences by the commission of a fresh offence for which a sentence of imprisonment could be imposed; 75 per cent of these offenders received an immediate custodial sentence (Home Office 1979b: 142 and 148).

Bottoms (1981) reviewed the impact of the introduction of the suspended sentence for the years 1967–78. He concluded, as have others, that the use of the suspended sentence may have increased rather than reduced the size of the prison population. It was introduced at a time when it was important to cut back

[6] Strictly speaking, suspended sentences are custodial measures, but as the aim is for the offender to remain in the community, it seems appropriate to consider them here.

the rate of imprisonment in the short term, but the 'practical effect [was] much less than it [seemed] at first sight (because of what may be described as the "kickback" effects of breached suspended sentences)' (Bottoms 1981: 24–5). Under the Criminal Law Act 1977 (Section 47) there is a new provision, namely the introduction of a different type of suspended imprisonment. A specified part of the sentence will be served in prison, the remainder will be served in the community. This has now been implemented.

DEFERRED SENTENCE

The Criminal Justice Act 1972 empowered courts to defer sentence on an offender so that account might be taken of his behaviour and circumstances after conviction. A sentence may be deferred on one occasion only for up to six months. In 1978, a deferred sentence was used for about 1 per cent of persons sentenced for indictable offences in the Magistrates' Courts and for about 2.5 per cent of those sentenced at the Crown Courts. Of those appearing after deferment of sentence in 1978, 12 per cent of those so sentenced in the Magistrates' Courts and 30 per cent of those so sentenced in the Crown Court received a sentence of suspended or immediate imprisonment (Home Office 1979b: 143). In a study of the use made of deferred sentences by all courts in West Yorkshire, Corden and Nott found that the offender who agreed (as he must) to the deferment of his sentence could usually expect to avoid a custodial sentence and that the 'courts [were] prepared to use this measure on offenders for whom a custodial alternative may have been seriously considered' (Corden and Nott 1980: 366). The authors also found that in almost half of the cases the offender faced a completely different bench at the adjourned hearing. They suggest that this raises serious questions about how well informed the 'second' bench might be about the intention of the 'first' in deferring sentence.

COMMUNITY SERVICE ORDERS

Of all the innovations introduced by the Criminal Justice Act 1972, the community service order was probably the most forward looking. It marked a new departure in penal thinking and policy in that it aimed to forge links between offenders and those offended against; it also implied that an offender might make indirect personal reparation for his offences. Like many of the other innovations of the 1972 Act, community service orders were based upon the recommendations of a Report of the Advisory Council on the Penal System into non-custodial and semi-custodial penalties chaired by Lady Wootton (Home Office 1970a). The Act provides that a community service order can be made in respect of an offender aged seventeen or over who is convicted of an offence punishable with imprisonment. The number of hours are to be specified in the order (not fewer than 40 or more than 240) and must normally be completed within one year of the making of the order. In addition, a court cannot make such an order unless the offender consents and arrangements have been made for such unpaid work and service in the area in which the offender will reside. The court must also be satisfied after considering a probation officer's report that the person is a suitable person to undertake such service. The probation service is charged with the responsibility of organizing the scheme, screening offenders for suitability, placing them, and monitoring their progress in consultation with those organizations responsible for offering them work and other opportunities. An offender may be brought back to court for breaching the order.

There have been a number of research studies into the working of community service. It was initially mounted in five parts of the country, monitored, and is now available throughout the country. The research studies demonstrate the need for careful planning and the need to obtain the good will and support of courts, the local community, and those whose help is being sought for suitable placements for offenders (see Prins 1976, Pease *et al.* 1975, Pease 1977, and Pease and McWilliams 1980). Most probation areas have managed to make available an impressive array of opportunities; many offenders, having completed their orders satisfactorily, have stayed on to continue their work afterwards on a voluntary basis. In 1978, 11,781 offenders were made subject to community service orders for indictable offences, 961 for motoring offences, and 1413 for other non-indictable offences – 2374 altogether for non-indictable offences (Home Office 1979b: 120).

In a major recent study of the use of community service orders in five probation and after-care areas in England, Young (1979) found that there were wide variations between areas in the frequency with which community service was used. A low use was associated with a low use of other non-custodial measures and a high use of custodial sentences. There were also marked variations in the use of the penalty amongst courts *within areas*. Young reaches the somewhat gloomy conclusion that 'the Community service order is evidently no nearer to achieving coherence and consistency, in its application as a tariff sentence and in its penal objectives, than it was when it was first introduced' (Young 1979: 135). Young fears that unless there is a clarification of objectives in the use of community service, enthusiasm for what is basically a very progressive measure 'will give way to pessimism and disillusion' (Young 1979: 142; see also Prins 1976: 75–6).

DAY TRAINING AND OTHER CENTRES

Day training centres were also brought into being by the Criminal Justice Act 1972. However, they were the only major non-custodial provision that did not stem from the Wootton Report (Bottoms 1973). Although they have already been mentioned under the section dealing with the duties of proba-tion officers, such centres can be run by a person other than a probation officer. Attendance at a day centre can be made a requirement of a probation order and the centres aim to provide intensive supervision and social re-education for offenders with a history of short custodial sentences who seem to be lacking in social skills. The training period lasts up to sixty days, and attendance is on a daily basis. As with community service orders, a cautious beginning was made in one or two probation and after-care areas. The day centre idea has now caught on more widely; probation officers are finding that it provides them not only with a unique opportunity to observe offenders in a semi-controlled environment, but also with many opportunities for innovative work in the area of social skills development and a chance to assess offenders in a small group setting. In 1978 the courts made day centre attendance a requirement in 182 cases

(Home Office 1979b: 438–39). The Act also provides for probation committees to set up a variety of other day activity,
community, and support centres; in these, attendance is voluntary and is not a requirement of a probation order. Again, as
with the day centres, considerable opportunities have been
provided for innovation. Mention has already been made of the
long-standing power to provide residence in a probation home
or hostel as a requirement of a probation order. In fact, the
range of semi-custodial facilities now available is quite considerable.

### ATTENDANCE CENTRES

Attendance centres were introduced by the Criminal Justice
Act 1948. Under the auspices of the Home Office and normally,
but not exclusively, run by the police, most of them are for the
under-17 age group, but there are one or two centres for young
men aged 17–21. A *Magistrates'* Court may make an attendance
centre order if (a) it has been notified that such a centre is
available, (b) it knows that a centre is reasonably accessible, (c)
the defendant has not received a previous custodial sentence,
(d) the offence is one for which a court could have imposed a
sentence of imprisonment, or the offender has refused or neglected to pay a fine or compensation, or he has failed to comply
with the requirements of a probation order. Orders may be
made for up to twenty-four hours' attendance but lesser periods
are quite usual. Failure to attend or the commission of a serious
breach of the rules can involve the offender in being brought
back to court and dealt with for the original offence. Attendance
is usually required on Saturday afternoons – for maximum
inconvenience value to the offender! The young person is
usually provided with opportunities to develop physical skills,
to learn some craft, and to receive some basic instruction in
citizenship. One of the main aims is to encourage the constructive use of leisure pursuits once the offender has left the centre.
To this extent, they have been found to be marginally successful
(McClintock 1961, and Goodman 1965). In 1978, some 11,000
attendance centre orders were made in the Magistrates' Courts
(Home Office 1979b: 120). Since the attendance centre idea is
closely linked to more recent developments, such as intermedi-

ate treatment for young offenders, I shall return to this topic in Chapter 8.

FINES AND OTHER MONETARY PENALTIES

The fine is by far the commonest form of non-custodial penalty imposed by the courts. In the Magistrates' Courts about 90 per cent of those found guilty of non-indictable offences are fined; if motoring offences are also included, the figure climbs to 98 per cent. Those found guilty of indictable offences are fined in just under 60 per cent of cases. In the Crown Court the figure drops quite sharply: just under 40 per cent are fined for motoring offences, 9 per cent for other (non-indictable) offences, and some 14 per cent for indictable offences (Home Office 1979b: 120). In 1978, in all courts, some 213,436 persons were fined for indictable offences, 1,088,040 for motoring offences, and 354,356 were fined for other non-indictable offences (Home Office 1979b: 120). A Magistrates' Court has power to impose a maximum fine of £1000 for any of the more serious offences; by virtue of the Criminal Law Act 1977, the Home Secretary is given power to increase the maximum levels of fines in accordance with changes in the value of money. In the Crown Court, there are no set upper limits.

In most cases an offender must be allowed time to pay his fine; in the event of his not doing so, the court must normally enquire into his means before sentencing him to imprisonment in default. It is possible for courts to make orders for 'attachment of earnings', whereby arrangements are made with the offender's employer for periodical payments to be deducted from earnings. If an offender's circumstances warrant it, courts are empowered to remit all or part of a fine. Magistrates' Courts also have the power to make what is known as a money-payment supervision order, placing the offender under supervision with the aim of encouraging him to pay the fine. It has been necessary to remind courts from time to time that this is no substitute for a probation order and that the sole purpose of a money-payment supervision order is to encourage the payment of the fine so that imprisonment for default may be avoided. In most areas, ancillary workers employed by the Probation and After-Care

Service or fines enforcement officers deal with money-payment supervision cases.

Since 1972, all courts now have power to order compensation and costs; before that time there were certain limitations upon the higher courts to make such orders. The 1972 Act also clarified and widened the scope of the law that enables courts to make orders for restitution.

## MISCELLANEOUS NON-CUSTODIAL PENALTIES

Under the Criminal Justice Act 1972, courts may now order an offender to forfeit any property in his possession or control used for a facilitating a crime. The Crown Court may also disqualify

Table 7(5)   *Summary of main non-custodial measures available to the courts**

| age group | measure |
| --- | --- |
| *17 and under 21* | Absolute Discharge |
| | Conditional Discharge |
| | Bind Over |
| | Probation (with or without requirement for attendance and residence) |
| | Fine |
| | Costs, Compensation, Restitution |
| | Suspended Sentence with or without supervision. Partial Suspension of sentence of imprisonment. |
| | Attendance Centre |
| | Community Service |
| | Forfeiture, disqualification |
| | Criminal bankruptcy** |
| | Guardianship under the Mental Health Act 1959*** |
| *21 and over* | As above with the exception of Attendance Centre |

*Notes to Table 7(5)*

* The Powers of Criminal Courts Act 1973 brought together and codified in one enactment most of the law relating to the disposals referred to in this chapter. However, the earlier enactments have been referred to in order to provide a sequential account of the development of the various measures described.

** Unlikely for this age group.

*** See Chapter 9.

an offender from driving if the court is satisfied that a vehicle was used to facilitate the crime. The Act also introduced the power for the Crown Court to make a criminal bankruptcy order against an offender in addition to any other penalty (with the exception of a compensation order). In addition, the loss or damage to other parties must exceed £15,000.

## Conclusion

I have summarized the main non-custodial penalties in *Table 7(5)*. In this chapter readers have been required to absorb a large number of facts and much of the material has of necessity been more descriptive than critical. I have, however, included some references to research into the use of some of the penalties currently in use. Nevertheless, it is important to continue to view these measures and penalties not as static entities, but as reflections of, and responses to, the forces and pressures outlined in the earlier chapters of this book. Those wishing to pursue a more detailed critical examination of the tensions that exist within the penal system should consult the further reading listed at the end of this chapter. In Chapter 8, I consider some of the measures available for offenders under the age of seventeen.

## References

Atkinson, D. (1981) Nor Iron Bars a Cage: Open Prisons – Anomaly or Opportunity. *Prison Service Journal* **41** (New Series): 1–3, 10 and 12.

Bottoms, A.E. (1973) Day Training Centres. *Criminal Law Review* January: 21–3.

——— (1981) The Suspended Sentence in England, 1967–1978. *British Journal of Criminology* **21**: 1–26.

Choppen, V. (1970) The Origins of the Philosophy of Detention Centres. *British Journal of Criminology* **10**: 158–68.

Corden, J. and Nott, D. (1980) The Power to Defer Sentence. *British Journal of Criminology* **20**: 358–67.

Field, E. (1969) Research into Detention Centres. *British Journal of Criminology* **9**: 62–71.

Fox, L. (1952) *The English Prison and Borstal Systems*. London: Routledge and Kegan Paul.

Goodman, N. (1965) Manchester Senior Attendance Centre. *British Journal of Criminology* **5**: 275–88.

*Guardian, The*, 2 September 1981.

Haxby, D. (1978) *Probation: A Changing Service*. London: Constable.

Home Office (1966) *Report of the Inquiry into Prison Escapes and Security* (Mountbatten Report). Cmnd. 3175. London: HMSO.

—— (1968) *The Regime for Long Term Prisoners in Conditions of Maximum Security*. Report of the Advisory Council on the Penal System. London: HMSO.

—— (1969) *People in Prison*. Cmnd. 4214. London: HMSO.

—— (1970a) *Non-Custodial and Semi-Custodial Penalties*. Report of the Advisory Council on the Penal System. (Wootton Report). London: HMSO.

—— (1970b) *Detention Centres*. Report of the Advisory Council on the Penal System. London: HMSO.

—— (1977) *Prisons and the Prisoner: The Work of the Prison Service in England and Wales*. London: HMSO.

—— (1978) *The Sentence of the Court: A Handbook for Courts on the Treatment of Offenders*. London: HMSO.

Home Office, Scottish Office, and Northern Ireland Office (1979a) *Committee of Inquiry into the United Kingdom Prison Services* (May Report). Cmnd. 7673. London: HMSO.

Home Office (1979b) *Criminal Statistics, England and Wales, 1978*. Cmnd. 7670. London: HMSO.

—— (1980a) *Report on the Work of the Prison Department, 1979*. Cmnd. 7965. London: HMSO.

Home Office, Scottish Home and Health Department, Welsh Office, and DHSS (1980b) *The Reduction of Pressure on the Prison System: Observations on the Fifteenth Report from the Expenditure Committee*. Cmnd. 7948. London: HMSO.

Home Office (1980c) *Probation and After-Care Statistics, England and Wales, 1979*. London: Home Office.

Howard, D.L. (1960) *The English Prisons*. London: Methuen.

Jellicoe, Earl (Chairman) (1975) *Boards of Visitors of Penal Institutions*. Joint Committee of Justice, Howard League and NACRO. London.

Maguire, M. (1980) The Impact of Burglary Upon Victims. *British Journal of Criminology* **20**: 261–75.

McClintock, F.H. (1961) *Attendance Centres*. London: Macmillan.

*Observer, The*, 16 August 1981.

Parliamentary All-Party Penal Affairs Group (1980) *Too Many Prisoners: An Examination of Ways of Reducing the Prison Population*. Chichester: Barry Rose.

—— (1981) *Still Too Many Prisoners*. Chichester: Barry Rose.

Parsloe, P. (1979) After-Custody: Supervision in the Community in England, Wales and Scotland. In H. Parker *Social Work and the Courts*. London: Edward Arnold.

Pease, K. (1977) *Community Service Assessed in 1976*. Home Office Research Studies. No. 39. London: HMSO.

—— (1981) The Size of the Prison Population. *British Journal of Criminology* **21**: 70–4.

Pease, K. and McWilliams, W. (1980) (eds) *Community Service by Order*. Edinburgh: Scottish Academic Press.

Pease, K., Durkin, P., Earnshaw, I., Payne, D., and Thorpe, J. (1975) *Community Service Orders*. Home Office Research Studies. No. 29. London: HMSO.

Prins, H. (1976) Whither Community Service? *British Journal of Criminology* **16**: 73–7.

Rawls, J. (1969) Two Concepts of Rules. In H.B. Acton (ed.) *The Philosophy of Punishment*. London: Macmillan.

Rutherford, A. (1980) Report of the Inquiry into the United Kingdom Prison Services. *British Journal of Criminology* **20**: 166–70.

Sparks, R.F. (1971) *Local Prisons: The Crisis in the English Penal System*. London: Heinemann.

Walker, N. (1966) *The Aims of a Penal System: The James Seth Memorial Lecture 1966*. Edinburgh: Edinburgh University Press.

—— (1969) *Sentencing in a Rational Society*. London: Allen Lane. The Penguin Press.

—— (1980) *Punishment, Danger and Stigma: The Morality of Criminal Justice*. Oxford: Basil Blackwell.

Wright, M. (1977) Nobody Came: Criminal Justice and the Needs of Victims. *Howard Journal of Penology and Crime Prevention*. **16**: 22–31.

Young, W. (1979) *Community Service Orders: The Development and Use of a New Penal Measure*. London: Heinemann.

FURTHER READING

*On legal, judicial, and ethical aspects of punishment see:*
Grunhut, M. (1972) *Penal Reform* (reprint). New Jersey: Patterson Smith.
Hibbert, C. (1966) *The Roots of Evil: A Social History of Crime and Punishment.* Harmondsworth: Penguin Books.
Honderich, T. (1971) *Punishment: The Supposed Justifications.* Harmondsworth: Penguin Books.
Moberly, W. (1968) *The Ethics of Punishment.* London: Faber and Faber.
Rennie, Y. (1978) *The Search for Criminal Man: A Conceptual History of the Dangerous Offender.* Lexington, Massachusetts: D.C. Heath.
Rose, G. (1961) *The Struggle for Penal Reform.* London: Stevens.

*On psychological and social aspects see:*
Stephenson, G.M. (1966) *The Development of Conscience.* London: Routledge and Kegan Paul.
Walters, R.H., Cheyne, J.A., and Banks, R.K. (1972) *Punishment: Selected Readings.* Harmondsworth: Penguin Books.
Wright, D. (1971) *The Psychology of Moral Behaviour.* Harmondsworth: Penguin Books.

*For autobiographical accounts of penal experiences see:*
Behan, B. (1961) *Borstal Boy.* London: Corgi Books.
Boyle, J. (1977) *A Sense of Freedom.* London: Pan Books.
Norman, F. (1958) *Bang to Rights.* London: Secker and Warburg.
Zeno, (1968) *Life.* London: Pan Books.

*For semi-autobiographical accounts see:*
Parker, T. (1963) *The Unknown Citizen.* London: Hutchinson.
Parker, T. (with Allerton, R.) (1962) *The Courage of His Convictions.* London: Hutchinson.

*For general accounts of prisons, prisoners, and prison life see:*
Cohen, S. and Taylor, L. (1972) *Psychological Survival: The Experience of Long-Term Imprisonment.* Harmondsworth: Penguin Books.

Emery, F.M. (1970) *Freedom and Justice within Walls: The Bristol Prison Experiment*. London: Tavistock Publications.

Fitzgerald, M. (1977) *Prisoners in Revolt*. Harmondsworth: Penguin Books.

Jones, H. and Cornes, P. (1977) *Open Prisons*. London: Routledge and Kegan Paul.

King, R.D. and Morgan R. (1980) *The Future of the Prison System*. Farnborough: Gower.

Klare, H. (1962) *The Anatomy of Prison*. Harmondsworth: Penguin Books.

Mathieson, T. (1965) *The Defences of the Weak*. London: Tavistock Publications.

McConville, S. (1981) *A History of English Prison Administration 1750–1877*. London: Routledge and Kegan Paul.

Morris, N. (1974) *The Future of Imprisonment*. Chicago: University of Chicago Press.

Parker, T. (1971) *The Frying Pan*. London: Panther Books. (On Grendon Underwood Psychiatric Prison.)

Thomas, J.E. (1972) *The English Prison Officer since 1850*. London: Routledge and Kegan Paul.

*On after-care and parole see:*

Davies, M. (1974) *Prisoners of Society: Attitudes and After-Care*. London: Routledge and Kegan Paul.

Morris, P. and Beverly, F. (1975) *On Licence: A Study of Parole*. London: Wiley.

Nuttall, C.P., Barnard, E.E., Fowles, A.J., Frost, A., Hammond, W.H., Mayhew, P., Pease, K., Tarling, R., and Weatheritt, M.J. (1977) *Parole in England and Wales*. Home Office Research Studies. No. 38. London: HMSO.

Thomas, D.A. (ed.) (1974) *Parole: Its Implications for the Criminal Justice and Penal Systems*. Cambridge: University of Cambridge.

*On the probation service more generally see:*

King, J.F.S. (ed.) (1979) *Pressures and Change in the Probation Service*. Cambridge: (Institute of Criminology) University of Cambridge.

Monger, M. (1972) *Casework in Probation* (second edition). London: Butterworths.

# CHAPTER EIGHT

# *Measures for young offenders (under seventeen)*[1]

> Our youths love luxury; they have bad manners, contempt for authority and disrespect of older people. Children nowadays are tyrants, they contradict their parents and tyrannize their teachers.
>
> SOCRATES

> I would there were no age between sixteen and three and twenty, or that youth would sleep out the rest; for there is nothing in the between but getting wenches with child, wronging the ancientry, stealing, fighting.
>
> THE WINTER'S TALE

> Youth and age will never agree.
>
> SIXTEENTH-CENTURY PROVERB

## Perspective

A sense of history helps to lend perspective to contemporary issues, especially if they are concerned with a problem as emotive as the misbehaviour of young people. The quotations at

---

[1] For the purposes of the criminal law, a 'child' is a person under the age of 14, a 'young person' is over 14 but under 17. In this chapter I use the terms synonymously unless I state otherwise. In addition the statement of law and practice is as it applies in England and Wales; the Scottish system of more informal hearings for dealing with youthful offenders is very different and, although interesting and innovative, cannot be discussed here.

the head of this chapter reflect an age-old concern; today's problems are by no means new. Despite this, there are today one or two additional factors that should be taken into account as a background to any discussion of the problem of the antisocial behaviour of the young. First, as I have already indicated in Chapter 3, the social pressures on the young people of today are enormous; not only do we have at the present time a massive scale of unemployment, but we are also faced with not having adequately understood, or come to grips with, the wider problems of young people in a multiracial society. Second, it is probably true to say that today many young people show, superficially at least, a degree of *apparent* sophistication and worldly wisdom that was not commonly observed fifty years ago. It would appear that young people today are more 'knowledgeable' than their parents (the word is used here in its wider and older sense: to have experience of).

Both history and social anthropology reveal that there has always been a degree of tension between young and old; indeed zoologists and ethologists would suggest that such tension is necessary for human survival. Thus it may well be a good thing for young people to have something against which to rebel: the periods of rebelliousness may enable them to work out for themselves their personal solutions and ethical values. It seems likely that the children of firm but just parents, as long as they are not overwhelmed, can identify with their parents' strengths and face life the better. Over the last 40 to 50 years many parents have become overwhelmed by conflicting advice from a plethora of experts on how to bring up their children, and some of them have been forced to give up the struggle and abrogate their responsibilities; others have become so uncertain in their handling that their children are left in a kind of emotional 'limbo'. Clinical experience tells us that such an abrogation of responsibilities or emotional limbo can produce fertile ground for the growth of delinquency. If we add these considerations to some of the social pressures referred to in Chapter 3, it is not hard to see that many young people have problems in coming to terms with persons in authority, whether these be parents, teachers, employers, or more direct representatives of law and order.

## Brief historical background

From earliest times, the law has attempted to have special regard for the needs of the young offender. (See for example Walker 1968, Chapter 1). The early English Poor Law, to which reference was made in Chapter 7, continued this regard for these special needs. However, as history shows, the law was applied unevenly and was also harsh and paternalistic (see Cohen 1949: 19–43). In effect, society tended to regard children as adults in miniature, an attitude which significantly influenced the attitudes towards and the treatment of children until the beginning of the twentieth century. Previous centuries had witnessed both exploitation and ill-treatment of children, and this despite various attempts to legislate for their protection and despite the work of outstanding pioneers in children's welfare such as Coram, Barnardo, and Shaftsbury. However, it was not until the beginning of the twentieth century that the first *substantial* legislative reforms for the treatment of young *offenders* were introduced. As I showed in Chapter 7, the time was then ripe for legislation to make an impact.

In 1933, the Children and Young Persons Act of that year helped to consolidate provisions available to the Juvenile Court for the treatment of both the delinquent and the deprived child. The problems of the latter were highlighted during the Second World War when many problems arose as a result of children being separated from their parents and because of difficulties involved in providing good substitute care. A grim account of these is given in the report of the Curtis Committee (Home Office 1946). The Children Act 1948 implemented the recommendations of the Curtis Committee. It established a single local-authority committee to be responsible for all deprived children, whether delinquent or not, and it made the appointment of a children's committee and a children's officer obligatory. In the early 1950s, further attention was directed to the problems of delinquent children in two important central government circulars, whose message to both local authorities and voluntary organizations was that the emphasis wherever possible should be on the prevention of juvenile delinquency. This need for preventive work was given the force of law in the provisions of the Children and Young Persons (Amendment)

Act 1952, which suggested, but did not instruct, children's committees to investigate all cases where children might be in need of care. Despite these measures and proposals, the steady rise in juvenile delinquency continued to cause concern. In 1960, a government committee under the chairmanship of Viscount Ingleby reported, *inter alia*, on two important matters: first, the problems presented by the delinquent child, and second, the deprivations suffered by the child subjected to neglect (Home Office 1960). The Children and Young Persons Act 1963, which implemented a number of the committee's proposals, went some way towards making improvements, but many people were still particularly unhappy about the role of the courts in the treatment of youthful delinquents. Underlying this unhappiness was the age-old problem of trying to reconcile the conflicting welfare needs of children on the one hand, and the need to protect society from their depredations on the other. It is this dilemma that has bedevilled law and policy-making in this area since the nineteenth century. As I shall show shortly, even with the rather more adventurous and benign approach to the problem of more recent years, the difficulty remains and is likely to do so. Nowhere is the general problem of reconciling the conflicting aims of punishment thrown up more clearly than in the treatment of the youthful offender.

In the mid-1960s, and largely as a result of the continuing concern just described, two now famous White Papers appeared. The first of these, *The Child, The Family and The Young Offender*, which appeared in 1965 (Home Office 1965), met with a considerable degree of opposition and criticism, largely because it was considered to be poorly thought out, too radical, and based more upon sentiment than upon any real appreciation of the needs of young delinquents. Three years later, a second White Paper appeared, entitled *Children in Trouble* (Home Office 1968a). This contained a number of rather less radical proposals for reform of the law and practice concerning young offenders. The proposals may be summarized baldly as follows:

(1) The introduction of new legal procedures for dealing with the under-14 age group.

(2) Provision for the restriction of prosecution of offenders aged 14 and under 17.

(3) Proposals for merging and rationalizing the various existing forms of residential provision, such as the existing approved schools, children's homes, and hostels.

(4) The introduction of a new form of disposal: 'intermediate treatment'.

(5) The introduction of regional planning to further the rationalization in (3) above.

Very shortly after the appearance of the second White Paper, the Report of the Committee on Local Authority and Allied Personal Social Services (Seebohm Report) was published (Home Office, Department of Education and Science, Ministry of Local Government, and Ministry of Health 1968b). Appearing as it did at this particular point in time, it probably deflected some attention from a number of important issues in the White Paper. The Seebohm Committee's proposals for restructuring the local authority personal social services were nearly all implemented in the Local Authority Social Services Act of 1970. As a result of this legislation, the children's committees and children's officers set up by the 1948 Act disappeared and were incorporated into the new Departments of Social Services headed by a director, who might or might not have had special experience of, and an interest in, the needs of children. To complicate matters still further, local authority social services departments also had to take on the additional work of implementing the Chronically Sick and Disabled Persons Act of 1970. Not long afterwards, they also had to cope not only with boundary changes in local government areas, but with the social-work implications of the reorganization of the National Health Service.

Many of the changes proposed in the White Paper were incorporated into the Children and Young Persons Act 1969. A number of the recommended changes still have to be implemented and, as we shall shortly see, in the past few years there have been calls for yet a further review of the legislation. This has arisen mainly because of dissatisfaction with the way the system has been working, because of lack of resources, and because many people consider that current legislation does not give sufficient protection to the rights of the child. (See for example Freeman 1981.) Before proceeding to make some critical comment upon current provisions and recent proposals for reform, it is necessary to describe briefly first of all the legislation prior to the 1969 Act, and then the new legislation it implemented.

## Summary of provisions prior to 1969

### CRIMINAL RESPONSIBILITY

The age of criminal responsibility was ten. Proceedings in respect of criminal offences could not be taken against children below that age, although such children could be brought before the juvenile court as in need of care or protection. Children below the age of fourteen were subject to the rule of *doli incapax* (legal presumption of a lack of guilty intent), and it was up to the prosecution to prove that the child possessed guilty intent.

### CRIMINAL PROCEEDINGS

Juvenile courts had always been able to make use of many of the provisions available for adults, such as fines, discharge, and probation (with or without a requirement as to residence). In the case of fining, the parents could, in certain circumstances, be ordered to pay the fine instead of the child. In addition to these more general powers, the juvenile court could order attendance at an attendance centre, commit to an approved school, to the care of the local authority under a fit person order, or commit (if male and over fourteen) to a detention centre. They were also able to commit to the then Quarter Sessions with a view to the imposition of a sentence of borstal training. In addition, if a young offender was found guilty of murder he could be ordered by the then Assize Court to be detained 'during Her Majesty's pleasure'. A young person convicted of any other grave crime (which, if committed by an adult, might carry a sentence of fourteen years' imprisonment or more) could also be ordered to be detained under such conditions as the Home Secretary might from time to time determine.

NON-CRIMINAL PROCEEDINGS

(These are mentioned here briefly in order to fill out the picture, though they are not in themselves of direct concern to us in this book.)

Children and young persons could be brought before the Juvenile Court as in need of care or protection as, for example, when they were considered to be falling into bad associations, were beyond the control of their parents, had persistently failed to attend school regularly, or had been the victims of offences committed against them. In all such cases, the child or young person could be placed under the supervision of a probation officer or other person selected by the court, or committed to the care of the local authority or to an approved school.

## Current legal and administrative provisions

The White Paper, *Children in Trouble*, recognized the ubiquity and wide range of delinquent behaviour and the diversity of explanations for it. It also recognized the conflicts in trying to reconcile justice and welfare.

> 'An important object of the criminal law is to protect society . . . but the community also recognizes the importance of caring for those who are too young to protect themselves. Over recent years these two quite distinct grounds for action by society in relation to young people have been moving steadily closer together. It has become increasingly clear that social control of harmful behaviour by the young, and social measures to help and protect the young, are not distinct and separate processes. The aims of protecting society from juvenile delinquency, and of helping children to grow up into mature and law abiding citizens, are complementary and not contradictory.'                          (Home Office 1968a: 3–4)

The implementation of the White Paper proposals in the 1969 Act was based upon the assumption that deprivation and delinquency are so closely related that it was not necessary to provide separate forms of treatment (see also Chapter 5). In sum:

> 'the legislators and those advising them . . . had to contrive to

reconcile two apparently opposing points of view; first, the view that regards children who break the law as children whose parents need help in bringing them up, and secondly, the view that regards children as primarily offenders from whose activities the community must protect itself.'

(Prins 1970: 76)

PROCEEDINGS PRIOR TO COURT APPEARANCE

The Act aims to keep as many children and young persons out of court as possible. Before youngsters can be brought before the court, there must be consultation between the police, the local authority and, if appropriate, the probation service, with a view to finding alternative remedies. In addition, in the new 'care proceedings' which the Act introduced, the commission of a criminal offence itself *can be taken into account*, but is *not of itself* a sufficient justification for intervention. Once proceedings have been taken, the court has to be guided by the following provisions:

*Section 1(2)* of the 1969 Act provides that:
The court before which a child or young person is brought under this section has to be satisfied that any of the following conditions are met with respect to him, namely that:

(a) His proper development is being avoidably prevented or neglected or his health is being avoidably impaired or neglected or he is being ill-treated; or,

(b) It is probable that the condition set out in (a) above will be satisfied in his case, having regard to the fact that the court or another court has found that that condition is or was satisfied in the case of another child or young person who is or was a member of the household to which he belongs; or,

(c) He is exposed to moral danger; or,

(d) He is beyond the control of his parent or guardian; or,

(e) He is not attending school within the meaning of the Education Act 1944; or,

(f) He is guilty of an offence (excluding homicide[2]) *and also* that he is in need of care or control which he is unlikely to receive

---

[2] Such cases can only be dealt with by the Crown Court.

unless the court makes an order under this section in respect of him.

It is made clear in the Act that two sides of an 'equation' have to be proved, namely the existence of one of the conditions listed above *and* the care or control requirement; to establish one without the other is not sufficient. Space precludes a detailed discussion here of the various interpretations that can be placed upon some of the conditions described above, but they have been subjected to a good deal of criticism and comment in recent years. (See for example McClean 1980, Freeman 1981, and Tutt 1981.) In the event of the court finding the conditions proved they have power in the case of offences to make the following orders.

PRESENT POWERS

*Non-residential measures*

In the case of criminal proceedings the Court may make a *supervision order* for not more than three years. Until the Criminal Law Act 1977, it was not possible to insert specific requirements in such an order or to impose sanctions for breaching it. The 1977 Act now makes both of these possible providing more 'bite' and bringing the supervision order more into line with the sanctions of a probation order. The Court may bind over the offender or his parents or guardian for a maximum period of three years and a maximum sum of £300. It may give the offender an absolute or conditional discharge, fine him, make an order for restitution or compensation, or make a guardianship order under the Mental Health Act 1959 (see Chapter 9). As already noted, the Court may order attendance at an attendance centre. The architects of the 1968 White Paper had anticipated that when schemes of intermediate treatment got under way (see below) it would be possible to phase out attendance centres. Far from this being the case, the numbers and use of attendance centres for the junior age groups has increased over the years. At the beginning of 1979, there were 71 junior attendance centres for boys (aged 10 and under 17), 6 for girls under 17, and 3 for boys *and* girls under 17 (Home Office,

Welsh Office, and DHSS 1980). (See also discussion under adult offenders in Chapter 7.)

### Intermediate treatment

Intermediate treatment was envisaged by the drafters of the 1968 White Paper with the aim of introducing a high degree of variety and flexibility into the treatment measures available for young offenders.

The idea of some form of treatment that stood midway between institutional and community care was first put forward in 1962 in a report on non-residential treatment of offenders under twenty-one (Home Office 1962). The committee was anxious that such experiments should be conducted within the framework of existing services that were designed to provide for the social education of young people generally (Home Office 1962). It is of interest to note two things here. First, the idea itself was not new, even in 1962. As long ago as 1927, the Moloney Committee on the Treatment of Young Offenders (Home Office 1927) considered that the best hope of reducing juvenile offences lay in developing and strengthening educational measures. Second, the notion was put forward that intermediate treatment should use and forge links with the community's general services for young people and that it should aim to diminish the gap between the young offender and the community. (In this respect, the thinking behind it has something in common with the ideas behind community service that I discussed in Chapter 7.) The term intermediate treatment was not used in the Act itself, but provisions for it were contained in Section 12 where powers to make supervision orders were discussed. When first introduced, provision was made for a form of treatment which *might* involve residence of up to ninety days (so that to this extent it can be regarded as a semi-residential measure). This provision has now been removed by the amendment provided by the Criminal Law Act referred to above. The effect of this is that:

'intermediate treatment is essentially participation under the charge of the supervisor or other responsible person, and as far as possible in the company of children who are taking part voluntarily, in activities of a recreational, educational or cultural nature or of social value.'

(McClean 1980: 131)

Attendance still remains at ninety days, but the court may specify attendance for shorter periods.

When first introduced, intermediate treatment as a form of semi-residential provision was hailed as something of a panacea for the ills caused by juvenile delinquency. Gradually, a more cautious stance has been adopted and as schemes have developed in various parts of the country and attempts made to evaluate them, so their merits have been discerned more objectively. Thorpe and his colleagues at the University of Lancaster have conducted a series of research studies into the provision of intermediate treatment. They have concluded that it has much to offer, but only if schemes are well researched, well planned, and executed with clearly defined objectives (Thorpe *et al.* 1980). For, as has been pointed out:

'Intermediate Treatment is *not* 'revolutionary' in the sense that it provides a system of care and involvement that has never been used before. It seeks rather to stimulate the use of existing resources, makes payment specifically available for them, and provides opportunities for their assessment. Moreover, its provisions help to blur boundaries.'

(Prins 1972: 5)

*Residential measures – care orders*

Under the provisions of the 1969 Act, approved school orders and fit person orders disappeared and were replaced by one single *care order*. This places the responsibility for determining what kind of residential care is appropriate solely in the hands of the local authority social services department. Not a few magistrates and some social workers have been critical of this new power. Magistrates consider that it removed from them the power of deciding what kind of residential care would be best and that it placed too much control in the hands of the executive. Following the disappearance of the approved school and fit person orders, the previous system of approved schools, remand homes, children's homes, and hostels was gradually replaced by a network of community homes. Under the 1969 Act, a *care order* commits a child to the care of the local authority in whose area he resides until he reaches the age of 18, or, if the child was already 16 when the order was made, until he reaches the age of 19. The regulations concerning the duties of a local authority towards children in its care (for whatever reason) are complex and cannot be discussed here. Suffice it to say that provisions are being introduced increasingly to safeguard the rights and interests of children in care. This is being achieved through the provision of 'independent' visitors who can watch over the welfare of those children in particular who have no contact with or are without parents, or those who are held in 'secure accommodation' because of their unruly or difficult behaviour (Child Care Act 1980). In 1978, 5364 care orders were made for indictable offences and 402 for non-indictable offences (Home Office 1979: 120).

*Other residential provisions*

Reference was made in Chapter 7 to the means whereby young adult offenders could be sent to borstal or to a detention centre. These provisions are also available for the young offender. In addition, as already mentioned, from time to time a few young people are convicted of very grave crimes. Under the provisions of the Children and Young Persons Act 1933, such young people may be detained in such institutions as the Home Secretary may from time to time decide. For example, a youthful murderer may start his institutional career in community-home education (formerly called an approved school) and subsequently be transferred to borstal or at a later stage to prison. In such cases, the Parole Board advises the Home Secretary on matters concerning release into the community. From time to time, other young offenders become too disturbed or disruptive to be handled in the ordinary community-home system. They may then have to be catered for either in special 'secure units' – in community homes or hospitals – or in one of the two specialist high security youth treatment centres (St Charles in Essex and Glenthorne in Birmingham). *Table 8(1)* provides a summary of the measures available for children and young persons found guilty of offences.

Table 8(1)   *Summary of main measures available for dealing with children and young persons involved in criminal proceedings*

| | |
|---|---|
| residential provision | care order |
| | detention centre (1) |
| | borstal (2) |
| | hospital order (3) |
| | detention for grave crimes only by order of the Secretary of State |
| non-residential and semi-residential provision | supervision order (4) |
| | binding over (of parents, guardian, or offender) |
| | absolute or conditional discharge |
| | fine and/or compensation (5) |
| | attendance centre |

*Notes to Table 8(1)*

(1) Only if aged 14 and over.

(2) 15 and over – committed by the Crown Court (there are one or two exceptions: absconders from borstal may be recommitted by magistrates).

(3) See Chapter 9.

(4) With or without requirements for good behaviour, residence, psychiatric treatment, or intermediate treatment. Supervision is undertaken by the probation service or the local authority social services department. Local authority social workers are responsible for the supervision of children under the age of 13 *unless the probation service is already involved with the family*. However, responsibility for the supervision of juvenile offenders aged 13–16 may be allocated by the court to *either* the probation service *or* to the local authority in the light of individual circumstances and any arrangements made between the probation and after-care committee and the local authority. (Those wishing to familiarize themselves with the functions and duties of local authority social services departments in more detail should consult Sainsbury 1977.)

(5) For a child, the maximum fine is £50, normally on parent or guardian. For a young person it is £200. (Criminal Law Act, 1977.)

   In respect of compensation, the maximum is £100 (Children and Young Persons Act 1969).

## Recent criticisms and proposals for the future

Some of the concern expressed by those who have been involved in, or who have had to operate, the new system has already been touched upon. We must now consider this concern in a little more detail. As already mentioned, magistrates think that the new Act removed from them the judicial discretion to direct a placement they had exercised previously. Before the 1969 Act, they had been able to determine, after taking advice, whether or not a young offender needed the somewhat more stringent training regime of an approved school, or the somewhat softer, more intimate provisions of, say, a small local authority children's home. But now the distinctions are blurred (at least in theory), for the balance of opinion has come down in favour of treating deprived and delinquent children in the same manner – a decision based on the somewhat dubious belief that, as the root causes were the same, the remedy could also be generalized. (For a compelling argument against this belief, see Sparks 1968 and 1969.) The decision failed to recognize that before such a realignment of institutional and community provisions could occur, staffs would need to be helped to develop special skills in handling difficult and disruptive children; in addition, special accommodation would need to be provided. Contrary to the belief of those who pioneered the 1969 Act that fewer children would need to be 'locked up', the reverse has proved to be the case. Some youngsters proved far too difficult for the smaller children's establishments to handle, with the result that some of them, placed by the courts on care orders, were allowed to remain at home by local authority social services departments. The further consequence of this was that they soon re-offended. This re-offending, and the fact that a number of these youngsters also absconded from the more open facilities to which they were eventually sent, meant that a not insignificant proportion of them found their way prematurely into the penal system – to borstals, detention centres, and to prison on remand. This last measure was a result of Juvenile Courts being persuaded to issue a 'certificate of unruly character' because of inadequate alternative provision. (See Thorpe *et al.* 1980 for a detailed discussion of this matter.) In addition, individual local authorities, despite the provisions in the 1969 Act for regional planning, had to make increasing provision for 'secure accommodation' for those youngsters who were proving too disruptive or disturbed to be contained in more open accommodation. To monitor this, local authority personal social services committees have had to set up special secure accommodation subcommittees whose membership must include a specially appointed 'independent' member whose job it is to help safeguard the interests of such children (see earlier discussion). At the risk of over-simplifying a very complex problem, one is compelled to ask what has really been achieved by some of the so-called more progressive residential measures provided by the 1969 Act. The fundamental dilemmas of welfare versus justice and care versus control still exist, and no amount of 'window-dressing' by renaming court orders and establishments is likely to resolve them. As with adult offenders, so with the young, we often fail to distinguish effectively between the social nuisance and the social menace. Such failure means that our provisions hover precariously over both, so that neither group is catered for adequately. Since society is always anxious about even minor law-breaking, and since the young (especially if they are working class or anti-establishment) are often viewed with suspicion by the majority of so-called law-abiding adults, such conflicts are likely to remain. More recent proposals to deal with some of these problems and to rationalize the disparate facilities for the young *adult* offender and the *young* offender provide yet further illustration.

The recent White Paper entitled *Young Offenders* (Home Office, Welsh Office, and DHSS 1980) makes a number of proposals for further reform.[3] The most significant of these seems to be a proposal to exert more control over young offenders in the community by means of a new 'supervised activity order'. In addition to this, it is also proposed that the courts should be able to make a specific 'intermediate treatment order' and that they should have a more active role in determining the requirements of supervision. These measures would be buttressed by the proposal to make community service available to those aged 16. If a juvenile already in care as an offender is found guilty of a further imprisonable offence, it is also proposed that the courts should be able to add a 'residential care order', with the effect that for a fixed period not exceeding six months he will not be allowed to remain at home. This is aimed

[3] This latest White Paper reflects and brings together a number of proposals that have been mooted for the reform of the law and of provisions for the 14–21 age group since 1974. (See Home Office 1974, Home Office *et al.* 1976, and Home Office 1978.)

no doubt at dealing with some of the criticisms voiced by the magistrates and referred to earlier. It is proposed to retain the detention centre for males aged 14 and under 17, but the minimum and maximum periods of detention will be shorter (from 3 weeks to 4 months). Sentences of borstal training and imprisonment for those aged 17 and under 21 will be replaced by a single determinate sentence, to be named 'youth custody'; those serving a medium-length youth-custody sentence will be catered for in designated training centres. Supervision of all young adult offenders on discharge from youth custody or detention will be for a period of not less than 3 or more than 12 months.

The proposal for youth custody as a sentence would require repeal of the relevant section of the Criminal Justice Act 1961. This placed severe restrictions on a court's powers to pass a sentence of imprisonment on young adult offenders aged 17 and under 21. Normally, if a court wished to pass a sentence of more than six months' imprisonment but less than three years, it had to pass a borstal sentence. At the time of writing, all these new proposals, both for the 17–21 age group and for those aged under 17, are still under discussion (see also notes to *Table 8(2)*). One cannot help thinking that useful though some of

Table 8(2)  *White paper proposals for new and rationalized measures for young adult and young offenders* *

| | |
|---|---|
| *custodial/institutional proposals* | |
| 14 and under 21 (males only) | detention centre (3 weeks to 4 months) |
| 15 and under 21 | 'youth custody' order (1) |
| 10 and under 17 | 'residential care order' (not to exceed 6 months) (2) |
| | |
| *non-custodial proposals* | |
| young persons aged 16 | community service order |
| 10 and under 17 | 'supervised activities order' |

*Notes to Table 8(2)*
* For further analysis of the impact of these proposals see Rutherford (1981). They are currently before Parliament in the Criminal Justice Bill 1981.
(1) For those aged 15 and 16, maximum term to be 12 months.
(2) For juvenile offenders already on a care order.

them may be, they are to a large extent a further 'tinkering' with a system that, as I have already indicated, continues to fail to reconcile conflicting needs. Tutt (1981) highlights the problem very cogently when he suggests that one of the outcomes of the proposals in the White Paper would be to 'suck in' more young offenders to the penal system. He also suggests that an expansion of disposals available to magistrates 'far from acting as an alternative to custody, acts as an addition with new offenders being recruited into the system' (Tutt 1981: 255). He also suggests that 'although a system based on overt social control may not be attractive, it must be the responsibility of its critics to offer a different philosophy – currently there is little agreement on what this should be' (Tutt 1981: 256).

The proposed new measures are outlined briefly in *Table 8(2)*.

From the more general considerations discussed in this chapter and the previous one, we move on in Chapters 9 and 10 to discuss more specific problem areas.

## References

Cohen, E.W. (1949) *English Social Services*. London: Allen and Unwin.

Freeman, M.D.A. (1981) The Rights of Children When They Do 'Wrong'. *British Journal of Criminology* **21**: 210–29.

Home Office (1927) *Report of the Committee on the Treatment of Young Offenders*. (Moloney Committee) Cmnd. 2381. London: HMSO.

—— (1946) *Report of the Care of Children Committee*. (Curtis Committee) Cmnd. 6922. London: HMSO.

—— (1960) *Report of the Committee on Children and Young Persons*. (Ingleby Committee) Cmnd. 1191. London: HMSO.

—— (1962) *Advisory Council on the Treatment of Offenders*. Non Residential Treatment of Offenders Under 21. London: HMSO.

—— (1965) *The Child, The Family and The Young Offender*. Cmnd. 2742. London: HMSO.

—— (1968a) *Children in Trouble*. Cmnd. 3601. London: HMSO.

Home Office, Department of Education and Science, Ministry of Local Government, and Ministry of Health (1968b) *Report of the Committee on Local Authority and Allied Personal Social Services*. (Seebohm Committee) Cmnd. 3703. London: HMSO.

Home Office (1974) *Young Adult Offenders*. Report of the Advisory Council on the Penal System. London: HMSO.

—— (1978) *Youth Custody and Supervision. A New Sentence*. Cmnd. 7406. London: HMSO.

—— (1979) *Criminal Statistics: England and Wales, 1978*. Cmnd. 7670. London: HMSO.

Home Office, Welsh Office, DHSS, and Department of Education and Science (1976) *Children and Young Person's Act, 1969. Observations on the Eleventh Report from the Expenditure Committee*. Cmnd. 6494. London: HMSO.

Home Office, Welsh Office, and DHSS (1980) *Young Offenders*. Cmnd. 8045. London: HMSO.

McClean, J.D. (1980) *The Legal Context of Social Work* (second edition). London: Butterworths.

Prins, H. (1970) Children Out of Trouble. *British Journal of Criminology* **10**: 73–8.

—— (1972) An Example of Compulsory Benevolence: Intermediate Treatment Examined. *Social Work Today* **4**: 2–5.

Rutherford, A. (1981) Young Offenders: Comments on the White Paper on Young Adult and Juvenile Offenders. *British Journal of Criminology* **21**: 74–8.

Sainsbury, E. (1977) *The Personal Social Services*. London: Pitman Publishing.

Sparks, R.F. (1968) 'Children in Trouble' Attacked. *New Society* 26.9.68.

—— (1969) The Depraved Are Not Just Deprived. *New Society* 24.7.69.

Thorpe, D.H., Smith, D., Green, C.J., and Paley, J.H. (1980) *Out of Care: The Community Support of Juvenile Offenders*. London: George Allen and Unwin.

Tutt, N. (1981) A Decade of Policy. *British Journal of Criminology* **21**: 246–56.

Walker, N. (1968) *Crime and Insanity in England*. Edinburgh: Edinburgh University Press.

FURTHER READING

*Residential provision*

*There is a vast literature on all aspects of residential provision. The following are useful surveys and afford an introduction:*

Berry, J.H. (1975) *Daily Experience in Residential Life*. London: Routledge and Kegan Paul.

Carlebach, J. (1970) *Caring for Children in Trouble*. London: Routledge and Kegan Paul.

Heywood, J. (1959) *Children in Care*. London: Routledge and Kegan Paul. (On historical developments generally)

Millham, S., Bullock, R., and Hosie, K. (1978) *Locking Up Children*. London: Saxon House.

Rose, G. (1967) *Schools for Young Offenders*. London: Tavistock Publications.

Wills, D. (1971) *Spare the Child: The Story of an Experimental Approved School*. Harmondsworth: Penguin Books.


*Social policy issues and current developments:*

Berlins, G. and Wansell, M. (1975) *Caught in the Act*. Harmondsworth: Penguin Books.

Boss, P. (1967) *Social Policy and the Young Delinquent*. London: Routledge and Kegan Paul.

Holt, J. (1975) *Escape from Childhood*. Harmondsworth: Penguin Books.

Morris, A. and McIssac, M. (1978) *Juvenile Justice?* London: Heinemann.

Parsloe, P. (1978) *Juvenile Justice in Britain and the United States*. London: Routledge and Kegan Paul.

Priestley, P., Fears, D., and Fuller, R. (1977) *Justice for Juveniles*. London: Routledge and Kegan Paul.


*On intermediate treatment specifically see:*

Jones, R. and Kerslake, A. (1979) *Intermediate Treatment and Social Work*. London: Heinemann Educational Books.

Leggett, E. (1979) *Wandsworth – A Multi-Disciplinary Approach to Intermediate Treatment*. Leicester: National Youth Bureau.
Paley, J. and Thorpe, D. (1974) *Children: Handle with Care*. Leicester: National Youth Bureau.

# CHAPTER NINE

## The mentally disordered (abnormal) offender

Canst thou not minister to a mind diseas'd,
Pluck from the memory a rooted sorrow,
Raze out the written troubles of the brain,
And with some sweet oblivious antidote
Cleanse the stuff'd bosom of that perilous stuff
Which weighs upon the heart?

MACBETH

In Chapters 1 and 5 brief reference was made to criminal responsibility and the relationship between mental disorder and criminal behaviour. We must now consider further aspects of these as they relate to the powers of the courts and the penal and hospital systems to deal with mentally disordered offenders. In addition, we shall refer briefly to the problems presented by those mentally disordered offenders thought to be dangerous.

### Definition of terms

It is necessary to explain the choice of title for this chapter. The term mentally disordered is used here as it is in the Mental Health Act 1959, namely to include mental illness (which is not defined in the Act), mental subnormality (including severe subnormality), psychopathy, and any other disorder or disability of mind. This enables us to deal with a broad range of mental states and conditions under one all-embracing title. The use of the term 'abnormal' is also useful for two reasons. First, because it includes persons who can be said to be mentally abnormal in the sense of departing from the statistical norm of mental functioning, although not necessarily mentally disordered. Second, it enables us to refer to persons who have committed offences under the influence of alcohol and other drugs, without begging the question whether such offences involve mental disorder as such. (See the Report of the Butler Committee for a further discussion of this important issue, Home Office and DHSS 1975: 4.)

## Brief historical context

Generally speaking, men and women are held responsible in law for their actions. However, over the centuries, exceptions to this principle have been noted. In Biblical times, although justice was severe, if a crime was unintentional some mitigation of penalty was available, as for example in the cities of refuge that existed for those who killed unintentionally. In Roman times, the beginnings of an attempt to introduce some notion of diminishment of responsibility in criminal matters can be discerned and Walker has identified similar attempts in the Saxon era (Walker 1968). In the thirteenth century it was generally held that neither the 'child nor the madman' should be held criminally liable and these ideas gathered momentum in the seventeenth and eighteenth centuries. However, it is probably safe to assume that in respect of mental illness the jurists of those days were concerned mainly with cases of frank insanity ('raving lunacy') akin to what we would regard today as acute psychotic behaviour. Such a state of mind was pleaded occasionally as a means of exculpation from responsibility for offences such as murder. The case of the brain-injured Hadfield, who was tried in 1800 for shooting at George III, was probably one of the first occasions on which brain injury had been used to plead diminishment of responsibility.

The trial of Daniel M'Naghten[1] in 1843 for attempting to murder Peel, the Prime Minister, is probably the most famous of all the early cases in which insanity was pleaded as a defence. M'Naghten probably suffered from what would today be regarded as paranoid delusions; he was eventually found not guilty by reason of insanity. Queen Victoria, who had herself

---

[1] The spelling of his name has varied over the years; I have adopted that in use currently.

been the victim of several attempted assaults upon her person, expressed dissatisfaction with the verdict; it was probably this dissatisfaction, amongst other matters, that led to the decision of the House of Lords to call the judges before them to clarify matters of law and practice concerning insanity. Two of the answers given by the judges eventually came to be known as the 'M'Naghten Rules'. Without going into the detail of these rules here, we can say that they state that a man shall have a defence if, first, he did not know the nature and quality of his act or, second, if he did know it but did not know it was wrong in law. The rules only really cover cases of extreme delusional insanity. Since the introduction of the Homicide Act 1957, 'M'Naghten madness' is rarely pleaded today (*see Table 9(1)*). (I have only provided a very summary account of the history here; those wishing to pursue it further should consult Walker (1968), West and Walk (1977), and Prins (1980).

Dissatisfaction with the 'Rules' had been expressed for many years, and the matter was re-examined in the Report of the Royal Commission on Capital Punishment in 1953. Partly as a result of this re-examination, and borrowing also from Scottish precedent and practice, the concept of diminished responsibility was introduced by the Homicide Act 1957. The advantage of this Act was that it reduced what would otherwise be murder to manslaughter; in so doing it enabled the courts to take into consideration a far greater range of disorders than the more restrictive 'M'Naghten Rules'. Murder is now reduced to manslaughter if the accused 'was suffering from such abnormality of mind (whether arising from a condition of arrested or retarded development of mind or any inherent causes or induced by disease or injury) as substantially impaired his mental responsibility' (Homicide Act, Section 2).[2]

## Present legal provisions

The law makes general provision for what I call 'erosions' of criminal responsibility in a variety of ways (see Prins 1980,

[2] It should also be noted that the Murder (Abolition of Death Penalty) Act 1965 suspended capital punishment for five years. This suspension is now continued permanently by virtue of affirmative resolution made by both Houses of Parliament in 1969. Murder is now punishable by a mandatory sentence of life imprisonment.

Chapter 2 for a detailed discussion). In Chapter 8 we saw what can happen in the case of children and young persons. In certain cases, it has been held that involuntary conduct (caused for example by sleep or physical illness) may allow exculpation from criminal responsibility; in other very rare cases a state of automatism will be accepted and occasionally intoxication may provide a defence in cases where a specific intent has to be proved. We must now turn to more detailed examination of the way in which mental disorder may impinge upon criminal responsibility and the means whereby such impingement is dealt with through the administrative, penal, and hospital systems. In attempting to summarize the rather complicated provisions, I have followed the divisions provided in the Butler Report (Home Office and DHSS 1975).

PRE-TRIAL ACTION, I.E., THE DECISION TO PROSECUTE

In Chapter 2, I referred to the wide discretionary powers exercised by the police and other authorities in deciding whether or not to prosecute an alleged offender. This discretion is not infrequently exercised in relation to patients in psychiatric and subnormality hospitals who may commit fairly minor offences, either when on town parole or during brief absconsions. In such cases they are often merely returned to the hospital. Under Section 136 of the Mental Health Act 1959, the police are enabled to take persons found in a place to which the public have access and *who seem to them* to be seriously mentally disordered to a place of safety, and to detain them for up to seventy-two hours so that they may be examined and assessed with a view to their being hospitalized. In a number of these cases it is clear that this procedure may obviate the need for prosecution for such fairly minor offences as breach of the peace, threatening behaviour, or some non-serious assaults. Some organizations concerned with the rights of the mentally disordered, for example MIND and the National Council for Civil Liberties, have questioned the advisability of the police being allowed the responsibility of determining the presence of serious mental disorder. However, the Butler Committee considered the matter in some detail and concluded that these procedures and other informal action (relief from prosecution) could usefully be extended in cases where there was no risk to members of the public and where there was urgent need for psychiatric treatment.

## DISABILITY IN RELATION TO THE TRIAL (FITNESS TO PLEAD)

In a brief review of some of the historical aspects of criminal responsibility, in some cases the accused seemed to be quite clearly mad. Sometimes this 'madness' may be highly relevant to the degree of the accused's responsibility at the time of the *offence*, at others it may only be in issue at the time of the *trial*. By tradition, the court has to determine whether a person's mental abnormality is so severe that he cannot even be tried. This means, in effect, can he understand the charge, can he challenge jurors, can he follow the evidence, and can he instruct counsel? These criteria were used at one time to determine whether or not the accused was 'insane on arraignment' or 'unfit to plead'. The Butler Committee suggested that the term 'under disability' instead of 'unfit to plead' be adopted as being more in keeping with modern thought and practice. The plea is not entered with any frequency today, mainly because the person concerned has to be very seriously disabled psychiatrically to satisfy the stringent criteria. However, the consequences that can flow from such a finding can be very serious for the accused and are productive of some anxiety concerning his civil liberties. If found to be 'under disability', the accused can currently be detained without limit of time under Section 65 of the Mental Health Act 1959. (See also below.) In effect, this means that he may be detained without ever having had the chance to rebut the charges against him. The Butler Committee made a number of suggestions for improving this state of affairs, one of the most important being that the question of 'disability' should be decided at the outset of the trial or as soon as it was raised as an issue. Where disability was found, and where the medical evidence suggested prospects of an early recovery, the judge should be able to adjourn the trial for up to three months with renewal of a month at a time for a maximum of six months. If the accused recovered within the six-month period, the normal trial would proceed immediately. *A trial of the facts* (i.e., the substance of the case against him) should take place as soon as disability had been found and there was no prospect of the accused recovering, or as soon during the six-month period as he might recover or prove to be unresponsive to treatment. If the accused was found to be under disability, there should nevertheless be a trial of the facts at the appropriate time. In cases where a finding of not guilty cannot be returned, the Committee recommended that the jury should be directed to find that the defendant be dealt with as a person under disability. This new form of verdict would not count as a conviction, neither, said the Committee, should it be followed by custodial punishment; the court should have wide discretion as to what penalty be imposed. The procedures just outlined would apply only to the Crown Court at present, but the Committee recommended that Magistrates' Courts should in future also have the power to determine and act upon the issue of disability.

## THE SPECIAL VERDICT

We now have to consider the situation that arises when an accused claims he should not be held criminally responsible because he was suffering from mental disorder at the *time of the offence*. The court has to decide two difficult questions. Did the accused commit the act or make the omission charged, and was he so insane at the time as not to be responsible in law for his actions? We saw how the M'Naghten Rules were introduced in order to deal with this kind of situation. This was at a time when the disciplines of psychology and psychiatry were relatively unadvanced and knowledge about states of mind somewhat unsophisticated. As can be seen from *Table 9(1)*, today the rules are only invoked in a handful of cases each year, largely because of the introduction of the concept of diminished responsibility and subsequently the abolition of the death penalty for murder. (For discussion of some of the Butler Committee's detailed proposals concerning the special verdict, see Prins 1980: 32–3.)

## DIMINISHED RESPONSIBILITY

We saw earlier how the statutory provision of diminished responsibility was introduced to reduce liability for murder to manslaughter, and how it enabled the courts to take into account a much wider range of disabilities than under the M'Naghten Rules. There are, however, many problems concerning the determination of what constitutes an abnormality of mind and the meaning of the word substantial in relation to impairment of responsibility. In the now famous case of Byrne,[3] a sexual psychopath, in 1960, it was held that abnormality should be construed as 'a state of mind so different from that of ordinary human beings that a reasonable man would term it abnormal'. But one may well ask, who is to define a reasonable man, and what are to be regarded as abnormalities? Samuels (1975) suggests that the more bizarre and horrible the nature of a killing the more likely will be the chance that diminished responsibility will be established, though the jury may well reject this and go for murder. (This seems to have happened in the Sutcliffe case (1981); further comment is not permissible at this point in time as the case is *sub judice* pending an appeal.)[4] It seems clear, however, that although psychiatric experts may be able to suggest that someone's responsibility is diminished by an 'abnormality of mind', it will be for the jury – those ordinary citizens on 'the Clapham Omnibus' so beloved of lawyers – to endeavour to determine what seems reasonable in all the circumstances. Bizarre and horrible behaviour may well seem to be beyond our 'ken', but it does not *necessarily* follow that it should be equated with, or be due to, an abnormality of mind in a more restricted psychiatric sense. For after all, may not some people be just evil or, if they are terrorists and hijackers, motivated perhaps by a fanaticism which, if hard to comprehend, may not necessarily be equated with mental disorder? It is far too easy to embrace the more comfortable notion, 'he must have been mad' to behave in such a fashion. The Butler Committee was aware of many of these problems and was in no doubt that the present provisions relating to diminished responsibility were unsatisfactory. It suggested that the provision was needed only because the offence of murder currently carries a mandatory life sentence. It recommended that the mandatory life sentence for murder be abolished. As a consequence the

[3] R. v. Byrne (1960), 2, Q.B. 396.
[4] Appeal subsequently dismissed, 25 May 1982.

provision of diminished responsibility would not be necessary and the courts would be able to apply a range of penalties according to the circumstances of individual cases. However, the Criminal Law Revision Committee (1980) and some very experienced forensic psychiatrists, for example Bluglass (1980), have indicated their reservations about such a proposal. They point out that many mentally disordered offenders dealt with currently as cases of diminished responsibility would be excluded, unless a wide interpretation of mental illness, which as I have already mentioned is undefined in the Mental Health Act, were allowed.

INFANTICIDE

In Chapter 4, I made reference to the special offence of infanticide. This was introduced in order to relieve a woman of a murder charge who had caused the death of her child under the age of twelve months by reason of disturbance of mind following the birth or by reason of the effect of lactation consequent upon the birth. The Act (first passed in 1922 but amended in 1938) was introduced at a time when more emphasis than was probably justified was placed upon what were thought to be the adverse effects of childbirth and lactation upon a woman's mental state. However, when one examines these comparatively rare cases, there are usually significant factors operating other than psychiatric abnormality arising directly as a result of the birth, for example the kind of adverse social circumstances outlined in Chapter 3. The Butler Committee doubted that the special offence of infanticide needed to be retained and that it could be subsumed under the defence of diminished responsibility.

We can see from the foregoing brief analysis that there are a variety of ways in which the issue of mental disorder may be raised. In *Figure 9(1)*, I have tried to present the relationship between the courts and methods of disposal in outline form. In *Tables 9(1)–9(6)*, I indicate how some such cases were dealt with during the ten-year period 1968–78.

*Figure 9(1)*    Disposal of mentally disordered offenders

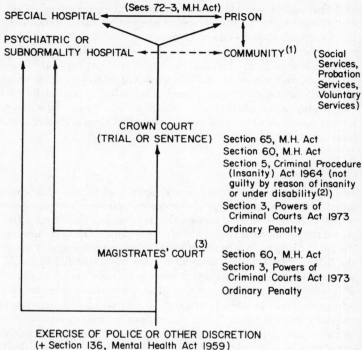

*Notes to Figure 9(1)*

(1) The provision for guardianship orders (under Section 60 of the Mental Health Act) is not shown separately in this figure as it is used so infrequently.

(2) A person admitted to hospital under this procedure is treated as if he had been ordered to be detained under a hospital order together with a restriction order detaining him without limit of time. The responsibility in such cases for finding a hospital bed is the Home Secretary's.

(3) A *Juvenile Court* may also make an order under Section 60 of the Mental Health Act, but may not commit an offender *under fourteen* to the Crown Court with a view to the making of a hospital order with restrictions. The Juvenile Court is no longer empowered to make probation orders, but may make a supervision order with a requirement for psychiatric treatment (see Chapter 8). A care order may be combined with a hospital order.

Table 9(1)   *Number of findings of 'under disability' and not guilty by reason of insanity, 1968–78*

| under disability | 1968 | 1969 | 1970 | 1971 | 1972 | 1973 | 1974 | 1975 | 1976 | 1977 | 1978 |
|---|---|---|---|---|---|---|---|---|---|---|---|
| | 3 | 9 | 3 | 7 | 6 | 4 | 3 | 4 | 3 | – | 2 |
| not guilty by reason of insanity ('M'Naghten mad') | 3 | – | 2 | 1 | 2 | 1 | 2 | 1 | 2 | 1 | – |

Table 9(2)   *Number of Section 2 Homicide Act (manslaughter) convictions, 1968–78*

| 1968 | 1969 | 1970 | 1971 | 1972 | 1973 | 1974 | 1975 | 1976 | 1977 | 1978 |
|---|---|---|---|---|---|---|---|---|---|---|
| 49 | 58 | 65 | 72 | 85 | 77 | 96 | 76 | 93 | 92 | 78 |

Table 9(3)   *Number of corresponding convictions for murder*

| 1968 | 1969 | 1970 | 1971 | 1972 | 1973 | 1974 | 1975 | 1976 | 1977 | 1978 |
|---|---|---|---|---|---|---|---|---|---|---|
| 76 | 78 | 99 | 91 | 85 | 83 | 135* | 98 | 108 | 115 | 110 |

* The peak figure is accounted for by convictions for increased terrorist activity in this year.

Table 9(4)   *Breakdown of disposal of Section 2 manslaughter cases for the year 1978*

| | |
|---|---|
| life imprisonment | 18 |
| over 10 years' imprisonment | 1 |
| 4–10 years' imprisonment | 8 |
| 4 years and under | 16 |
| *Section 65, Mental Health Act 1959 | 18 |
| *Section 60, Mental Health Act 1959 | 4 |
| probation and supervision orders | 9 |
| suspended sentence | 3 |
| other | 1 |
| total | 78 |

* hospital order disposals represent about 30 per cent of the total.

Table 9(5)  *Comparison with Butler Committee figures for Section 2 cases for the years 1970–73 (aggregated)*

| | |
|---|---:|
| life imprisonment | 40 |
| other terms of imprisonment | 52 |
| *Section 65, Mental Health Act 1959 | 126 |
| *Section 60, Mental Health Act 1959 | 27 |
| probation | 35 |
| other | 10 |
| total | 290 |

* hospital order disposals represent some 50 per cent of the total for this three-year period.
(Home Office and DHSS 1975: 243.)

Table 9(6)  *Number of infanticide convictions 1968–78*

| 1968 | 1969 | 1970 | 1971 | 1972 | 1973 | 1974 | 1975 | 1976 | 1977 | 1978 |
|------|------|------|------|------|------|------|------|------|------|------|
| 25 | 13 | 15 | 18 | 17 | 9 | 15 | 5 | 6 | 6 | 8 |

(Source for *Tables 9(1), 9(2), 9(3), 9(4), and 9(6)* Home Office 1979: 176–77.)

## Powers of the courts to order treatment for mental disorder

If an accused is found guilty of an offence and his mental state is successfully pleaded in mitigation, the court may proceed to make one of the orders listed below, or it may choose to deal with the defendant in such a way as to facilitate arrangements for voluntary treatment (for example by way of a fine or a discharge). Alternatively, the court may decide, whatever the psychiatric factors in mitigation may be, that a custodial penalty is the only appropriate course of action and impose a sentence of imprisonment. It is relevant to point out here that, in addition to Grendon Underwood special psychiatric prison, there are other prisons that cater for mentally disturbed offenders (for example Wormwood Scrubs and Wakefield). In some of these establishments, treatment is offered to special categories of prisoners (for example sex offenders) or special modes of treatment are offered, such as group and individual psychotherapy or behaviour modification. (See also Chapter 11.) Unhappily, such facilities can in no way cater for the numbers of mentally disordered offenders now being detained in prison because the National Health Service is unwilling or unable to cope with them. The most recent report of the Parliamentary All-Party Penal Affairs Group (1981) indicates that there were at least 400 mentally disordered offenders in prison who would have warranted treatment under the Mental Health Act alone. Some further aspects of this problem will be dealt with later in the chapter.

As can be seen from *Figure 9(1)*, the powers of the courts to make formal psychiatric disposals derive mainly from the Mental Health Act 1959 and the Powers of Criminal Courts Act 1973. These are summarized briefly below.

## HOSPITAL AND GUARDIANSHIP ORDERS

Section 60 (1) of the Mental Health Act 1959 enables courts to make hospital or guardianship orders when a person is convicted on indictment of any offence (other than an offence the penalty for which is fixed by law) or, in the case of Magistrates' Courts, if a person is convicted of an offence which is punishable on summary conviction with imprisonment. In addition, under Section 60 (2) of the Act, a *Magistrates' Court* may make an order in respect of a person suffering from *mental illness* or *severe subnormality* without first convicting him, if it is satisfied that the accused committed the act or made the omission charged. Before making a hospital or guardianship order, the court must be satisfied:

(a) On the evidence of two doctors, at least one of whom is approved by an area health authority under Section 28 of the Act as having special experience in the diagnosis and treatment of mental disorder, that the offender is suffering from mental illness, psychopathic disorder, subnormality, or severe subnormality of a nature or a degree which warrants detention in hospital for medical treatment or his reception into guardianship. ('Medical treatment' is further defined in the Act to include nursing and other care and training under medical supervision.)

(b) That a particular hospital is willing to admit the patient within 28 days, or that the local authority or other person approved by the local authority is willing to receive the patient into guardianship.

(c) That the circumstances are such that a hospital order or guardianship order is the most suitable method of dealing with the case.

A hospital or guardianship order may *not* be made unless the offender is described by each of the two doctors as suffering from the same sort of disorder, whether or not he is also described by either of them as suffering from another of the disorders specified in (a) above. For the purposes of obtaining reports, the offender may be remanded in custody or on bail (see also Chapter 6). If a person is committed in *custody* for trial there is no power for the court to order the preparation of medical reports, but the prison medical officer can arrange for such reports to be available to the court of trial and the committing court can suggest that this be done. In order to reduce the numbers of persons in custody awaiting disposal, some prisons have made facilities available for medical and psychiatric reports to be obtained on bail on an 'out-patient' basis, the offender attending the prison for examination in the same way as he had been required to attend a hospital psychiatric out-patients department. Although this facility has now been available for some years, the indications are that it is not used as frequently as it might be.

ORDERS FOR RESTRICTION

The Crown Court may make an order under Section 65 of the Act subjecting the offender to special restrictions for a specified period or without limit of time. The Court may do this if it thinks it necessary for the protection of the public, having regard to the nature of the offence, the antecedents of the offender, and the risk of his committing further offences if set at large prematurely. The offender must not be set at liberty without the consent of the Home Secretary. Mental Health Review Tribunals, which exist to safeguard the interests of compulsorily detained patients (whether detained by court or civil order), have limited powers at present in respect to patients detained under Section 65. A restriction order cannot be made by the court unless at least one of the two doctors providing the report (see (a) and (c) above) gives oral evidence. A restriction order has serious implications for an offender and we shall examine some of these later in this chapter.[5]

## POWERS TO TRANSFER FROM PRISON TO HOSPITAL

A person already in custody (either awaiting trial or undergoing sentence), whose mental state becomes such that he requires compulsory detention in hospital, may be transferred under the provisions of Sections 72 and 73 of the Act. Before doing so, the Home Secretary has to be satisfied that the same criteria apply as for the making of a hospital order by a court. For all practical purposes, the making of such an order under Section 72 or 73 has similar effects to the making of a restriction order under Section 65 of the Act. If the offender recovers before the term of his sentence has expired he may be returned from hospital to prison.

## PROBATION AND MENTAL TREATMENT

Section 3 of the Powers of the Criminal Courts Act 1973 empowers a court to make a probation order, with a requirement that the offender submit to in-patient or out-patient treatment. The requirement may be made for the whole of the probation period or for such part of it as the court may specify. Such orders can only be made if:

(a) The offender consents. (Note that an offender's consent is *not* required in the case of a hospital or guardianship order.)
(b) A hospital (or other approved establishment) will receive him and is able to provide the treatment.
(c) The oral or written evidence of one doctor (approved under Section 28) indicates that the offender's condition requires and may be susceptible to treatment, but is not such as to warrant detention in pursuance of a hospital order.

---

[5] The interests of compulsorily detained offender/patients are likely to be safeguarded by new provisions in the Mental Health (Amendment) Bill, now before Parliament. (See also pp. 197–98.)

## Statistics

Over the years there has been a decline in the number of hospital orders and psychiatric probation orders made by the courts. In 1978, fewer than 1000 hospital orders were made (131 of these were made with a restriction under Section 65) and only 8 guardianship orders (Home Office 1979: 442–43). In 1978, the courts made 1334 psychiatric probation orders; 944 of these were for non-residential treatment and 390 for residential treatment. This decline has been due in part to the unwillingness of the ordinary psychiatric and mental hospitals to take difficult or disruptive patients, with the result that the prisons have had to receive them, or they have had to be admitted to one of the special hospitals, which are already overcrowded. It will be noted how few guardianship orders are made. These give the local authority the same rights over the person subject to the order as those exercised by a father over a child under the age of fourteen. The Butler Committee suggested that more use should be made of such orders and encouraged local authorities to view their use more positively.

## Current problems and future developments

There are a number of issues that arise out of our attempts to cater for mentally disordered offenders within the administrative, judicial, penal, and health care systems. There are, for example, the age-old arguments over the differences between what behaviours should be considered to be crimes as distinct from acts of moral transgression. What should rightfully be regarded as sickness and what should be regarded as sin? How much emphasis should we place upon the protection and cure (if possible) of the individual – particularly if he seems to be severely deranged – and how much priority of emphasis should be placed upon the protection of the community? It is easy to see that the law and its machinery may be somewhat clumsy instruments for trying to serve all these conflicting purposes, many of them being not only finely poised but also likely to generate strong emotions. For example it seems to many observers, particularly those concerned with the protection of the liberty of the individual, that there exists a curious paradox whereby a man may be found 'not guilty by reason of insanity' and yet ordered to be detained without limit of time in a special hospital under conditions, which if recent accounts are anything to go by, may seem to both the patient and his family to differ only marginally from imprisonment (Cohen 1981).

Some offender/patients may be detained in hospital, ostensibly in their 'best interests', for periods of time far longer than the fixed (determinate) sentence of imprisonment with which their depredations would normally be punished. In effect, the person adjudged to be 'mad' and 'bad' may be doubly disadvantaged. First, by the opprobrium that attaches to these dual labels (see also Chapter 3), and second, because he may feel that he is being doubly punished. This seems a far cry from early Roman law, which held that a man visited by madness who committed crime was punished enough by his condition without the law needing to add to his punishment. All these difficulties are exacerbated by the almost arbitrary fashion in which a mentally disordered offender may be dealt with through the various systems of disposal now in use. Since the publication of the Butler Report, the government has more recently asked for comment from various organizations on possible reforms of the Mental Health Act 1959 (see for example DHSS *et al.* 1978). Proposed reforms would include changes in the existing provisions for the detention of mentally disordered offenders. In particular, Section 65 would be reworded to make more clear the essential purpose of a restriction order, namely to protect the public from *serious harm*. This is a helpful proposal and would go some way towards making a clearer distinction between the offender who is really a serious threat to persons or property and the offender who merely has a high nuisance value and is disruptive rather than dangerous. The present powers that afford flexibility in the care of Section 65 patients are likely to be retained, but it has been recommended that hospital Responsible Medical Officers (RMOs) should, in future, be required *by statute* to make an annual report on each of their restricted patients. It is also anticipated that any revision of the 1959 Act will include facilities to give Mental Health Review Tribunals themselves more power than they have at present to review and to dispose of Section 65 cases. Currently, such tribunals can only make *recommendations* to the Home Secretary for discharge or change of status of offender/patients. It is anticipated that in strengthening the powers of tribunals, other compulsorily detained patients (not necessarily offender/patients) will also have their interests further safeguarded. Such improvements include the limitation of the range of 'irreversible' treatments that may be imposed upon non-consenting patients and opportunities for more frequent access to tribunals.

The Mental Health (Amendment) Bill, currently being debated in Parliament, contains, amongst others, a number of proposals for amending the law relating to mentally disordered offenders. The following would appear to be the most important:

(1) Courts will only be permitted to make a hospital order in respect of persons suffering from psychopathic disorder or from mental subnormality (to be called mental handicap in future) if there is evidence that medical treatment in hospital is likely to alleviate or prevent a deterioration in the offender's condition.

(2) Detained offender/patients will benefit from more frequent access to Mental Health Review Tribunals and from the general oversight of the proposed Mental Health Act Commission; the latter is envisaged as a powerful 'watch-dog' over the rights of *all* detained mental patients.

(3) In future, it will only be possible for Crown Courts to make a restriction order if the public needs protection 'from serious harm'.

(4) The Bill makes provisions for direct remands to hospital and for 'interim' hospital orders for the purposes of assessment; such interim orders would be made for periods of up to 12 weeks, renewable for up to 6 months.

It is hoped that these (and other wide-ranging proposals for non-offender/patients) may become law by the summer of 1982, but a number of them are unlikely to be fully implemented before late 1983. At this time it is hoped to pass a Mental Health Consolidation Bill that will bring together the provisions of the 1959 Act and the Amendment Act. It is quite clear from the provisions of the Bill and from the government's guidelines accompanying it (Reform of Mental Health Legislation: DHSS *et al.* 1981) that a considerable investment of funds and of extra manpower will be required if the proposals are to be implemented in any effective manner.

## Dangerous behaviour

However far-reaching and humanitarian such legislative reforms may prove to be, they will not of themselves necessarily assuage the anxieties of both the general public and some professionals over the past and possible future dangerous behaviour of many offender/patients. In some cases, it may well be possible to establish a very close link between an offender's mentally disordered state and his propensity to commit acts of serious physical violence towards persons or property. In others, the relationship may not be nearly so clear-cut. It may also be the case that the alleviation of the mental disorder may not necessarily deal with the propensity to commit crime. In Chapter 5 I pointed out that the relationship between mental disorder and crime was for the most part equivocal. The same can also be said of the relationship between mental disorder and dangerous behaviour (see also Tennent 1975). The term dangerous has an age-old and pejorative connotation in relation to criminality. The early Poor Law attempted to deal with both mendicancy and crime and was based upon assumptions about the 'perishing and dangerous' classes. Vagrants, beggars, and criminals were all viewed as a great danger to society (see Rennie 1978). Such assumptions die hard in the minds of men. The Butler Committee spent a great deal of effort in trying to classify the concept of dangerousness. As it rightly pointed out:

> 'Dangerousness depends in the majority of cases not only on the personality of the potentially dangerous offender, but also on the circumstances in which he finds himself. The practice of referring to some individuals as "dangerous" without qualification creates the impression that the word refers to a more or less constantly exhibited disposition, like left-handedness or restlessness . . . The situation and circumstances which are potentially dangerous can often be defined, and sometimes foreseen and avoided or prevented. The individual who spontaneously "looks for a fight" or feels

a need to inflict pain or searches for an unknown sexual victim is fortunately rare, although such people undoubtedly exist.'                         (Home Office and DHSS 1975: 57–8)

The Butler Committee was right to suggest that in a number of instances a person's dangerous behaviour might have been predicted and perhaps avoided. I have drawn attention else-where to the possibilities of this and to the means through which such intervention might best be carried out (see Prins 1975, 1980 (Chapter 6), 1981, and 1982). Nevertheless, it is all too easy to be 'wise after the event'; as the Butler Committee suggested, there are some people for whom it is wellnigh impossible to make predictions on the basis of past behaviour or anticipated future conduct. Such people may therefore need to be detained for long periods of time for their own protection and for the protection of others. Sometimes this detention may need to be for the rest of their lives, for there are no foolproof actuarial devices that can enable us to make predictions of future be-haviour with any certainty (see Prins 1980 (Chapter 6) and Monahan 1981). We are thus left with one group of people who need to be detained for a long time in conditions of maximum security and another group whose behaviour may give cause for concern either because of its oddness or because of its *disruptive* as distinct from its dangerous nature. At this point we need to examine some of the resources currently available and also some of their deficiencies.

## Resources

Reference has already been made to the decline of National Health Service involvement in the control and management of the mentally disordered offender. Detailed confirmation of this decline is available in a study by Parker and Tennent (1979). They examined the operation of Sections 60 and 65 of the Mental Health Act for the periods 1962–64 and 1972–74. They showed clearly that the intention built into the Act of investing the care of the mentally disordered in the NHS was not being fulfilled. As I showed earlier, this trend has continued beyond the period surveyed by Parker and Tennent. There are at least four reasons to account for this trend.

First, more patients are now admitted to psychiatric hospitals informally and for much shorter periods. Few hospitals now have locked wards or, if they do, they use them only occasionally (Bluglass 1978).

Second, in the light of these developments, staff have become increasingly reluctant to treat patients they fear may be violent or disruptive and for whom they do not have the necessary secure facilities. Some of this reluctance springs from a very real concern amongst nursing staff that they may not have the skills needed for such a task, but it is also true to say that their reluctance has been used as a spring-board for arguments about improvements in general pay and working conditions.

Third, some consultants are reluctant to accept restricted patients because of the additional controls they are expected to exercise over home leave or discharge. They have also felt that such orders result in their having to continue to be responsible for offender/patients for whom they feel they can offer no effective treatment (Gostin 1977 and Bowden 1977).

Fourth, there is the problem of obtaining beds in the special hospitals. There are four special hospitals in England and Wales (Broadmoor, Rampton, Moss Side, and Park Lane) and one in Scotland (Carstairs). Those interested in examining the history and development of the hospitals in England and Wales should consult Greenland (1969), Walker and McCabe (1973), Gostin (1977), DHSS (1980), and Cohen (1981). Some account of the history of Carstairs may be found in a report of a recent committee of enquiry into that institution (Scottish Home Department 1977). Under Section 40 of the National Health Service Reorganization Act 1973, the Secretary of State for Social Services (and not the regional health authority) is responsible for providing and maintaining establishments for persons subject to detention under the Mental Health Act 1959 who, in his opinion, require treatment under conditions of special security on account of their dangerous, violent, or criminal propensities. It should be noted that about one-third of all special hospital patients are not offenders, but have been admitted under civil proceedings (under Part IV of the Act). Unlike all other hospitals, the special hospitals are controlled directly by the DHSS. Because of the geographical isolation of some of them (for example Broadmoor in Berkshire and Rampton in Nottinghamshire) they tend to suffer from insularity and isolation. This isolation has led to a degree of staff 'inbreeding'. This in turn has resulted in complacency about outdated treatment methods, and abuses of some patients' rights have been more readily condoned. Until very recently, Rampton had no single person designated as its medical director and control lay in the hands of DHSS Headquarters in London. Following the enquiry of a committee set up to investigate allegations of ill-treatment, abuses, and other matters (DHSS 1980), a medical director has recently been appointed. The committee (chaired by Sir John Boynton) made a number of very serious criticisms indicating that 'The Hospital appears to have been in a backwater and the main currents of thought about the care of mental patients have passed it by' (DHSS 1980, iii). Despite the serious criticisms of Rampton and similar criticisms over the years of other special hospitals, even the severest critics acknowledge that these hospitals have a tremendously difficult task in trying to combine containment, clinical treatment, and rehabilitation in a climate of opinion that puts the 'mad' and the 'bad' at the bottom of the economic priority list. They also have to operate in a society that prefers not to know or care too much about its more disturbed and difficult members.

There is no doubt that the special hospitals have to contain some highly dangerous individuals, but, as suggested earlier, they also have to contain far too many patients whose potential for dangerous behaviour is minimal. This state of affairs was recognized almost from the outset by the Butler Committee, which was so concerned that it issued an Interim Report (Home Office and DHSS 1974) reiterating suggestions made by a government committee some *thirteen years earlier* (Ministry of Health 1961) that regional secure units should be established for the assessment and management of especially difficult cases. In its Interim Report the Committee recommended that urgent priority should be given to establishing such NHS Regional Secure Units offering some 2000 places overall. It is a scandal that in the years since these recommendations for urgent priority were made, hardly any units have been established, and this despite the 'earmarking' of special funds by the government. It is equally disturbing to find that there still seems to be some doubt as to the types of patients these units should cater for.

They are clearly not intended for the potentially dangerous offender/patient needing maximum security, but for the difficult and disruptive. But how is disruptive to be defined and by whom? There is the danger that such units may be asked to take patients who have merely been transiently difficult or towards whom some staff have taken a strong dislike. This could result in the units becoming as 'silted up' as the special hospitals, while continuing to allow the ordinary psychiatric hospitals to evade their responsibilities under the Mental Health Act. In future, one would hope that such units would cater for those patients who had committed a fairly serious offence and upon whom the court required a psychiatric opinion, with the circumstances being such that a report could best be provided in the specialist regime of a secure unit rather than in prison. (See earlier discussion on remands for reports.) Such units could also cater for offender/patients who had responded successfully to treatment in a special hospital, but who could benefit from the 'transitional' care that such a unit could provide before eventual return to the community. Secure units could also provide a useful regime of treatment for persons suffering from mental disorder who had persistently failed to take advantage of out-patient facilities or opportunities on an open ward.

The widespread provision of regional secure units would go a considerable way towards providing a more effective and humane system of care for some mentally disordered offenders. However, this will not be enough. We need to provide also a much greater degree of flexibility within the whole system to promote interchange between a range of facilitating environments such as hostels, half-way houses, and day centres. There needs to be a far greater degree of co-operation and joint usage between health service and penal provision. For example, more use could be made of facilities that already exist for non-mentally disordered offenders, such as the day centres and hostels organized and staffed by the probation and after-care service. In addition, more community-based projects might help to lessen the public anxiety and antipathy referred to earlier.

## Conclusions

In this chapter I have tried to demonstrate the circumstances and situations in which those suffering from mental disorder may be dealt with by the courts and the penal and health care systems. The problems of determining the extent to which mental disorder may provide full or partial exculpation from criminal responsibility are fundamental and perhaps insoluble; but, as the Butler Committee indicated, it would seem possible to make the law and its machinery a little less archaic and cumbersome. The measures of disposal could be made more flexible and some quite simple but essential steps could be taken to improve the protection of the rights of compulsorily detained offender/patients. Existing resources are inadequate and can only be improved in the long term if the public can be induced to take a more humane and less fear-ridden view of those who are adjudged to be both 'mad' and 'bad'. In the *short term*, better use could be made of the limited resources already available, and there should be more joint use of such resources between the penal and health care systems. Such blurring of boundaries would not only be in the interests of offender/patients, but would enhance the knowledge and experience of those concerned with their care. It would also help to reduce the isolation of those who work in the special hospitals, and the restricted vision that such isolation inevitably induces.

## References

Bluglass, R. (1978) Regional Secure Units and Interim Security for Psychiatric Patients. *British Medical Journal* **1**: 489–93.

—— (1980) *Psychiatry, the Law and the Offender – Present Dilemmas and Future Prospects.* Seventh Denis Carroll Memorial Lecture, Croydon: Institute for the Study and Treatment of Delinquency.

Bowden, P. (1977) The NHS Practice of Forensic Psychiatry in One Region. *Psychological Medicine* **7**: 141–48.

Cohen, D. (1981) *Broadmoor.* London: Psychology News Press.

Criminal Law Revision Committee (1980) *Offences Against the Person.* Cmnd. 7844. London: HMSO.

DHSS (1980) *Report of the Review of Rampton Hospital*. (Boynton Report) Cmnd. 8073. London: HMSO.

DHSS, Home Office, Welsh Office, and Lord Chancellor's Department (1978) *Review of the Mental Health Act, 1959*. Cmnd. 7320. London: HMSO.

—— (1981) *Reform of Mental Health Legislation*. Cmnd. 8405. London: HMSO.

Gostin, L.O. (1977) *A Human Condition (Volume 2)*. London: MIND (NAMH).

Greenland, C. (1969) The Three Special Hospitals in England and Wales and Patients With Dangerous, Violent or Criminal Propensities. *Medicine, Science and the Law* 9: 253–64.

Home Office (1979) *Criminal Statistics for England and Wales, 1978*. Cmnd. 7670. London: HMSO.

Home Office and DHSS (1974) *Interim Report of the Committee on Mentally Abnormal Offenders*. Cmnd. 5698. London: HMSO.

—— (1975) *Report of the Committee on Mentally Abnormal Offenders*. (Butler Committee) Cmnd. 6244. London: HMSO.

Ministry of Health (1961) *Treatment of Psychiatric Patients Under Security Conditions*. HM (61) 69. London: HMSO.

Monahan, J. (1981) *Predicting Violent Behaviour: An Assessment of Clinical Techniques*. London: Sage Publications.

Parker, E. and Tennent, G. (1979) The 1959 Mental Health Act and Mentally Abnormal Offenders: A Comparative Study. *Medicine, Science and the Law* 19: 29–38.

Parliamentary All-Party Penal Affairs Group (1981) *Still Too Many Prisoners*. Chichester: Barry Rose.

Prins, H. (1975) A Danger to Themselves and to Others (Social Workers and Potentially Dangerous Clients). *British Journal of Social Work* 5: 297–309.

—— (1980) *Offenders, Deviants, or Patients: An Introduction to the Study of Socio-Forensic Problems*. London: Tavistock Publications.

—— (1981) Dangerous People or Dangerous Situations: Some Implications for Assessment and Management. *Medicine, Science and the Law* 21: 125–33.

—— (1982) Dangerous Behaviour: Some Implications for Mental Health Professionals. In P. Bean (ed.) *Key Issues in Mental Illness*. Chichester: John Wiley. (In press.)

Rennie, Y. (1978) *The Search for Criminal Man. A Conceptual*

*History of the Dangerous Offender*. Lexington, Mass. D.C.: Heath.

Samuels, A. (1975) Mental Illness and Criminal Liability. *Medicine, Science and the Law* **15**: 198–204.

Scottish Home Department (1977) *State Hospital, Carstairs: Report of Public Local Inquiry Into the Circumstances Surrounding the Escape of Two Patients on 30 November, 1976 and into Security and Other Arrangements at the Hospital.* Edinburgh: HMSO.

Tennent, T.G. (1975) The Dangerous Offender. In T. Silverstone and B. Barraclough (eds) *Contemporary Psychiatry* (pp. 308–15). Ashford, Kent. Headley Brothers.

Walker, N. (1968) *Crime and Insanity in England (Volume 1)* (especially Chapters 1–5). Edinburgh: Edinburgh University Press.

Walker, N. and McCabe, S. (1973) *Crime and Insanity in England and Wales (Volume 2)*. Edinburgh: Edinburgh University Press.

West, D.J. and Walk, A. (1977) *Daniel McNaughten: His Trial and the Aftermath*. Ashford, Kent: Gaskell Books, for the Royal College of Psychiatrists.

FURTHER READING

*On criminal responsibility and related matters see:*

Bromberg, W. (1979) *The Uses of Psychiatry in the Law: A Clinical View of Forensic Psychiatry*. Quorum Books: London and Westport.

Fingarette, H. and Hasse, A.F. (1979) *Mental Disabilities and Criminal Responsibility*. Berkeley and London: University of California Press.

Flew, A. (1973) *Crime or Disease?* London: Macmillan.

Floud, J. and Young, W. (1981) *Dangerousness and Criminal Justice*. London: Heinemann Educational Books.

Glueck, S. (1966) *Law and Psychiatry: Cold War or Entente Cordiale?* Baltimore: Johns Hopkins,

Jacobs, F.G. (1971) *Criminal Responsibility*. London: London School of Economics/Weidenfeld and Nicolson.

Walker, N. (1980) *Punishment, Danger and Stigma: The Morality of Criminal Justice*. Oxford: Basil Blackwell.

*On assessment and management (with special reference to the dangerous offender) see:*

Brody, S. and Tarling, R. (1980) *Taking Offenders Out of Circulation*. Home Office Research Studies. No. 64. London: HMSO (Home Office).

Devon Probation and After Care Committee (1981) *Report of the Working Party on Serious Offenders*. Exeter.

Gunn, J. and Farrington, D.P. (1982) (eds) *Abnormal Offenders, Delinquency, and the Criminal Justice System* (Part 3). Chichester: John Wiley.

Halleck, S.L. and Bromberg, W. (1968) *Psychiatric Aspects of Criminology*. Illinois: Charles C. Thomas.

King, J.F.S. (1976) *Control Without Custody?* Institute of Criminology, Cambridge: Cambridge University. (Especially papers by Fullwood, Brewer, Woodside, and Fowler.)

Pasternack, S.A. (ed.) (1975) *Violence and Victims*. New York: Spectrum Publications.

Royal College of Psychiatrists (1980) Report of a Special Committee of the College. *Secure Facilities for Psychiatric Patients: A Comprehensive Policy*. London.

Scott, P.D. (1975) *Has Psychiatry Failed in the Treatment of Offenders?* Fifth Denis Carroll Memorial Lecture. London: Institute for the Study and Treatment of Delinquency.

Stürup, G. (1968) *Treating the 'Untreatable': Chronic Criminals at Herstedvester*. Baltimore: Johns Hopkins.

Tutt, N. (1976) (ed.) *Violence*. London: HMSO (DHSS).

# CHAPTER TEN

# Other categories of offenders

In this chapter, which is divided into three sections, I discuss two specific offender categories – female offenders and sexual offenders; I also consider the relationship between criminal behaviour and alcohol and other drugs. None of these can be considered at length; the interested reader can pursue the subject in greater depth by consulting the references and further reading listed at the end of the chapter for each section.

## Section one – Female offenders

> If men behaved like women, the courts would be
> idle and the prisons empty.
>
> BARONESS WOOTTON

The situation may not be quite so dramatic as Baroness Wootton suggests, but it is true that numerically women constitute a very small percentage of the total offender population. Why then, the critical reader may ask, should I devote a section of this chapter to them? There are two good reasons for doing so. In the first place, female offenders have, until recently, received fairly scant attention in the criminological and penological literature. Two quite recent examples illustrate this point. The revised edition of *Prisons and the Prisoner* (Home Office 1977) devotes some 5½ out of its 188 pages specifically to the problems of women and girls in prison. The Butler Committee, in a footnote in their report, state 'throughout the report, we refer to offenders as male except where specific reference to women is appropriate. Apart from convenience, this is justified by the statistics, for women are a small minority of offenders'. (Home Office and DHSS 1975: 7). Second, female crime has been the subject of a somewhat polemical debate between those who see it mainly in deterministic terms and those (notably feminists, such as Smart 1976) who see the phenomenon not only from a more broadly based perspective, but who also suggest that a *male view* of female criminality will inevitably be distorted. The truth about female offending probably lies somewhere between an extreme psychological deterministic interpretation and one that is excessively sociological. No one can deny that there are quite vital physiological and psychological differences between men and women, but it is also true to say that some of these fundamental differences are exaggerated by socially determined attitudes that may well be heavily prejudiced in favour of men. For all these reasons, female offending merits some special consideration in this book.

STATISTICS RELATING TO FEMALE CRIME

Overall, the proportion of male to female offenders is about 8:1, though there are obviously variations in the figures depending upon the type and seriousness of the offence. In respect of police cautioning, the ratio is about 4:1 (see also Chapter 2). In 1978, some 388,126 males were found guilty by all courts of indictable offences compared with some 65,757 females (Home Office 1979). In the last few years, the proportion of women found guilty of indictable offences has been about 15 per cent and for non-indictable offences about 8 per cent. If we take recent criminal statistics at their face value there does indeed appear to have been a sharp increase in known female crime. Smart (1979) calculated that the total of all indictable offences committed by women had doubled in the period 1965–75, with the greatest proportionate increase being in offences of violence against the person. Similar increases have been noted in the United States (Kestenbaum 1977). However, Smart suggests that this increase in female offending is not as *new* a phenomenon as the oft-quoted statistics would suggest. By using the criminal statistics for earlier periods (for example for the years 1935–46) there was an increase of some 365 per cent. In addition, she suggests that the interpretation of current statistics can also be misleading. Taking the statistics for murder by women in England and Wales as one example, it would appear that there has been an increase of 500 per cent in the years 1965–75, but the actual numbers of *individuals* involved are 1 and 5 respectively (Smart 1979)!

We can conclude, therefore, that not only do changes in the offence rates of women need to be seen in a much longer historical context, but current statistics must also be interpreted with caution. Such an examination suggests that female criminality is but one response by women to a number of forces that have been operating for change during the last 40 to 50 years. It may be that until fairly recently women have been prosecuted for criminal activity less often than men on the grounds of chivalry, because of a reluctance of the police to prosecute the 'weaker' of the species. Mawby (1980) concludes that this may now no longer be the case. He administered a self-report questionnaire to 340 boys and 266 girls in a Sheffield secondary school. He deduced from his findings that the absence of female involvement in delinquency was not so much a product of the chivalry of agencies reluctant to prosecute, but that girls seemed actually less delinquent than boys except in areas where their opportunity was the same as boys – thefts from home or school for example.

When women are actually taken to court, it is sometimes pleaded in extenuation that the woman was an unwilling or unwitting accomplice under the influence of a dominant male. Some authorities have suggested that, until recently, women had less opportunity for criminal activity. Today, it appears that more women are involved in crimes of serious assault, hijacking, and other forms of terrorism. Modern technological advances and enhanced equal opportunities with men are seen by some as providing more opportunities for female involvement in business frauds, forgeries, and other offences of deception (Smith 1974). Some doubt has been cast upon this assertion in recent work by Morris and Gelsthorpe (1981) and Widom (1981). These writers suggest that it is erroneous to place such emphasis upon the effects of so-called female emancipation.

It has also been observed that (with the exception of soliciting for prostitution) the law has unfairly discriminated against men until fairly recently. There is also evidence to suggest that the antisocial behaviour of women takes mainly non-criminal forms such as promiscuity (which, in men, is often not considered to be antisocial conduct at all), and that psychiatric explanations for criminal conduct may be invoked more frequently in women. This has resulted in the diversion of women from the judicial and penal systems into psychiatric and allied areas of care. However, there is a good deal of overlap between sexual misconduct and other forms of delinquency (Gibbens 1959). It has also been suggested that the courts may tend to find fewer women *guilty* of offences (Pollak 1961), but the evidence for this is conflicting (Jones 1965 and Mannheim 1965). In respect of *penalties*, until very recently it was considered that women were dealt with more leniently by the courts. However, May (1977), in a study of the sentencing practices for *juvenile* offenders in Aberdeen, found that girls were more severely dealt with, and Mawby (1977), in a study which included adult offenders, found that when *previous record* was taken into consideration females were more likely to be imprisoned than males.

EXPLANATIONS OF FEMALE CRIMINALITY

It will be apparent that the explanations for the criminality of women are complex and there are many imponderable factors that may determine the extent to which females are dealt with through the judicial and penal systems. We shall now examine briefly some of these explanations. A number of studies have shown a high degree of psychiatric morbidity in female offenders (for example, Gibbens 1971, Goodman and Price 1967, Home Office and DHSS 1975: 41–2, Guze 1976, and Barack and Widom 1978). This may merely mean, however, as already suggested, that women tend to get diverted towards psychiatric systems of referral and treatment. Epps and Parnell (1952) found that female delinquents tended to be more mesomorphic than non-delinquents, a finding similar to that established for male delinquents (see Chapter 4). Smith (1962), in her study of women in prison, found evidence of more precocious physical sexual development. She suggested that, when this was not accompanied by equal development of personality, it might lead to restless or rebellious behaviour and make a girl vulnerable to the development of promiscuity and antisocial conduct. In Chapter 4, I referred to endocrine disturbance and crime and I noted that the menstrual cycle was considered to be of importance. A study of women detained in a special hospital, by Hands, Herbert, and Tennent (1974) noted *some* association between phases of the menstrual cycle and aggressive behaviour. However, the evidence from this and other studies is inconclusive; all we can deduce from studies of endocrine and related functioning is that there *may* be instances in which these factors are of importance in the individual case.

Many workers have noted the unstable and impoverished backgrounds from which younger female offenders are drawn (Epps 1951 and 1954, Cockburn and Maclay 1965, Goodman and Price 1967, Cowie, Cowie, and Slater 1968, and Caplan *et al.* 1980). The evidence from these studies suggests that the psychopathological elements in such backgrounds tend to be more florid and traumatic than in those of young male delinquents. It may be that reactions to female delinquency within the home are more melodramatic and that the memories of these reactions tend to persist in the minds of those most closely involved. One quite striking factor that seems to emerge from a number of studies is the extent to which an impoverished relationship with father or his absence seems to be significant (Riege 1972, Gilbert 1972, and Felice and Offord 1972).

SOME OFFENCES PECULIAR TO WOMEN

There is one crime which is only committed by women, and for which the law makes specific provision, namely the crime of infanticide (see Chapter 9). There are certain other offences that are found to be committed by women more than men – examples are the procuration of criminal abortion (very rare these days since the Abortion Act 1967), shop-lifting, soliciting for prostitution, and baby stealing. Instances of non-accidental injury to children tend to be attributed more frequently to mothers than to fathers, but in many cases it is often hard to discern who really struck the first blow or to what extent one partner was covering up for the other. I now deal briefly with shop-lifting, soliciting for prostitution, and baby stealing.

*Shop-lifting*

The current, though admittedly changing, roles and occupations of women provide them with a greater degree of opportunity for stealing from shops than men. However, as Smart (1976) has shown, men seem to be catching up on them. The major studies of shop-lifting have been carried out by Gibbens and Prince (1962) and Gibbens, Palmer, and Prince (1971). They reported that shop-lifting was very much an offence of women over the age of forty and that when women of this age did engage in shop-lifting there was a fairly high degree of recidivism. Quite a high proportion of female shop-lifters show psychiatric disorder in one form or another – nearly 30 per cent in the case of recidivists. The studies also found a high proportion of physical ailments or disabilities, many of which were gynaecological conditions.

*Soliciting for prostitution*

Prostitution itself is not a criminal offence; the only unlawful elements are soliciting in public and keeping a brothel. A disturbing number of prostitutes are still sent to prison (about 10 per cent). Some studies of prostitutes demonstrate a high concentration of mental and personality disorders; at the same time it would be unwise to over-emphasize these psychopathological elements for there seems to be very good evidence that the offence is also largely culturally determined. As Smart (1976) and other feminist writers have rightly pointed out, there is an apparent double standard of morality for men and for women. The man who 'kerb crawls' for service gets little of the attention and opprobrium reserved for the 'common' prostitute who provides it. Very little research has been carried out on the clients of prostitutes, but a study by Gibbens and Silberman (1960) showed that many of these men had poor and shallow social relationships, while their backgrounds had much in common with the women whose services they sought. Apart from any possible affront to public decency, it is very doubtful whether the law should involve itself in this kind of behaviour; it is as much a matter of moral judgement and public health as of criminality. It is encouraging to see that in order to protect their interests some prostitutes have now formed 'collectives'. The public attitude towards prostitutes also seems to be less hypo-critical and punitive now than it was fifty years ago.

## *Baby stealing*

Although child stealing in various forms figures prominently in folklore and legend, and was known in Victorian times, it has only become a matter of concern to the courts and penal system in more recent years. Baby stealing is almost exclusively a female offence, whereas child stealing more often involves males in the abduction of young children of either sex. D'Orbán (1972 and 1976) notes an increase in the more pathological forms of baby stealing in recent years; he records that for the period 1950–57 there was an average of 9 cases, but in 1973 61 cases were reported. Such cases attract a good deal of publicity; Hunter (1973) has suggested that prosecution may only make matters worse for all concerned. D'Orbán considers that the offence usually seems to be an attempt to seek compensation for emotional deprivation or frustrated maternal feelings. The offence rarely seems to be premeditated, though in some cases there is evidence of previous planning. In his studies of 24 cases D'Orbán (1972 and 1976) suggests a fourfold classification: (1) girls of subnormal intelligence who steal a baby to play with; (2) psychotic offenders whose offence is motivated by delusional ideas; (3) psychopathic personalities preoccupied with a desire to have children; (4) a manipulative group in which the motive for baby stealing is an attempt to influence a man by whom the offender had become pregnant and with whom the relationship had become insecure. In this latter group offences were precipitated by a crisis (such as a miscarriage) or the threat of desertion. Such women presented the stolen baby to their partner pretending the child was his. D'Orbán found that the stolen babies were generally well cared for and their where-abouts ascertained quite quickly. However, he suggests that the motivation was highly pathological.

### TREATMENT AND ALLIED ISSUES

Generally speaking, women seem to benefit more than men do from many of our penal treatment measures. Thus they seem to respond better to probation, to fines, or to imprisonment or care in a psychiatric institution, at least as far as reconviction is concerned. When in an institution, however, they seem much harder to manage than men (Goodman and Price 1967, Walker and McCabe 1973, and Campbell 1981). Gibbs (1971) and Smith (1974) have noted how traumatic the effects of a prison sentence may be, not only for the woman offender but also for her family. Richardson (1969), Hall Williams (1970), and Smart (1976) have all pointed to the lack of realistic rehabilitation programmes in most of our penal and allied institutions for women. So many of the work opportunities appear to be confined to the drudgery of domestic and similar roles. The regimes in many institutions for women lack imagination and purpose, so it is hardly surprising that when they return to the community they are as ill equipped as ever to cope with a complex and ever-changing society. The fact that such a large proportion of female offenders have, or have had, a poor relationship with father or a father figure prompts the suggestion that we have not capitalized sufficiently on the use of male staff to work with them in the past. Happily, this is now occurring more frequently, both within penal establishments and in the community. In this latter connection, Parsloe (1972) has pointed out the advantages of male probation officers supervising female offenders. It can be beneficial for some women offenders to have a relationship with a member of the opposite sex that is caring, persistent, consistent, and non-exploitive.

CONCLUSION

A study of the criminological and allied literature suggests that there is no single simple theory that can adequately account for the apparent differences in female/male offending. A complex web of bio-psycho-social influences impinges to bring these about. It is because female offending is such a complex and, one might add, emotive subject that there is good reason for studying it in its own right.

## Section two – Sexual offenders

> A private sin is not so prejudicial in the world as
> a public indecency.
>
> CERVANTES

### SEXUAL BEHAVIOUR AND SEXUAL OFFENDING

The understanding and management of those who commit sexual offences are closely associated with wider attitudes to sexual behaviour and society's views about it. Few subjects are more emotive, and productive of so many blind spots and prejudices. Despite much-publicized programmes of sex education and more open discussion, it is doubtful whether people are less guilt-ridden today in their attitudes towards sex than in the days of the book of Leviticus with its solemn injunctions about sexual conduct.

Not all deviant sexual behaviours constitute offences, and indeed, what seems to one person to be a perverse or abnormal sexual activity may be regarded as normal by another. In recent years, the law has attempted to be less concerned with private sexual acts, only seeking to intervene when the young or specially vulnerable might be involved, where opportunities for coercion exist or where public decency might be affronted. It is also important to remember that there is no such thing as exclusive maleness or femaleness: all of us carry attributes and feelings of the opposite sex within us. Those who work with sexually deviant or delinquent people need to bear in mind this vital but uncomfortable notion if they are to offer informed and compassionate help. This is all the more important in work with certain offenders whose crimes may engender very real feelings of revulsion and horror (Prins 1980).

I first provide both a clinical and a legal classification of sexual deviation and offending. I then discuss the size of the problem before examining some specific offences.

### CLINICAL CLASSIFICATION

*Sexual Deviations (Variations)* (after Prins 1980)

Only some of the following will come within the purview of the criminal law.

(1) *Sexual activity not requiring a human partner.* For example, the use of animals (bestio-sexuality, zoophilia), objects, or materials (fetishism).

(2) *Sexual activity not requiring a willing partner.* Rape (both heterosexual and homosexual), being a 'Peeping Tom' (voyeurism), rubbing (frotteurism), exhibitionism, necrophilia (use of a dead partner).

(3) *Requiring willing partners.*
   (a) Masturbatory activities of various kinds without proceeding to copulation (mutual masturbation, fellatio, cunnilingus, anal sex).
   (b) Requiring unusual conditions, for example a partner of the same sex, involvement of three persons in simultaneous sexual activity (troilism), a child (paedophilia), an old person (gerontophilia), a forbidden partner (incest), or requiring punishment or suffering (masochism and sadism).

(4) *Others.* In the following cases there may be sexual motivations for the behaviour.
   (a) Kleptomania – a tenuous relationship has been suggested between some forms of stealing and repressed sexual impulses.
   (b) Pyromania – certain cases of fire-raising seem to have a strong sexual element.
   (c) Coprophagia, coprophilia, saliromania (terms used to indicate the derivation of sexual pleasure from contact with, or sight of, body wastes or other secretions).

LEGAL CLASSIFICATION (SEXUAL OFFENCES)

Most sexual offences are covered by the following enactments: the Vagrancy Act 1824, the Sexual Offences Act 1956, the Indecency with Children Act 1960, the Sexual Offences Act 1967, the Sexual Offences (Amendment) Act 1976, and the Criminal Law Act 1977. The following classification has been modified from that suggested by James (1964).

(1) *Offences in which the sex drive is distorted.*
   (a) Rape and attempts to rape.

    (b)  Indecent assault on females.
    (c)  Some forms of sexual murder.
    (d)  Molestation of children of the opposite sex.
    (e)  Soliciting for prostitution. *(See earlier discussion under female offenders.)*

(2)  *Offences in which the sexual drive seems to be more clearly deviant.*
    (a)  Punishable male homosexuality (buggery and attempts, gross indecency, indecent assault, and male soliciting).[1]
    (b)  'Peeping Tom' activities.
    (c)  Indecent exposure.
    (d)  Buggery with animals (bestiality).
    (e)  Molestation of, or interference with, corpses (necrophilia).

The offences listed above would be regarded by most people as being fairly obvious sexual crimes. However, to these must be added some others which are perhaps less obvious, but whose inclusion is necessary in order to complete the picture. They include the following:

(1)  Pornography offences, particularly where these involve children as participants.
(2)  Making obscene telephone calls.
(3)  Conspiracy to corrupt public morals, such as publishing advertisements for the solicitation of illicit sexual acts.
(4)  Bigamy. This is best regarded as an offence against family life rather than as a sexual offence.
(5)  Adultery. This is still a punishable offence in some countries.
(6)  Abduction of females.
(7)  Procuration of others for the commission of sexual offences.
(8)  Certain 'masked' offences in which the accompanying or underlying motivation may be sexual. Stealing to satisfy

---

[1] The Sexual Offences Act 1967 removed consenting male homosexual acts in private from the statute book (it is left to the courts to decide what constitutes a public place, but a public lavatory would be so regarded). (See also Chapter 2.) However, this only applies when (i) both parties are over twenty-one; (ii) two people only are involved; (iii) the act is in private (in England and Wales, but not Northern Ireland). Nothing in the Act prevents homosexual acts from still being held to be offences when committed by serving members of Her Majesty's Armed Services or of the Merchant Service.

fetishistic desires (for example, larceny of ladies' underwear from clothes lines). Some murders or other serious assaults, certain 'proving' offences arising out of displaced sexual desires (an example being motor cycle thefts by some types of youth in order to prove their virility).

## THE SIZE OF THE PROBLEM

Sexual offences constitute less than 3 per cent of all crimes. There is also a wide discrepancy between the numbers of these offences *known* to the police and the numbers *dealt with or prosecuted* (see also Chapter 2). Most sexual offences are dealt with by non-custodial penalties, but rape, buggery, incest, and serious indecent assaults are dealt with most frequently by imprisonment. *Table 10(1)* shows the total number of indictable sexual offences known to the police for the years 1975–78, and *Table 10(2)* provides details of the more serious of these.

Table 10(1)   *Indictable sexual offences known to the police – 1975–78\**

| 1975 | 1976 | 1977 | 1978 |
|---|---|---|---|
| 23,731 | 22,203 | 21,313 | 22,367 |

Table 10(2)   *Selection of the more serious indictable sexual offences known to the police – 1975–78*

| | 1975 | 1976 | 1977 | 1978 |
|---|---|---|---|---|
| rape | 1040 | 1094 | 1015 | 1243 |
| buggery | 720 | 662 | 594 | 697 |
| Indecent assault on a male | 2885 | 2689 | 2633 | 2455 |
| Indecent assault on a female | 11,809 | 10,901 | 11,048 | 11,814 |
| Incest | 349 | 338 | 295 | 329 |
| unlawful sexual intercourse with a girl *under* 13 | 327 | 295 | 243 | 214 |
| unlawful sexual intercourse with a girl *under* 16 | 4533 | 4313 | 3681 | 3491 |

\* Source for all statistical material, *Criminal Statistics, England and Wales* (Home Office 1979).

*Notes to Table 10(2)*

(1) The figures reveal that females are the predominant victims. It is quite likely that a not inconsiderable proportion of men and youths fail to report sexual attacks, largely because of the shame and embarrassment involved.

(2) Before 1978, indecent assault on a male included attempts to commit buggery. From 1978, attempts to commit buggery are included with buggery.

(3) Each year, there are also some 2500 convictions for indecent exposure, 3000 for soliciting for prostitution, about 600 for male importuning, and over 100 for living on immoral earnings. With the exception of the latter, almost all of them are dealt with in the Magistrates' Courts.

The figures in *Tables 10(1)* and *10(2)* indicate that the number of offences remains much the same from year to year; such fluctuations as occur are often the result of changes in the legislation or in offence classification (*see note (2) to Table 10(2)*). Although reported and prosecuted sexual offences constitute but a small proportion of those that actually take place, some sexual offenders cause considerable distress to their victims, and others are the hapless victims of their own misdirected desires and impulses. A small minority cause grave physical and psychological harm to their victims and pose a serious threat to the public. I now give more detailed consideration to some specific sexual offences. This implies that motivations and explanations are distinct for each group, which of course is not necessarily the case; the distinction is arbitrary and made only for convenience.

INDECENT EXPOSURE

This is the commonest of all the sexual offences. Although the rates of offending remain more or less static there seems to have been an increase in the number of prosecutions for those aged *twenty-one and under* in recent years (Rooth 1972). It is exclusively a male offence, though doubtless if women exposed their genitals they might be prosecuted for a breach of the peace. Although the display and emphasis of the male genitalia has been commonly recorded in art, history, and literature, the law did not appear to make specific provision against it before the Vagrancy Act of 1824. To substantiate the offence, there must be wilful intent to insult a female by exhibiting the penis. Indecent exposure (the offence) must be distinguished from exhibitionism (a clinical pattern of sexual behaviour) (Rooth 1975). Most victims are adult females or children of either sex. Not infrequently, as with other sexual offences, there is a marked reluctance to report the occurrence (see Gittleson, Eacott, and Mehta 1978 and Cox and McMahon 1978). Sometimes the offender will merely expose himself, or make gestures or verbal suggestions. Those who have a history of both sexual and non-sexual offences, who engage in some physical activity at the time of the offence, and who also expose predominantly to adult women, are most likely to have the worst prognosis (Bluglass 1980). Various attempts have been made to classify indecent exposers (see, for example, Maclay 1952, Pollock 1960, and Rooth 1975) with varying degrees of success. The following is a fairly rudimentary classification.

(1) The inhibited and possibly latently homosexual young man who struggles against his impulses to expose. He usually exposes with a flaccid penis and feels anxious about his behaviour. Where such behaviour occurs in adolescence, counselling and guidance on sex matters are usually helpful.

(2) A less inhibited type who feels little guilt. He exposes with an erect penis and may masturbate at the same time. He may also engage in physical overtures; if this is the case it is a somewhat ominous sign, as it may be a precursor of further seriously deviant sexual behaviour.

(3) Exposure as a result of a dementing process or because of organic disease. Here medical treatment and care are clearly indicated.

(4) Situational exposure. Here, the offence may be the result of some concurrent stress, such as marital disharmony. Counselling with the offender and/or spouse can be helpful in such cases.

(5) Exposure committed by dull and subnormal individuals and by the psychotically disturbed. Care and treatment in hospital or at a clinic may be needed in such cases (see Chapters 5 and 9).

(6) Cases in which the exposure is facilitated by overindulgence in alcohol, or where the sexual drive is very strong and accompanied by a broader pattern of deviant

and aggressive sexuality. This can be a potentially dangerous group of offenders.

## Explanations

The classification listed above provides some clues as to aetiology. Other explanations include a need to assert a wavering or undeveloped masculinity and a feeling of unattractiveness to females. In some cases, there may be a need to assert power over or to insult and shock women; such behaviour may be a suppressed wish to commit rape. In these cases, women may be viewed as dangerous powerful creatures, and it is not surprising that impotence and latent or overt homosexuality are found in the backgrounds of some of these indecent exposers. A sensitive account of a persistent exposer is that given by Harry Mills in Parker's book *The Twisting Lane* (Parker 1970).

## Treatment Considerations

Some of these have already been touched upon. Sometimes the shock of a court appearance will suffice, in other cases counselling the offender and his family will help, as will some training in elementary social skills, such as learning how to approach girls (Burgess *et al.* 1980). Some workers have found that group counselling is successful because the offender gains benefit from not feeling he carries his burden alone (Mathis and Cullens 1971 and Milo 1976). The use of feminizing hormones has been tried in some cases, as has behaviour modification (Rooth 1975, Jones and Frei 1977, Perkins 1980, Gayford 1981, and Snaith and Collins 1981). Overall, it would appear that treatment aimed at helping the offender to control his offending behaviour quickly holds out the best hope. Thus behavioural methods and social skills training are probably to be preferred to long-term psychotherapy, except in those cases where the offence behaviour seems to be closely related to deep-rooted interpersonal conflicts and stresses (Cox 1980). As for all sex offenders, the communication of genuineness and warmth by the therapist is more important than the particular school of thought he espouses or the model of practice he adopts.

SEXUAL ASSAULTS ON CHILDREN (PAEDOPHILIA,
CHILD MOLESTATION)

Sexual offences against children and young persons vary considerably in their form and in their intensity. For example, incest can be regarded as one kind of sexual offence against a child; similarly, buggery and attempted buggery are often committed against children, but the criminal statistics do not distinguish these acts from those committed against adults. Those who commit sexual offences against children (almost always men) are usually referred to as paedophiles, although pederasty is the term sometimes employed for those who commit sexual offences against male children or youths.

Gordon (1976) and Lambert (1976) have analysed the history of paedophilia and tried to place it in context. The physical love of children has always been a fairly universal phenomenon and there are probably many people who are attracted in this way towards children but who manage to keep their inclinations in check. However, such love may be harmful for two reasons. First, it may become over-possessive, smothering, and selfish. This may result in the child never growing towards the independence of adulthood, remaining a child, and carrying over the sexual games of childhood into adult life. Second, such love may go beyond the limits of normal care and protection and become inappropriate in situations that then become both physically and emotionally traumatizing to the victim. It should therefore come as no surprise that a large number of sexual offences against children are committed by those who are in positions of tutelage or trust. Many such offenders give accounts of disordered family relationships or, as might be expected from the earlier discussion, of their own corruption in youth. However, too much reliance should not be placed upon tales of corruption. Not all alleged victims are as innocent as they may appear; indeed, some have been known to be the corrupters, behaving seductively, both covertly and overtly. Some are also quite unscrupulous in their behaviour, not being averse to offering favours for financial reward and occasionally indulging in blackmail. Virkkunen (1975), Elwell (1979), Ingram (1979), and Burgess, Groth, and McCausland (1981) have all placed varying degrees of emphasis upon the seductive or precipitating role of the so-called victim.

It is difficult to estimate the actual harm that is caused to children by sexual assault. Where the assault is both violent *and unexpected*, the effects can be very damaging both physically and emotionally. Paul (1975 and 1977), Tilelli, Turek, and Jaffe (1980), Herjanic and Wilbois (1980), and Ellerstein and Cavanagh (1980) provide ample evidence of the physical and emotional damage that may be caused by serious sexual assault on young children. As with many forms of sexual assault, the offence behaviour may take many forms. It may include exhibitionism, attempts to put the hand up the knickers of small girls, feeling the breasts or genitalia, touching the penis, masturbatory activities of various kinds, or attempts at sexual intercourse – both heterosexual and homosexual.

## Classification

The following rudimentary classification may be helpful. The advice I gave earlier that classification is always arbitrary and overlapping should still be borne in mind.

(1) Bisexual (rather than homosexual) inadequate adolescents, who are able to bribe children. They may have been placed in positions of trust towards them by adults.

(2) A more dangerous adolescent offender, who makes serious assaults; he often has a history of having been assaulted in his own childhood (see above).

(3) The middle-aged paedophile; lonely and isolated, he may seek out the company of little girls in order to find solace.

(4) The senile pederast, whose inclinations have not been dulled even if his sexual ability has.

(5) The paedophile of low or subnormal intelligence, who lacks social skills and an appreciation of social norms (see also Chapter 5).

(6) Those whose offending seems to be a reaction against sexual or emotional frustration at an adult level (see also discussion of indecent exposers).

(7) The exclusively homosexual paedophile (pederast), who sees himself as the protector of disadvantaged boys; he

cannot see that his behaviour is wrong and is quite impervious to treatment.

## Treatment considerations

Treatment will be determined to a large extent by the kind of classification suggested above. Exclusive sexual interest in young children is a very difficult condition to treat. This is partly because sexual predilection becomes firmly fixed at an early age; thus techniques based upon insight-giving psychotherapy do not seem to be very helpful. In adolescent cases, sex counselling may help, as will assistance in developing social skills (Brodsky 1980). In cases where the behaviour seems to be temporary or situationally determined, efforts to locate and treat the particular stresses offer some hope of success. For the exclusively homosexual paedophile, the only treatment likely to prove beneficial will be that which will serve to damp down sexual desires. Various methods have been tried, with equally varying claims for success. These include the use of feminizing hormones and anti-hormones and other drugs (see Field and Williams 1970, Field 1973, and Tennent, Bancroft, and Casse 1974). Aversion therapy has been advocated by some workers (McGuire and Vallance 1964, McGuire, Carlisle, and Young 1965, Mather 1966, and Bancroft 1969). Useful and more recent accounts of assessment procedures in such cases can be found in Crawford (1980) and Matthews (1980). In some cases, castration and surgical interference with parts of the brain (notably the hypothalamus) have been tried (Roeder, Orthner, and Muller 1972 and Ortmann 1980). The irreversible nature of these procedures presents ethical problems of some magnitude, even though the informed consent of the offender/ patient may be sought. There are also ethical implications in the use of reversible procedures such as hormone injections or implants. It may be tempting for the pederast serving a long sentence of imprisonment to accelerate his chances of parole by agreeing to subject himself to these treatments even though his real motivation for change may be slight. There are arguments against this line of thinking. *If* his informed consent has been given without coercion, *if* he is fully aware of the implications, and *if* he is prepared to make himself available for follow-up after release, not only is he less likely to be a menace to children, but he may be able to make a useful contribution to society and enjoy the benefits of freedom.

## INCEST

Incest is the sexual crime that probably provokes the most emotive reaction. In general, taboos have existed against its practice from time immemorial, although history reveals some notable exceptions (for example in ancient Egyptian culture). Mythology and literature are replete with allusions to incestuous conduct or to incestuous themes. There are, of course, many reasons for the strict prohibitions against incestuous behaviour. First, there are the religious injunctions, more particularly in the Old Testament. Second, there appears to be a deeply held and primitive horror of consanguinous sexual relationships between parents and their offspring. Third, there is the Freudian belief (stemming from Darwin's theory of the primal horde) which suggests that in primitive societies the incest taboo was erected to preserve the power of the paternal tyrant, in order that he might prevent the younger males from banding together to deprive him of his sexual rights over the females. Fourth, taboos are said to be strong because of the serious role confusion that can occur when close kin have sexual relationships. Fifth, there is evidence that incestuous relationships produce a higher incidence of genetic weakness than those found in normal sexual unions. (Roberts 1967, Nakashima and Zakus 1977, and Browning and Boatman 1977.) However, it seems more likely that it is the *combination* of poor antenatal care, poor nurturing, environment, *and* the incestuous relationships that occur in these socially disordered families that produces these results rather than genetic transmission alone.

Incest did not become a specific criminal offence until 1908, and the present law is now incorporated into the Sexual Offences Act 1956 and the Criminal Law Act 1977. (See also Bluglass 1979.) Simply put, the law states that a man who has sexual intercourse with a woman he *knows* to be his granddaughter, daughter, sister, or mother is guilty of incest, as is a woman of or above the age of sixteen who, with consent, permits her grandfather, father, brother, or son to have sexual intercourse with her. It is also an offence to incite a girl under the age of sixteen to have incestuous sexual intercourse. Incest is punishable with a maximum sentence of imprisonment for seven years; in the case of the offence being committed against a girl under thirteen, it is punishable with imprisonment for life. Comparatively few cases come to the attention of the police (*see Table 10(2)*), and even fewer are prosecuted. Generally, a veil of extreme secrecy is preserved within the family. Not infrequently, the case may only come to light because of pregnancy, because of an attempt at blackmail, through the investigation of some non-related offence behaviour, or as a result of a confession by one of the parties.

The most outstanding characteristic in the background in a large proportion of incestuous families is that of social and emotional disorder (see Canepa and Bandini 1980, Connell 1980, Dietz and Craft 1980, Selby *et al.* 1980). Lukianowicz (1972) found a 4 per cent incidence of incest among an unselected group of psychiatric patients in Northern Ireland. Hall Williams (1974) found a high incidence of subnormality and previous criminal convictions, and Virkkunen (1974) found alcohol to be heavily associated with the offence. In over half the cases, the victim seems to be the man's own child or children (Maisch 1973 and Hall Williams, 1974). More recently, Gibbens, Way, and Soothill (1978) have made a comparative study of *sibling* and *parent-child* incest cases. 61 per cent of the fathers were first offenders, and 12 per cent had subsequent convictions; some 13 per cent of these fathers had prior sexual offences. 72 per cent of the parent-incest cases were forty at the time of the offence and 90 per cent of them went to prison. Of the sibling offenders, 60 per cent were aged twenty or less; 54 per cent of them had previous findings of guilt or convictions, but few were for sexual offences. However, over the next twelve years, they continued to be heavily convicted; 49 per cent for property offences and 14 per cent for violence. In indicating possible reasons for these different profiles, the authors make three suggestions. First, incest behaviour may come to light more readily where the family is already under surveillance by social workers. Second, sibling incest may well be more common in large overcrowded families where a high rate of ordinary criminal behaviour is common. Third, their sample may have comprised a group of young recidivists who continued offending wholly or partly because of sexual maladjustment which was not always revealed in *convictions* for sexual offences. (See also discussion of 'masked' sexual offences above.)

It is not hard to see that family composition and life-style are highly significant in creating conditions for the occurrence of incestuous behaviour. These conditions may be classified broadly as follows.

*Classification*

(1) Incest occurring in large, overcrowded families, where the participants almost slip into an incestuous pattern of behaviour.

(2) Incestuous relations developing because of intellectual impairment or psychotic illness in either or both of the parties.

(3) Cases where the wife is absent either through death or separation and where the daughter(s) may take over the wife's role. It may also occur in cases where the wife is still physically present but where she has abrogated her sexual role. In such cases she is often not only quite aware of what is occurring but also prepared to collude in the practice.

(4) Cases in which the father is a dominant individual who uses threats of violence to get his way in the full knowledge that such behaviour is wrong. Such men may indulge in alcohol abuse.

(5) Occasional instances where the parties do not know that they are in a consanguinous relationship. For example, a brother and sister who have been separated from each other very early in life may meet much later and unknowingly enter into a sexual relationship.

(6) Cases of 'object fixation incest' (Bagley 1969). Bagley suggests that incest may occur in those instances where the dominant partner was sexually fixated on an earlier object of sexual gratification, a child or an adolescent with whom he had his first sexual experience when he was a child himself. (See discussion of aetiology of paedophilia above.)

*Treatment considerations*

In work with incest cases, it is important to have come to terms with one's own incest anxieties and fears. The courts, on the whole, deal severely with adult males convicted of incest with their children. Sometimes one wonders whether more harm than good is done by the additional stress created for the family by sentencing the father to a very long term in prison. However, the welfare of the children has to be protected, particularly in those cases where multiple incestuous relationships have occurred. These days, elaborate precautions are taken by both the probation service and the local authority social services departments in all cases where children have been, or are likely to be, the subject of injury or attack from whatever cause. In view of this, some have argued for the removal of the crime of incest from the statute book, because it would still be possible to take the necessary prosecutory and precautionary steps under existing sex offence legislation (Morris and Hawkins 1970). In this way, the special abhorrence with which the offence is viewed might be diminished to some extent. It could then be seen for what it really is, an offence connected with adverse family attitudes and living conditions, calling for social and psychiatric intervention rather than punitive wrath born of irrational feelings. In addition, the global use of the term incest means that we link together all its variants and treat them all alike. In order to offer more effective treatment we need to discriminate more carefully. Perhaps the law should only intervene most heavily in cases under (4) above. In other instances, arrangements would have to be made for the withdrawal of the offending party from the family (perhaps by means of a probation order with a requirement of residence) while the complexities of the situation were clarified. The local authorities have adequate powers already to supervise younger members of the family and to effect their removal should the situation escalate. The overall aim of treatment should be to restore family functioning rather than to disrupt it further by the imposition of inflexible and punitive sanctions.

SERIOUS SEXUAL ATTACK (RAPE)

*Background*

Reference to *Table 10(1)* indicates that serious sexual assaults on females not only constitute a large proportion of known sexual offences, but that their frequency seems to remain fairly constant. For reasons we shall examine later, the figures for serious sexual attack (rape) have shown a small but steady increase in the last few years. As already indicated, the statistical classification of an offence may give no real indication of its severity. Thus there are many gradations of rape and of incest assault, ranging from fairly minor attempts at rape to serious indecent assaults that only just fall short of it. Stereotypes of the rapist abound, and the act of rape, like incest, has its place in myth and legend. Mistaken interpretations of anthropology and history have encouraged men in their chauvinistic belief that manhood and virility can only be demonstrated by taking a woman against her will. Such mistaken interpretations lead to the belief that a woman may 'enjoy' the act of rape while failing to recognize the horror and distress experienced by rape victims. Much of the more recent literature on rape victimology helps to present the picture in its true light. However, it is also true that a few women may unwittingly make themselves vulnerable by hitch-hiking alone, leaving doors and windows open at night, or by wearing provocative clothes. Those familiar with court proceedings will have observed how the allegedly provocatively dressed schoolgirl may impress quite differently when clad in school gym slip in court. Imprudent though the behaviour of some victims may be, this cannot condone the conduct of the offender. Carried to their logical conclusion, such arguments would suggest that we *deserve* to lose our cars if we leave them unlocked or have our houses burgled if we leave doors unfastened.

It is not surprising that much rape has, until recently, been under-reported. A woman may be understandably reluctant to go through the ordeal of a searching medical examination and a public exploration of the circumstances of the alleged assault. Some women are also reluctant to report the offence to their partners or other family members. They may suffer much torment and guilt as a result. The physical consequences, apart from any vaginal or anal injury that may have been caused, are very important. The victim may have become pregnant, have contracted venereal disease or one of the increasingly common genital herpes (HSV-2) infections (Burt 1979 and Catterall 1981); all this just compounds their distress. Many women feel so defiled by the experience that they go to extreme lengths to cleanse themselves, for example by scrubbing their genitalia with strong disinfectants repeatedly. Gradually we are recognizing the importance of the emotional state of the victim and the need for post-rape counselling. The development of rape crisis centres is an encouraging development here, but *all* who come into contact with rape victims and their families require help to develop knowledge and skills in this area. (For some helpful account of what can be achieved see Abarbanel 1976, Hardgrove 1976, Hall 1977, Nadelson and Nutman 1979, and Holmes 1981.)

Far less attention has been given to cases of male rape. These are covered in the criminal statistics as acts of buggery or attempts thereat. Such acts are sometimes committed with great force and the person concerned (frequently a minor) may be put in great fear. Moreover, the reluctance to talk about it or to report it, is, if anything, greater than it is for women. The physical and emotional trauma (apart from pregnancy) and its sequelae are just as severe. Apart from accounts of rape in prison and allied institutions in the USA (for example, Sccaco 1975) we have few documented accounts of the incidence and effects of anal rape.

*Legal aspects*

It is only in recent years that the ingredients of the offence of rape have been fully defined by statute. Until then, rape was a crime at common law, the only statutory reference to it being in Section 1 of the Sexual Offences Act 1956. It is worth noting that it is still not a criminal offence for a man to rape his wife (unless a separation order is in force), though a husband who uses force in exercising his 'rights' against his wife may be found guilty of assault. Recent changes in the law owe much to the work of feminists who viewed the legal approach to the crime of rape as one example of discrimination by men against women (see Brownmiller 1975 and Toner 1977). In 1975, in the case of *DPP v. Morgan*, the Law Lords ruled that belief in a woman's consent, *even if unreasonable*, must exonerate the accused. This ruling resulted in the setting up of a government committee of enquiry into the law of rape. The Committee did not disagree with the Law Lords' decision, but made certain recommendations concerning the preservation of the anonymity of the parties in court proceedings and evidence of the victim's previous sexual history. They also recommended joint representation of the sexes on juries in rape cases. Most of the Committee's recommendations were incorporated into the Sexual Offences (Amendment) Act 1976. The law now holds that a man commits rape if (a) he has unlawful sexual intercourse with a woman who at the time of the intercourse does not consent to it; and (b) at that time he knows that she does not consent to the intercourse or is reckless as to whether she consents to it. Concerning consent, the law now states that, if at a trial for a rape offence the jury has to consider whether a man believed that a woman was consenting to sexual intercourse, the presence or absence of reasonable grounds for such a belief is a matter to which the jury should have regard, in conjunction with other relevant matters, in considering whether he so believed. As a result of this more adequate statement of the ingredients of the offence, the clarification of issues concerning consent and the preservation of anonymity, it appears that more women are prepared to risk court proceedings. However, as has already been pointed out, there is still reluctance to do so on other grounds.

*Characteristics of rape and rapists*

A number of studies have been made of what might loosely be described as the epidemiology of rape; of these, that by Amir (1971) is probably one of the most comprehensive. Amir found that, contrary to common belief, about a third of the victims had been in previous contact with their assailants. Alcohol was an important factor in two-thirds of his cases. In 75 per cent of cases, the rape had been planned and 50 per cent of the victims had failed to resist their attackers. He also found a high proportion of multiple rape cases (43 per cent). Schultz (1975) and Macdonald (1971) have both provided thoughtful reviews of the subject, and paid careful attention to the role of, and impact upon, the victim. Recent studies in this country have shown that a sizeable proportion of serious sex offenders (including rapists) are re-convicted *a long time after their first conviction* (Soothill, Jack, and Gibbens 1976, Soothill and Gibbens 1978, and Gibbens, Way, and Soothill 1981). Howells and Wright (1978) found that serious sex offenders scored significantly higher than controls on scales measuring sexual maladjustment and loss of control. In a more recent study Wright (1980) found further evidence that serious physical assault often accompanied the rape. This, he considers, puts the lie to the oft-repeated assertion that women either enjoy the experience or acquiesce in it too readily. He says, 'it becomes apparent that to the woman involved, the attack might justifiably be seen as a *life-threatening* situation' (Wright 1980: 112, italics in original).

The arbitrary nature of attempts at classification must again be acknowledged, as must be the degree of overlap between groups. Gibbens, Way, and Soothill (1977) discerned three groups: paedophiliac rapists, aggressive rapists, and isolated rape offences. Hall Williams (1977) divided serious sexual offenders into the following four groups: (a) the extensively aggressive; (b) a mixed aggressive group; (c) the use of serious sexual offences as a means of resolving personal problems or as reactions to stress; (d) essentially paedophiliac types. In attempting any classification, problems arise because we are sometimes describing the offence by the nature of the behaviour displayed (for example, aggressive or over-inhibited), sometimes by the choice of victim (for example, children), and sometimes by the presence of other features, such as mental disorder. With this cautionary thought in mind I will now attempt to make a more detailed classification of those who commit serious sexual attack (rape).

(1) The (in other respects) well-adjusted sexually virile young man, out for what he can get, whose hedonism is not counterbalanced by finer scruples or caution.
(2) The inhibited shy young man who is trying to overcome his feelings of sexual inferiority. He may mistake the responses

of his victim as a 'come-on'. Some such rapists are latently homosexual and their behaviour may be seen as a defence against their homosexuality. (See also classification of indecent exposers.)

(3) The sexually violent and aggressive. Such offenders have records of other forms of violence; alcohol often plays a large part in their offending since they may hold the mistaken belief that it improves performance. It may of course merely serve to narcotize inhibition.

(4) A group which is potentially highly dangerous, in that offenders need to gain reassurance for their masculinity by a show of force. In West's study of such men undergoing group psychotherapy for serious rape offences, one of the main features that emerged was that these men suffered severe feelings of inferiority concerning their masculinity (West, Roy, and Nichols 1978). This group includes those who set out to defile and denigrate their victims, forcing them to participate in acts of both vaginal and anal intercourse and in oral sex. These men are women-haters and some of them may eventually commit sadistic sexual murder (Brittain 1970).

(5) A sub-group of (4). These men have psychopathic tendencies and insatiable sexual appetites. They may in fact need the resistance of their victims to arouse their potency. These offenders may also engage in homosexual rape.

(6) Those suffering from mental disorder, such as organic psychosis, brain tumour, hypomania, or from subnormality.

(7) Those who rape in groups or packs. These rapists tend to be younger and may belong to groups such as the notorious 'Hell's Angels'. A high proportion are likely to have previous convictions for violence and a few of them for other sexual offences. They are also inclined to indulge in perverse sexual activities and, like the rapists in group (4), frequently seek to defile their victims. As with those in group (3), alcohol often plays a large part in their offending (Wright and West 1981).

## Treatment Considerations

In the rudimentary classification I have suggested, some clues will be found to the type of treatment that may be successful. Such a classification should also help us to discriminate between those whose offence is less likely to be repeated and those whose dangerousness is a constant threat. Some form of brief counselling or psychotherapy may be useful for groups (1) and (2). Those in group (3) are less likely to respond to treatment, but attempts to recognize their *multifaceted* disturbance are more likely to result in some chance of success. Prolonged group psychotherapy within a secure institution seems to be marginally successful with those I have assigned to groups (4) and (5) (West, Roy, and Nichols 1978). Those in group (6) may respond to treatment or management for their underlying mental disorder. Those in group (7) may outgrow their sexually deviant and other delinquent proclivities as they mature. However, they may need to be put out of circulation for a period, both for the protection of society and for the reinforcement of their own consciences.

### SEXUAL DEVIANCE AND OTHER CRIMES

As we have seen, a number of crimes may be committed in which the underlying motivation is sexual, for example the *crime passionel* or murder committed because of pathological sexual jealousy. In some cases, the sexual motivation may not be at all clear at first sight and only patient exploration will bring it to light (Hyatt Williams 1964). Brittain (1970) has provided a useful profile of the sadistic sexual killer. Both sexual deviants and sex offenders may of course commit suicide either as a result of fear of exposure or because of guilt feelings. Rupp (1970) suggests that indiscriminate homosexuals are more prone to sudden death than the average citizen. There are a variety of ways in which sexual deviance may end in death or serious injury. A man who makes his homosexual inclinations too obvious may be at the prey of 'queer bashers'. Finally, death may occur in the course of the sexually deviant act itself, as for example in strangulation caused as a result of pressure applied to the neck during anal intercourse. Sexual molestation of corpses (necrophilia) comes to light rarely. In some cases, it is difficult to ascertain whether a murder has been committed purely for the purposes of sexual molestation after death.[2] The literature on this subject, not surprisingly, is sparse, but readers who wish to explore it further should consult Bartholomew, Milte, and Galbally (1978) and Lancaster (1978).

CONCLUSION

The range of behaviours that constitute sexual offending is vast and complex. It is necessary to reiterate the need for us to overcome our prejudices, if we are to understand those who commit offences which are not infrequently bizarre and sometimes sickening. Despite many appearances to the contrary, a number of sexual offenders are very distressed and disturbed by their behaviour and its impact upon others. Only when they discern a dispassionate and compassionate recipient for their feelings can they unburden themselves; by so doing, they may be helped to ease some of the misperceptions and tensions that have contributed to their offending. Finally, a multi-method approach to management is likely to be the most successful. For this reason, close collaboration between all who are concerned with the care and management of such offenders is crucial in bringing about any improvement; it must be accepted, however, that such improvements may be minimal.

## Section three – Alcohol, other drugs, and crime

> Wine is an insolent fellow, and strong drink makes an uproar; no one addicted to their company grows wise.
>
> BOOK OF PROVERBS

> Habit is a great deadener.
>
> SAMUEL BECKETT

In this section no attempt is made to summarize the vast literature on the causes, epidemiology, or treatment of alcohol and other drug abuse; those wishing to seek a summarized

[2] Mather (1979) personal communication.

account should consult Prins (1980) and the further reading listed at the end of this section. There is some danger in discussing alcohol and other drugs as separate entities, but it seems appropriate to do so for the following reasons. First, it is legitimate to describe alcohol as just one of a number of drugs, hence the choice of title for this section. Second, it makes for easier presentation if the material is divided. Third, there are important differences between the sequence of events and processes involved in the abuse of, or addiction to, alcohol and the sequence with regard to other drugs. A notable difference is that, whereas in the case of drugs dependence is accompanied by a need for increased dosage, in the case of alcohol this is a transient feature, since the person heavily addicted to alcohol, in the latter stages of his addiction, tends to have a diminished tolerance. Fourth, there are a number of differences in the personal characteristics, behaviours, and social backgrounds in those involved in the abuse of alcohol and those involved in the abuse of other drugs. Finally, and by no means of least significance, is the fact that apart from certain limited exceptions it is not unlawful to imbibe or be in possession of alcohol. However, the controls on possession, consumption, and availability of many other drugs are very strict and their infringement can incur heavy penalties. This is not to say that there will never be characteristics in common, and some people abuse both alcohol and other drugs.

USE OF TERMS

The words addiction and abuse tend to be used somewhat loosely. There are good grounds for suggesting that addiction is a rather over-used and emotive word. Increasingly, the more accurate descriptive term 'dependence' is being used. We should note two aspects of dependence. First, *psychological* dependence, in which a drug produces feelings of satisfaction and a need for the continuance of its ingestion to produce pleasure and avoid discomfort. Second, *physical* dependence, a state that shows itself by extreme physical disturbance when the administration of a drug is discontinued (WHO 1974 and McCulloch and Prins 1978). We should also note that many of the studies which examine the relationship between alcohol, other drugs, and crime do not adequately define the use of terms such as alcoholic. This lack of precision should be borne in mind in assessing the validity of any research in this area.

## ATTITUDES

Society's attitudes to all forms of alcohol and other drug taking are decidedly ambivalent. There are those on the one hand who see alcohol abuse as a sign of moral turpitude and those on the other who see it as a purely medical problem. In addition, we regard indulgence in all these drugs as bad, but we advertise their benefits indiscriminately as a boost to self-esteem or personal attractiveness. As with smoking, strictures as to their use sit uneasily and hypocritically with the large tax revenues derived annually from both products. In respect of drugs other than alcohol, it is matter for much concern that there appears to be massive medical over-prescribing of many substances which serve to 'pep' people up, calm them down, or alleviate personal ills. Such personal difficulties are better dealt with by various forms of counselling (see Zacune and Hensman 1971).

## ALCOHOL AND CRIME

The association between the ingestion of alcohol and crime has already been noted elsewhere in this book. It is to be found particularly amongst recidivists (West 1963, Smith-Moorhouse and Lynn 1966, Hensman 1969, Edwards, Hensman, and Peto 1971, Edwards, Gattoni, and Hensman 1972, and Washbrook 1977). Glatt (1958 and 1965) suggests that both alcoholic and criminal behaviour have a multi-factorial aetiology, such as broken homes and parental disharmony. In a more recent American study, Guze (1976) found that 43 per cent of his male criminals and 47 per cent of the women satisfied the criteria for a diagnosis of alcoholism. In an earlier and smaller American study, Rubington (1969) gave an overall estimate of 24–40 per cent. He suggested that alcoholics were more likely to be involved in crimes against individuals than property. Similar findings are reported in an Australian survey (Bartholomew 1968). In this study, Bartholomew took the trouble to check the offender's own accounts by means of interviews with family members, for it is well known that heavy drinkers and alcoholics are notoriously unreliable in their own accounts of their drinking patterns.

In a recent Canadian study, Haines (1978) reports 60–80 per cent of crimes as being alcohol-related. The degree to which alcohol is associated with violent crimes seems to have been clearly demonstrated. Nicol *et al.* (1973) indicate that the use of alcohol, particularly in response to stress, facilitates violent behaviour in men with *already severe difficulties in interpersonal relationships* (my italics). (See also Roslund and Larson 1979.) All the studies quoted so far have concerned themselves with the extent of excessive drinking or alcoholism amongst *penal populations*. Very few studies have been made of the incidence of criminality amongst alcoholic patients. However, Bartholomew and Kelley (1965), in a study of 1000 alcoholics referred to a *psychiatric clinic*, found that 35 per cent of the male referrals and 10 per cent of the females had a criminal record. This study is much in accord with an earlier and smaller survey made by Glatt (1958). He found that about one-third of 120 male in-patients treated in an alcoholic unit had been before the courts for various offences. Much more recently, Edwards, Kyle, and Nicholls (1977), in a study of 935 hospitalized alcoholic patients, found that 32 per cent of the men and 17 per cent of the women had a criminal record. In summary, we may say that although we have clear indications of close *associations* between excessive drinking, alcoholism, and criminality, direct causal connections are less obvious (Sapsford and Fairhead 1980). We can now attempt to make some classification of alcohol-related offences.

*Classification*

(1) Serious offences against the person or property due directly to the disinhibiting effects of alcohol. (For example, murder, other serious assaults, and arson.)

(2) Other less serious forms of assault against persons or property.

(3) Offences against the Road Safety and Road Traffic Acts, notably driving whilst unfit through drink or drugs. In one of the very few studies made of the backgrounds of serious

motoring offenders, Willett (1964) found that 15 per cent of his sample had been charged with driving under the influence of drink or drugs. He also found in about 8 per cent of all the other serious motoring offences that alcohol was a contributing factor. He considered that this was probably an underestimate.

(4) Offences committed in order to obtain supplies of alcohol, for example acts of stealing or deception.

(5) Those who commit specific offences of drunkenness[3] (habitual drunken offenders).

### The habitual drunken offender

The number of convictions for drunkenness has risen steadily in recent years; in 1975 the figure stood at just under 100,000. Studies made by Parr (1962), Gath *et al.* (1968), and Hershon, Cook, and Foldes (1974) show that these offenders behave with a considerable degree of recidivism. Fines and imprisonment seem to be quite ineffective. As long ago as the nineteenth century, legislation was introduced to keep such offenders out of the penal system, but for various reasons it was never put into effect (see Prins 1980: 274–75). Current legislation now empowers a police constable, instead of arresting such persons, to take them to a medical treatment centre (detoxification) instead. To date, our record of making this alternative provision available has been very poor; indeed one centre has been closed prematurely and another highly successful centre in Leeds has run into considerable difficulties over funding. No doubt this lack of investment in what is generally recognized to be a most useful provision is a further reflection of society's ambivalent attitude to the problem.

### Treatment

For the person found drunk habitually in public places, treatment can best be afforded by detoxification, but only if it is followed up by intensive after-care and community support

[3] Drunkenness is not itself an offence in law. It becomes unlawful when exhibited in a highway or other public place. The law also penalizes a variety of behaviours which exacerbate the act itself, for example being drunk and disorderly, drunk and indecent, or drunk in charge of a child under the age of seven years (Licensing Acts 1872 and 1902 and Penalties for Drunkenness Act 1962).

(Hamilton *et al.* 1977). The offender who is alcoholic or who drinks to excess, or who commits crime *because* he drinks, presents rather different problems. There is a very high relapse rate for all alcohol abusers, and all workers (whether they be proponents of behavioural, psychoanalytic, or pharmacological methods) agree that treatment can only be effective if there is a real desire on the part of the person to change his life-style. Those who are both alcoholic and criminal and who are sentenced to longish periods of imprisonment gain at least one advantage, namely a defined period of enforced abstinence from alcohol. However, unless there is a concurrent attempt through group or individual counselling to help the individual to examine why he needs to offend *and* drink, enforced abstinence will only serve to prepare the individual for early relapse on discharge. Groups such as Alcoholics Anonymous now operate within many of our prisons and they have helped many offenders to review their life-styles. For the homeless offender with a drinking problem, the support of a good hostel can make an enormous difference, provided such care is backed up by firm but benign sanctions and coupled with active supervision by someone like a probation officer. The offender who *also* has a drink problem has two hurdles to surmount, his alcohol problem *and* the fact that he has been labelled and processed as an offender. Thus the opprobrium he draws upon his head is twice compounded and his problematic social and interpersonal relationships are that much more difficult to clarify and resolve.

## OTHER DRUGS

In the following discussion, we must bear in mind two aspects of the problem. First, the compulsive need to continue to take drugs and to obtain supplies by any means – particularly unlawful means. Second, the serious physical and social repercussions for the individual and society. In the last twenty years, there has been growing concern about the steady increase in illicit drug use, particularly amongst the young. Following a more recent period, in which the use of drugs appeared to be levelling off, a steady increase has again been noted in the last year or so. Of particular concern is the increase in illicit importation of hard drugs such as heroin. The number of registered addicts in 1979 stood at nearly 3000 (Home Office 1979), while the estimated number of non-registered addicts has recently been put at 20,000. In addition, abuse of other compounds, particularly glues and solvents, by young people has also been noted (Watson 1978 and 1979 and Barnes 1979).

## *Types of drug users, abusers, and addicts*

The largest group of drug users and abusers are young and predominantly male. In the main, drug abusers tend to be solitary people, to be somewhat immature and uncertain in their social relationships. They are often sadly lacking in confidence and turn to drugs to enhance their low self-esteem. The group with which we are most concerned are those who have marked problems with their interpersonal and social relationships; these are predominantly a personality-disordered group whose drug abusing or addictive behaviour may be associated with criminality.

### DRUG TAKING AND CRIMINALITY

We may make the following somewhat arbitrary classification. In doing so, readers should also refer to the classification concerning the relationship between alcohol and crime.

(1) Offences against the various acts which control the possession, distribution, and consumption of drugs.

(2) Offences committed in order to obtain drugs, for example breaking and entering and stealing from pharmacies, doctors' surgeries, and drug warehouses.

(3) Offences due to the ingestion of drugs. (See classification (1) and (2) under alcohol above.)

## *Hard drugs and crime*

In 1979, the number of persons found guilty or cautioned for offences involving controlled drugs was just over 14,000. From 1973–79, about 1 in 5 persons sentenced for drug offences received some form of custodial sentence; and by 30 June 1979, 772 persons were undergoing sentences in penal establishments for drug offences (Home Office 1979). There is a certain danger in drawing too fine a distinction between *addiction* and crime and drug *abuse* and crime since the literature does not always indicate that researchers themselves have always made this distinction clear. In addition, writers sometimes refer to opiates and sometimes to other drugs. The evidence as to association also appears to be conflicting. In a survey of heroin addicts in prison, Pierce-James (1969) found that 76 per cent had been convicted by a court *before* addiction; Hawks (1970) found that about half the known addicts in Great Britain committed offences *before* receiving opiates on prescription. Gordon (1973), in a study of 60 male multiple drug users who had started their drug taking before the age of 20, found that 92 per cent had court convictions. Following drug use, particularly heroin, the incidence of violence in his sample increased. He concluded that criminality and drug dependence emerged as a combined expression of deviancy in the population studied. Similar findings are reported in an American study by Cushman (1974). Later studies by Mott and Taylor (1974), Mott and Rathod (1976), and Mott (1978) tend to give confirmation to these earlier researches. Grimes (1977), in a study of addicts attending clinics during the years 1968–73, found that 23 per cent were on probation. During a four-year follow-up period, 73 per cent had obtained convictions. More recently, Wiepert, D'Orbán, and Bewley (1979) reported upon a study of 455 male and 120 female opiate addicts treated at drug dependency clinics. Treatment had no effect on the overall crime rate of these patients and the outcome of treatment was worse for the female addicts.

A number of workers have commented upon the hostility shown by hard drug addicts (Rosenberg 1971 and Gossop and Roy 1977). Bell and Champion (1979) compared two groups – a general cross-section of young people and a cross-section of antisocial deviants. They established that illicit drug use was more extensive amongst those who had suffered parental deprivation and whose parents were separated and/or divorced. The degree of antisocial deviancy correlated highly with illicit drug use.

The main conclusion to be drawn from this group of studies is that the web of interaction between opiate addiction and criminality is part of the addict's complex life-style. The compulsive element already referred to propels the addict towards obtaining drugs by any means at his disposal. In addition, his declining social performance and personal deterioration make him especially vulnerable to the attention of the medical, judicial, and penal authorities.

## Abuse of 'soft' drugs and delinquent behaviour

The relationship between abuse of 'soft' drugs (notably amphetamines) and crime has been investigated by Scott and Willcox (1965) and Scott and Buckle (1971). They compared amphetamine takers with those youths in which there was no evidence of amphetamine taking. They found no major differences in type of crime committed or in social and family background. They concluded that the taking of amphetamines appeared to be incidental to delinquency, most likely having similar roots in opportunity and predisposition (a finding not dissimilar to that described earlier in respect of opiate addiction and crime). Neither of these studies confirmed the commonly held belief that there is a progression from 'soft' to 'hard' drug use. However, Noble (1970) found, in a sample of remand home boys, that on a two-year follow-up 19 per cent of the 'soft' drug group had progressed to 'hard' drugs. It is important to note his other main finding that those in the 'hard' drug group showed a significantly greater incidence of abnormal personality, family history of psychiatric illness, and disturbed relationships within the family. (See also Ball 1967 and Kraus 1981.)

## Treatment

As with the alcoholic or excessive drinker, treatment for the drug abuser or drug addict must have regard to the individual's total life-style and not just his drug taking. The problems of those who are actually addicted are of course much greater than those of transient or occasional drug users. The prognosis for addicts is not good and the mortality rate is high. The latter is not necessarily due to the effects of the drugs themselves, but is more likely to be brought about by physical deterioration and damage from infection, as a result of repeatedly injecting with dirty equipment, and of course from suicide. As with alcohol abusers, a large number of drug addicts claim that they are not ill and therefore do not need treatment. Many of those who do start treatment discharge themselves from it prematurely. For any form of treatment to be effective, the fostering of a relationship which combines firmness with genuine concern is essential. This must be associated with a realistic appreciation that relapses are likely to be frequent and the drug abuser's or addict's attitudes are likely to be provocative, prevaricative, deceitful, and rejecting. As with the alcoholic, the fact that the drug addict has been also labelled as a delinquent adds to his problems. A number of studies have confirmed the need for insistence and persistence and for after-care on discharge from whatever kind of institutional care has been provided (Váillant and Rasor 1966, Melotte 1975, Wilson and Mandlebrote 1978a and 1978b).

# References

SECTION ONE — FEMALE OFFENDERS

Barack, L.I. and Widom, C.S. (1978) Eysenck's Theory of Criminality Applied to Women Awaiting Trial. *British Journal of Psychiatry* **133**: 452–56.

Campbell, A. (1981) *Girl Delinquents*. Oxford: Blackwell.

Caplan, P.J., Awad, G.A., Wilkes, C., and White, G. (1980) Sex Differences in a Delinquent Clinic Population. *British Journal of Criminology* **20**: 311–28.

Cockburn, J.J. and Maclay, I. (1965) Sex Differentials in Juvenile Delinquency. *British Journal of Criminology* **5**: 289–308.

Cowie, J., Cowie, V., and Slater, E.T.O. (1968) *Delinquency in Girls*. London: Heinemann.

D'Orbán, P.T. (1972) Baby Stealing. *British Medical Journal* 10 June: 635–39.

—— (1976) Child Stealing: A Typology of Female Offenders. *British Journal of Criminology* **16**: 275–81.

Epps, P. (1951) A Preliminary Survey of 300 Female Delinquents in Borstal Institutions. *British Journal of Delinquency* **1**: 187–97.

—— (1954) A Further Survey of Female Delinquents Undergoing Borstal Training. *British Journal of Delinquency* **4**: 265 –71.

Epps, P. and Parnell, R.W. (1952) Physique and Temperament of Women Delinquents Compared with Women Undergraduates. *British Journal of Medical Psychology* **25**: 249–55.

Felice, M. and Offord, D.R. (1972) Three Developmental Pathways to Delinquency in Girls. *British Journal of Criminology* **12**: 375–89.

Gibbens, T.C.N. (1959) Supervision and Probation of Adolescent Girls. *British Journal of Delinquency* **10**: 84–103.

—— (1971) *Female Offenders*. In T. Silverstone and B. Barraclough (eds) *Contemporary Psychiatry*. Ashford: Headley Brothers.

Gibbens, T.C.N. and Prince, J. (1962) *Shoplifting*. London: ISTD.

Gibbens, T.C.N. and Silberman, M. (1960) The Clients of Prostitutes. *British Journal of Venereal Diseases* **36**: 113–17.

Gibbens, T.C.N., Palmer, C., and Prince, J. (1971) Mental Health Aspects of Shoplifting. *British Medical Journal* **3**: 612 –15.

Gibbs, C. (1971) The Effect of the Imprisonment of Women upon their children. *British Journal of Criminology* **11**: 113– 30.

Gilbert, J. (1972) Delinquent (Approved School) and Non-Delinquent (Secondary Modern School) Girls. *British Journal of Criminology* **12**: 325–56.

Goodman, N. and Price, J. (1967) *Studies of Female Offenders. Home Office Studies in the Causes of Delinquency and the Treatment of Offenders*. Home Office Research Unit. London: HMSO.

Guze, S.B. (1976) *Criminality and Psychiatric Disorders*. Oxford: Oxford University Press.

Hall Williams, J.E. (1970) *The English Penal System in Transition*. London: Butterworths.

Hands, J., Herbert, V., and Tennent, G. (1974) Menstruation and Behaviour in a Special Hospital. *Medicine, Science and the Law* **14**: 32–5.

Home Office (1977) *Prisons and the Prisoner. The Work of the Prison Service in England and Wales*. London: HMSO.

—— (1979) *Criminal Statistics for England and Wales, 1978*. London: HMSO.

Home Office and DHSS (1975) *Report of the Committee on Mentally Abnormal Offenders*. (Butler Committee) Cmnd. 6244. London: HMSO.

Hunter, J. (1973) The Problem of Baby Stealing. *Social Work Today* **4**: 266–68.

Jones, H. (1965) *Crime and the Penal System* (third edition). London: University Tutorial Press.

Kestenbaum, S.E. (1977) Women's Liberation for Women Offenders. *Social Casework* **58**: 77–83.

Mannheim, H. (1965) *Comparative Criminology (Volume 2)*. London: Routledge and Kegan Paul.

Mawby, R.I. (1977) Sexual Discrimination and the Law. *Probation* **24**: 39–43.

—— (1980) Sex and Crime: The Results of a Self-Report Study. *British Journal of Sociology* **31**: 525–43.

May, D. (1977) Delinquent Girls before the Courts. *Medicine, Science and the Law* **17**: 203–12.

Morris, A. and Gelsthorpe, L. (1981) False Clues and Female Crime. In A. Morris and L. Gelsthorpe (eds) *Women and Crime*. Institute of Criminology. University of Cambridge: Cambridge.

Parsloe, P. (1972) Cross-Sex Supervision in the Probation and After-Care Service. *British Journal of Criminology* **12**: 269–79.

Pollak, O. (1961) *The Criminality of Women*. New York: S.A. Barnes.

Richardson, H. (1969) *Adolescent Girls in Approved Schools*. London: Routledge and Kegan Paul.

Riege, M.G. (1972) Parental Affection and Juvenile Delinquency. *British Journal of Criminology* **12**: 55–73.

Smart, C. (1976) *Women, Crime and Criminology. A Feminist Critique*. London: Routledge and Kegan Paul.

—— (1979) The New Female Criminal: Reality or Myth? *British Journal of Criminology* **19**: 50–9.

Smith, A.D. (1962) *Women in Prison*. London: Stevens.

—— (1974) The Woman Offender. In L. Blom-Cooper (ed.) *Progress in Penal Reform*. Oxford: Oxford University Press.

Walker N. and McCabe, S. (1973) *Crime and Insanity in England (Volume 2)*. Edinburgh: Edinburgh University Press.

Widom, C.S. (1981) Perspectives of Female Criminality: A Critical Examination of Assumptions. In A. Morris and L.

Gelsthorpe (eds) *Women and Crime*. Institute of Criminology. University of Cambridge: Cambridge.

**FURTHER READING**

*On imprisonment see:*

Arrowsmith, P. (1970) *Somewhere Like This*. London: W.H. Allen.

Kassebaum, G. (1966) *Women's Prison*. London: Weidenfeld and Nicolson.

*On violence in the family see:*

Carver, V. (ed.) (1978) *Child Abuse – A Study Text*. Milton Keynes: Open University Press.

Kempe, R.S. and Kempe, C.H. (1980) *Child Abuse*. London: Fontana/Open Books.

Lee, C.M. (ed.) (1978) *Child Abuse – A Reader and Source Book*. Milton Keynes: Open University Press.

Martin, J.P. (ed.) (1978) *Violence and the Family*. London: John Wiley.

*On prostitution and street offences see:*

Home Office (1974) *Report of the Working Party on Vagrancy and Street Offences*. London: HMSO.

McIntosh, M. (1977) Who Needs Prostitutes? The Ideology of Male Sexual Need. In C. Smart and B. Smart (eds) *Women, Sexuality and Social Control*. London: Routledge and Kegan Paul.

Sandford, J. (1975) *Prostitutes: Portraits of People in the Sexploitation Business*. London: Secker and Warburg.

West, D.J. (ed.) (1980) *Sex Offenders in the Criminal Justice System* (Part II, papers by Vickers, Cunnington, and Trott). Institute of Criminology. Cambridge: Cambridge University.

**SECTION TWO – SEXUAL OFFENDERS**

Abarbanel, G. (1976) Helping the Victims of Rape. *Social Work* November: 478–82.

Amir, M. (1971) *Patterns of Forcible Rape*. Chicago: Chicago University Press.

Bagley, C. (1969) The Varieties of Incest. *New Society* 21 August: 280–82.

Bancroft, J. (1969) Aversion Therapy of Homosexuality. *British Journal of Psychiatry* **115**: 1417–431.

Bartholomew, A.A., Milte, K.L., and Galbally, F. (1978) Homosexual Necrophilia. *Medicine, Science and the Law* **18**: 29–35.

Bluglass, R. (1979) Incest. *British Journal of Hospital Medicine* August: 152–57.

—— (1980) Indecent Exposure in the West Midlands. In D.J. West (ed.) *Sex Offenders in the Criminal Justice System*. Institute of Criminology. Cambridge University: Cambridge.

Brittain, R.P. (1970) The Sadistic Murderer. *Medicine, Science and the Law* **10**: 198–207.

Brodsky, S.L. (1980) Understanding and Treating Sexual Offenders. *The Howard Journal* **19**: 102–15.

Browning, D.H. and Boatman, B. (1977) Incest: Children at Risk. *American Journal of Psychiatry* **134**: 69–72.

Brownmiller, S. (1975) *Against Our Will: Men, Women and Rape*. London: Secker and Warburg.

Burgess, A.W., Groth, G.N., and McCausland, M.P. (1981) Child Sex Initiation Rings. *American Journal of Orthopsychiatry* **51**: 110–19.

Burgess, R., Jewitt, R., Sandham, J., and Hudson, B.L. (1980) Working with Sex Offenders: A Social Skills Training Group. *British Journal of Social Work* **10**: 133–42.

Burt, J.L. (1979) The Epidemiology of Genital Herpes (HSV-2) Infections. *Journal of the Royal Society of Health* **99**: 31.

Canepa, G. and Bandini, T. (1980) Incest and Family Dynamics – a Clinical Study. *International Journal of Law and Psychiatry* **3**: 453–60.

Catterall, R.D. (1981) Biological Aspects of Sexual Freedom. *The Lancet* 7 February: 315–19.

Connell, H. (1980) Incest, a Symptom of Family Pathology. *British Journal of Sexual Medicine* May: 24–7.

Cox, D.J. and McMahon, B. (1978) Incidents of Male Exhibitionism in the United States as Reported by Victimized Female College Students. *International Journal of Law and Psychiatry* **1**: 453–57.

Cox, M. (1980) Personal Reflections upon 3,000 Hours in

Therapeutic Groups with Sex Offenders. In D.J. West (ed.) *Sex Offenders in the Criminal Justice System*. Institute of Criminology. Cambridge: Cambridge University.

Crawford, D. (1980) Applications of Penile Response Monitoring to the Assessment of Sexual Offenders. In D.J. West (ed.) *Sex Offenders in the Criminal Justice System*. Institute of Criminology. Cambridge: Cambridge University.

Dietz, C.A. and Craft, J.L. (1980) Family Dynamics of Incest: A New Perspective. *Social Casework* **61**: 602–09.

Ellerstein, N.S. and Cavanagh, J.W. (1980) Sexual Abuse of Boys. *American Journal of Diseases of Children* **134**: 255–57.

Elwell, M.E. (1979) Sexually Assaulted Children and Their Families. *Social Casework* **60**: 227–35.

Field, L.H. (1973) Benperidol in the Treatment of Sexual Offenders. *Medicine, Science and the Law* **13**: 195–96.

Field, L.H. and Williams, M. (1970) The Hormonal Treatment of Sexual Offenders. *Medicine, Science and the Law* **10**: 27–34.

Gayford, J.J. (1981) Indecent Exposure: A Review of the Literature. *Medicine, Science and the Law* **21**: 233–42.

Gibbens, T.C.N., Way, C.K., and Soothill, K.L. (1977) Behavioural Types of Rape. *British Journal of Psychiatry* **130**: 32–42.

—— (1978) Sibling and Parent-Child Incest Offenders. *British Journal of Criminology* **18**: 40–52.

—— (1981) Sex Offences Against Young Girls: A Long Term Record Study. *Psychological Medicine* **11**: 351–57.

Gittleson, N., Eacott, S.E., and Mehta, B.M. (1978) Victims of Indecent Exposure. *British Journal of Psychiatry* **132**: 61–6.

Gordon, R. (1976) Paedophilia: Normal and Abnormal. In W. Kraemer (ed.) *The Forbidden Love*. London: Sheldon Press.

Hall, J. (1977) Rape and Some of Its Effects. *Midwife, Health Visitor and Community Nurse* **13**: 96–100.

Hall Williams, J.E. (1974) The Neglect of Incest: A Criminologist's View. *Medicine, Science and the Law* **14**: 64–7.

—— (1977) Serious Heterosexual Attack. *Medicine, Science and the Law* **17**: 140–46.

Hardgrove, G. (1976) An Inter-Agency Service Network to Meet the Needs of Rape Victims. *Social Casework* April: 245–53.

Herjanic, B. and Wilbois, R.P. (1980) Sexual Abuse of Children. *British Journal of Sexual Medicine* March: 37–42.

Holmes, K.A. (1981) Services for Victims of Rape: A Dualistic Practice Model. *Social Casework* **62**: 30–9.

Home Office (1979) *Criminal Statistics for England and Wales, 1978.* London: HMSO.

Howells, K. and Wright, E. (1978) The Sexual Attitudes of Aggressive Sexual Offenders. *British Journal of Criminology* **18**: 170–74.

Hyatt Williams, A. (1964) The Psychopathology and Treatment of Sexual Murderers. In I. Rosen (ed.) *The Pathology and Treatment of Sexual Deviation.* Oxford: Oxford University Press.

Ingram, Fr. M. (1979) The Participating Victim. *British Journal of Sexual Medicine* (parts 1 and 2) Jan: 22–5 and Feb: 24–6.

James, T.E. (1964) Law and the Sexual Offender. In I. Rosen (ed.) *The Pathology and Treatment of Sexual Deviation.* Oxford: Oxford University Press.

Jones, I.H. and Frei, D. (1977) Provoked Anxiety as a treatment of Exhibitionism. *British Journal of Psychiatry* **131**: 295–300.

Lambert, K. (1976) The Scope and Dimensions of Paedophilia. In W. Kraemer (ed.) *The Forbidden Love.* London: Sheldon Press.

Lancaster, N.P. (1978) Necrophilia, Murder and High Intelligence. *British Journal of Psychiatry* **132**: 605–08.

Lukianowicz, N. (1972) Incest, I – Paternal Incest, II – Other Types of Incest. *British Journal of Psychiatry* **120**: 301–13.

Macdonald, J.M. (1971) *Rape: Offenders and Their Victims.* Illinois: Charles C. Thomas.

Maclay, D.T. (1952) The Diagnosis and Treatment of Compensatory Types of Indecent Exposure. *British Journal of Delinquency* **III**: 34–45.

Maisch, H. (1973) *Incest* (trans. C. Bearne). London: Deutsch.

Mather, N.J. de V. (1966) The Treatment of Homosexuality by Aversion Therapy. *Medicine, Science and the Law* **6**: 200–05.

Mathis, J.C. and Cullens, M. (1971) Enforced Group Therapy in the Treatment of Exhibitionism. *Current Psychiatric Therapy* **11**: 139–45.

Matthews, R. (1980) Assessment of Sexual Offenders at Worm-wood Scrubs. In D.J. West (ed.) *Sex Offenders in the Criminal Justice System*. Institute of Criminology. Cambridge University: Cambridge.

McGuire, R.J. and Vallance, M. (1964) Aversion Therapy by Electric Shock. *British Medical Journal* **1**: 151–53.

McGuire, R.G., Carlisle, J.M., and Young, B.G. (1965) Sexual Deviations as Conditioned Behaviour. *Behaviour, Research and Therapy* **2**: 185–90.

Milo, B. (1976) Cui Bono – For Whose Benefit? *Prison Service Journal* **24**: 11–13.

Morris, N. and Hawkins, G. (1970) *The Honest Politician's Guide to Crime Control*. Chicago: Chicago University Press.

Nadelson, C.C. and Nutman, M.T. (1979) Psychoanalytic Considerations of the Response to Rape. *International Review of Psychoanalysis* **6**: 97–103.

Nakashima, I.I. and Zakus, G.E. (1977) Incest, Review and Clinical Experience. *Paediatrics for the Clinician* **60**: 696–701.

Ortmann, J. (1980) The Treatment of Sexual Offenders: Castration and Antihormone Therapy. *International Journal of Law and Psychiatry* **4**: 443–51.

Parker, T. (1970) *The Twisting Lane: Some Sex Offenders*. London: Panther Books.

Paul, D.M. (1975) The Medical Examination in Sexual Offences. *Medicine, Science and the Law* **15**: 154–62.

—— (1977) The Medical Examination in Sexual Offences Against Children. *Medicine, Science and the Law* **17**: 251–58.

Perkins, D. (1980) Psychological Treatment of Sexual Offenders. *Prison Service Journal* **39** (New Series): 15–17.

Pollock, C.B.R. (1960) A Case of Neurotic Exhibitionism. *British Journal of Criminology* **1**: 37–49.

Prins, H. (1980) *Offenders, Deviants, or Patients: An Introduction to the Study of Socio-Forensic Problems*. London: Tavistock Publications.

Roberts, D.F. (1967) Incest: Inbreeding and Mental Abilities. *British Medical Journal* **4**: 336.

Roeder, F., Orthner, H., and Muller, D. (1972) In A. Hithcock, L. Leitinen, and K. Vaernet (eds) *Psychosurgery*. Illinois: Charles C. Thomas.

Rooth, F.G. (1972) Changes in the Reconviction Rate for

Indecent Exposure. *British Journal of Psychiatry* **121**: 89–94.

—— (1975) *Indecent Exposure and Exhibitionism.* In T. Silverstone and B. Barraclough (eds) *Contemporary Psychiatry.* Ashford: Headley Brothers.

Rupp, J.C. (1970) Sudden Death in the Gay World. *Medicine, Science and the Law* **10**: 189–91.

Sccaco, A.M. (1975) *Rape in Prison.* Illinois: Charles C. Thomas.

Schultz, L.G. (ed.) (1975) *Rape Victimology.* Illinois: Charles C. Thomas.

Selby, J.W., Calhoun, L.G., Jones, J.M., and Matthews, L. (1980) Families of Incest: A Collation of Clinical Impressions. *International Journal of Social Psychiatry* April: 8–16.

Snaith, R.P. and Collins, S.A. (1981) Five Exhibitionists and a Method of Treatment. *British Journal of Psychiatry* **138**: 126–30.

Soothill, K.L. and Gibbens T.C.N. (1978) Recidivism of Sexual Offenders: A Reappraisal. *British Journal of Criminology* **18**: 267–76.

Soothill, K.L., Jack, A., and Gibbens, T.C.N. (1976) Rape: A 22 Year Cohort Study. *Medicine, Science and the Law* **16**: 62–9.

Tennent, G., Bancroft, J., and Casse, J. (1974) The Control of Deviant Sexual Behaviour by Drugs: A Double-Blind Study of Benperidol, Chlorpromazine and Placebo. *Archives of Sexual Behaviour* **3**: 261–71.

Tilelli, J.A., Turek, D., and Jaffe, A.C. (1980) Sexual Abuse of Children: Clinical Findings and Implications for Management. *The New England Journal of Medicine* **302**: 319–23.

Toner, B. (1977) *The Facts of Rape.* London: Arrow Books.

Virkkunen, M. (1974) Incest Offences and Alcoholism. *Medicine, Science and the Law* **14**: 124–28.

—— (1975) Victim-Precipitated Paedophilia Offences. *British Journal of Criminology* **15**: 175–80.

West, D.J., Roy, C., and Nichols, F.L. (1978) *Understanding Sexual Attacks.* London: Heinemann.

Wright, R. (1980) Rape and Physical Violence. In D.J. West (ed.) *Sex Offenders in the Criminal Justice System.* Institute of Criminology. Cambridge: Cambridge University.

Wright, R. and West, D.J. (1981) Rape – A Comparison of Group Offences and Lone Assaults. *Medicine, Science and the Law* **21**: 25–30.

FURTHER READING

*On anthropological and related aspects of sexual behaviour see:*

Cook, M. and Wilson, G. (1979) *Love and Attraction*. (Chapters 1–8). Oxford: Pergamon.

Ford, C.S. and Beach, F.A. (1965) *Patterns of Sexual Behaviour*. London: Methuen.

Kinsey, A.C., Pomeroy, W.B., and Martin, C.E. (1948) *Sexual Behaviour in the Human Male*. London: W.B. Saunders.

Kinsey, A.C., Pomeroy, W.B., Martin, C.E., and Gebhard, P.M. (1953) *Sexual Behaviour in the Human Female*. London: W.B. Saunders.

Masters, W.H. and Johnson, V. (1970) *Human Sexual Inadequacy*. New York: Little Brown.


*On homosexuality see:*

Ettore, E.M. (1980) *Lesbians, Women and Society*. London: Routledge and Kegan Paul.

Rosen, D.H. (1974) *Lesbianism. A Study of Female Homosexuality*. Illinois: Charles C. Thomas.

West. D.J. (1960) *Homosexuality*. Harmondsworth: Penguin.

Wolff, C. (1977) *Bisexuality: A Study*. London: Quartet Books.


*Sexual offenders, more specifically, see:*

Cook, M. and Wilson, G. (1979) *Love and Attraction* (Chapter 12). Oxford: Pergamon.

Cox, M. (1979) Dynamic Psychotherapy with Sex Offenders. In I. Rosen (ed.) *Sexual Deviation* (second edition). Oxford: Oxford University Press.

Delin, B. (1978) *The Sex Offender*. Boston: Beacon Press.

DHSS (1977) *Selected References on Paedophilia and Sexual Offences Against Children*. Bibliography Series. B.91. London: HMSO.

Forward, S. and Buck, C. (1981) *Betrayal of Innocence: Incest and Its Devastation*. Harmondsworth: Penguin.

Gebhard, P.H., Gagnon, J.H., Pomeroy, W.B., and Christenson, V.C. (1965) *Sex Offenders. An Analysis of Types*. New York: Harper and Row.

Gunn, J. (ed.) (1978) *Sex Offenders: A Symposium*. Special Hospitals Research Report No. 14. London: DHSS.

Macdonald, J.M. (1973) *Indecent Exposure*. Illinois: Charles C. Thomas.

Meiselman, K.C. (1978) *Incest*. San Francisco: Jossey-Bass.

Renvoize, J. (1982) *Incest: A Family Pattern*. London: Routledge & Kegan Paul.

Taylor, B. (ed.) (1981) *Perspectives on Paedophilia*. London: Batsford Academic and Educational.

*On legal aspects (including proposals for reform of the law) see:*

Hogan, B. (1980) Reform of the Law Relating to sexual offences – Various Proposals. In D.J. West (ed.) *Sex Offenders in the Criminal Justice System*. Institute of Criminology. Cambridge University: Cambridge.

SECTION THREE – ALCOHOL, OTHER DRUGS AND CRIME

Ball, J.C. (1967) Marijuana Smoking and the Onset of Heroin Use. *British Journal of Criminology* **7**: 408–13.

Barnes, G.E. (1979) Solvent Abuse: A Review. *International Journal of the Addictions* **14**: 1–26.

Bartholomew, A.A. (1968) Alcoholism and Crime. *Australian and New Zealand Journal of Criminology* **1**: 70–99.

Bartholomew, A.A. and Kelley, M.H. (1965) The Incidence of Criminal Record in 1,000 Consecutive Alcoholics. *British Journal of Criminology* **5**: 143–49.

Bell, D.S. and Champion, R.A. (1979) Deviancy, Delinquency and Drug Use. *British Journal of Psychiatry* **134**: 269–76.

Cushman, P. (1974) Relationship Between Narcotic Addiction and Crime. *Federal Probation* **28**: 38–43.

Edwards, G., Hensman, C., and Peto, J. (1971) Drinking Problems Among Recidivist Prisoners. *Psychological Medicine* **5**: 388–99.

Edwards, G., Gattoni, F., and Hensman, C. (1972) Correlates of Dependence Scores in a Prison Population. *Quarterly Journal of Studies in Alcoholism* **38**: 417–29.

Edwards, G., Kyle, E., and Nicholls, P. (1977) Alcoholics Admitted to Four Hospitals in England: III – Criminal Records. *Journal of Studies on Alcoholism* **38**: 1648–664.

Gath, D., Hensman, C., Hawker, A., Kelly, M., and Edwards, G. (1968) The Drunk in Court: A Survey of Drunkenness Offenders from Two London Courts. *British Medical Journal* **4**: 808–11.

Gibbens, T.C.N. and Silberman, M. (1970) Alcoholism Among Prisoners. *Psychological Medicine* **1**: 73–8.

Glatt, M. (1958) Alcoholism, Crime and Juvenile Delinquency. *British Journal of Delinquency* **IX**: 84–93.

—— (1965) Crime, Alcohol and Alcoholism. *Howard Journal of Penology and Crime Prevention* **IX**: 274–84.

Gordon, A.M. (1973) Patterns of Delinquency in Drug Addiction. *British Journal of Psychiatry* **122**: 205–10.

Gossop, M. and Roy, A. (1977) Hostility, Crime and Drug Dependence. *British Journal of Psychiatry* **130**: 272–80.

Grimes, J.A. (1977) *Drug Dependency Study: A Survey of Drug Addicts Attending for Treatment*. London: HMSO.

Guze, S.B. (1976) *Criminality and Psychiatric Disorders*. Oxford: Oxford University Press.

Haines, D. (1978) Alcoholism in Prisons. *International Journal of Offender Therapy and Comparative Criminology* **22**: 27–32.

Hamilton, J.R., Griffith, A., Ritson, E.B., and Aitken, R.C.B. (1977) A Detoxification Unit for Habitual Drunken Offenders. *Health Bulletin* May: 146–54.

Hawks, D.V. (1970) The Epidemiology of Drug Dependence in the United Kingdom. *Bulletin of Narcotics* **22**: 15.

Hensman, C. (1969) Problems of Drunkenness among Male Recidivists. In T. Cook, D. Gath, and C. Hensman (eds) *The Drunkenness Offence*. Oxford: Pergamon.

Hershon, H.I., Cook, T., and Foldes, P.A. (1974) What Shall We Do with the Drunkenness Offender? *British Journal of Psychiatry* **124**: 327–35.

Home Office (1979) *Statistics of the Misuse of Drugs in the United Kingdom, 1977*. London: HMSO.

Kraus, J. (1981) Juvenile Drug Abuse and Delinquency: Some Differential Associations. *British Journal of Psychiatry* **139**: 422–30.

McCulloch, J.W. and Prins, H.A. (1978) *Signs of Stress: The Social Problems of Psychiatric Illness*. London: Woburn Press.

Melotte, C. (1975) A Rehabilitation Hostel for Drug Users: One Year's Admissions. *British Journal of Criminology* **15**: 376–84.

Mott, J. (1978) A Long Term Follow-Up of Male Non-Therapeutic Opiate Users and Their Criminal Histories. In D.J. West (ed.) *Problems of Drug Abuse in Great Britain*.

Institute of Criminology. Cambridge: Cambridge University.

Mott, J. and Rathod, N.H. (1976) Heroin Misuse and Delinquency in a New Town. *British Journal of Psychiatry* **128**: 428–35.

Mott, J. and Taylor, M. (1974) *Delinquency Amongst Opiate Users.* Home Office Research Studies No. 23. London: HMSO.

Nicol. A., Gunn, J., Griswood, J., Foggitt, R., and Watson, J. (1973) The Relationship of Alcoholism to Violent Behaviour Resulting in Long-Term Imprisonment. *British Journal of Psychiatry* **123**: 47–51.

Noble, P.J. (1970) Drug Taking in Delinquent Boys. *British Medical Journal* 10 January: 102–05.

Parr, D. (1962) Offences of Drunkenness in the London Area: A Pilot Study. *British Journal of Criminology* **2**: 272–77.

Pierce-James, I. (1969) Delinquency and Heroin Addiction in Britain. *British Journal of Criminology* **9**: 108–24.

Prins, H. (1980) *Offenders, Deviants, or Patients: An Introduction to the Study of Socio-Forensic Problems.* London: Tavistock Publications.

Rosenberg, C.M. (1971) The Young Addict and His Family. *British Journal of Psychiatry* **118**: 469–70.

Roslund, B. and Larson, C.A. (1979) Crimes of Violence and Alcohol Abuse in Sweden. *International Journal of the Addictions* **14**: 1103–115.

Rubington, E. (1969) Types of Alcoholic Offenders. *Federal Probation* **33**: 28–35.

Sapsford, R.J. and Fairhead, S. (1980) Reconviction, Alcohol and Mental Disorder. *British Journal of Criminology* **20**: 157–65.

Scott, P.D. and Buckle, M. (1971) Delinquency and Amphetamines. *British Journal of Psychiatry* **119**: 179–82.

Scott, P.D. and Willcox, D.R.C. (1965) Delinquency and the Amphetamines. *British Journal of Addiction* **61**: 9–27.

Smith-Moorhouse, P.M. and Lynn, L. (1966) Drinking Before Detention. *Prison Service Journal* **5**: 29–39.

Vaillant, G.E. and Rasor, R.W. (1966) The Role of Compulsory Supervision and Compulsory Parole in the Treatment of Addicts. *Federal Probation* **30**: 53–9.

Washbrook, R.A.H. (1977) Alcoholism versus Crime in Birmingham, England. *International Journal of Offender Therapy and Comparative Criminology* **21**: 166–73.

Watson, J.M. (1978) Clinical and Laboratory Investigations in 132 Cases of Solvent Abuse. *Medicine, Science and the Law* **18**: 40–4.

—— (1979) Morbidity and Mortality Statistics on Solvent Abuse. *Medicine, Science and the Law* **19**: 246–52.

West, D.J. (1963) *The Habitual Prisoner.* London: Macmillan.

Wiepert, G.D., D'Orbán, P.T., and Bewley, T.H. (1979) Delinquency by Opiate Addicts Treated at Two London Clinics. *British Journal of Psychiatry* **134**: 14–23.

Willett, T.C. (1964) *The Criminal on the Road.* London: Tavistock Publications.

Wilson, S. and Mandlebrote, B. (1978a) Drug Rehabilitation and Criminality. *British Journal of Criminology* **18**: 381–85.

—— (1978b) The Relationship Between Duration of Treatment in a Therapeutic Community and Subsequent Criminality. *British Journal of Psychiatry* **132**: 487–91.

World Health Organisation (1974) *Expert Committee on Drug Dependence. Twentieth Report.* Geneva: WHO.

Zacune, J. and Hensman (1971) *Drugs, Alcohol and Tobacco in Britain.* London: Heinemann Medical Books.

FURTHER READING

*On alcoholism and alcohol abuse generally see:*

Edwards, G. and Grant, M. (eds) (1977) *Alcoholism. New Knowledge and New Responses.* London: Croom Helm.

Grant, M. and Gwinner, P. (1979) *Alcoholism in Perspective.* London: Croom Helm.

Home Office (1971) *Habitual Drunken Offenders. Report of the Working Party.* London: HMSO.

Jellinek, E.M. (1960) *The Disease Concept of Alcoholism.* Connecticut: Hillhouse Press.

Royal College of Psychiatrists (1979) *Alcohol and Alcoholism: The Report of a Special Committee.* London: Tavistock Publications.

*On other drugs see:*

Bean, P. (1974) *The Social Control of Drugs.* London: Martin Robertson.

Cockett, R. (1971) *Drug Abuse and Personality in Young Offenders.* London: Butterworths.

Glatt, M.M. (1974) *A Guide to Addiction and Its Treatment: Drugs, Society and Men.* Lancaster: Medical and Technical Publishing.

# CHAPTER ELEVEN

## The management of offenders

If I cry 'murder!' no one answers;
If I appeal for help, I get no justice.

BOOK OF JOB

Listen to me, but do but listen,
and let that be the comfort you offer me.

BOOK OF JOB

The management of offenders has already been touched upon at various points in this book. In this penultimate chapter, opportunity will be taken to expand upon the topic briefly. The term 'management' is preferred to 'treatment'; the latter is probably too restrictive a word and assumes a medical or clinical model which is not entirely appropriate in considering the needs and management of offenders. More generally, the word 'punishment' is also used by some as a convenient term for dealing with persons convicted of crime. Useful though such a shorthand term may be, it over-emphasizes the coercive or compulsory elements in the management of offenders in the interests of protecting society. It fails to do justice to notions of welfare and counselling, which are an essential part of the management equation. These opposing interests present dilemmas for probation officers and other penal workers who have to try and intervene in situations that call for the recognition of the interests of the offender on the one hand and society on the other. (For a perceptive discussion of these issues see two papers by my colleague Robert Harris, 1977 and 1980.)

In this chapter, it is not possible to review extensively all the methods that are available for the management and care of offenders; I shall merely indicate some general approaches and offer guidance to the reader who wishes to explore this area further.

There are a number of problems to be faced by those who would work with offenders, either in institutional settings or in the community. To begin with, it is worthwhile emphasizing an obvious but often forgotten point: the terms 'delinquent', 'offender', and 'criminal' have highly emotive connotations; they may introduce moral evaluations into our thinking, thus bringing us halfway to rejecting those we may be trying to help. In addition, persistent offenders appear to need to create an interaction characterized by attack and retaliation (see also Chapter 5). Because of this, society spends a good deal of time in locking people up, often for long periods. Many of these more persistent offenders are also adept at seducing us into rejecting them, trying frequently through their behaviour to test us out, to see whether we feel as negative about them as they feel about themselves. Such individuals have a very poor self-image and many of them lack social skills. If help is offered with a view to raising self-esteem and the enhancement of social skills, it often seems to bring about an improvement in social functioning with a consequent diminution of delinquent behaviour (see for example Priestley *et al.* 1978). Another important characteristic of many more persistent offenders is their inability to tolerate tension and their need to discharge such tension through action. They also show a lack of toleration of frustration and an inability to postpone gratification (an ability which is usually seen as the hallmark of the more mature person). In the seriously psychopathic, such inability is very marked indeed. Not infrequently there is also an intolerance of any unpleasant emotion and a pressing need to do something to get rid of it.

Central to the problem of managing offenders, whether in the community or in institutions, is the issue of authority. For whatever the causes of their conduct, and however we choose to classify offenders, one problem faced by almost all of them is their difficulty in coping with authority, whether exercised by their families, peers, or in the wider community. The origins of attitudes towards authority lie within the very roots of family life and within the wider community and its effects upon family life-style (see also Chapters 3 and 5). According to the psychoanalytically orientated, the infant 'takes in' the attitudes shown by the mother or mother substitute, even at the breast or bottle. If this early experience of 'mothering' is an harmonious one, and one in which the infant can come to terms with the conflict between his demands and their satisfaction, then later experiences at the hands of those who have 'power' over him may be much easier to cope with (see Salzberger-Wittenberg 1970 and Bowlby 1979). However, as has already been noted in this book (in Chapter 5), the role of the father in this context also seems to be critical; we also noted there that the importance of his role may have been overlooked in the past. The day-to-day attitudes of offenders towards those in authority over them (whether they be the police, magistrates, judges, probation officers, prison and nursing staffs, psychiatrists, or hostel wardens) will nearly always have been influenced by such early experiences, particularly if they have been of an adverse kind. Once the adverse pattern of reaction has been laid down in these early years, subsequent experiences at the hands of teachers and employers may tend to reinforce these early reactions. It requires much patience and skill on the part of those who have to deal with such persons (when they have become labelled as offenders) to help to unravel the origins of such attitudes. As a result their behaviour may become less provocative. Much of the work of those who deal with offenders consists of social education and re-education. However, this education and re-education can only be successful if it is based upon an adequate knowledge of the person's bio-psycho-social history. Such knowledge does not normally presuppose a psychoanalytic 'delving' into the offender's unconscious life, though in certain instances it may be necessary to help an offender look back upon, and re-integrate, early and painful experiences if these are still influencing his present behaviour (Cox 1978 a and b and West, Roy, and Nichols 1978). Those whose work gives them power over offenders need to bear in mind three very important requirements.

(1) Clarity as to the nature of the task required.
(2) Competence in undertaking the task (i.e., being trained for it).
(3) The resolution of one's own feelings of conflict implicit in

the exercise of authority over others. (See Foren and Bailey 1969 and Prins 1969.)

There are many dangers when power is placed in the hands of the wrongly motivated, when authority is exercised merely for the pleasure of power over others, or when the person in authority is not mature enough for the task. In recent years numerous enquiries into the workings of some of our institutions for offenders and the disadvantaged have shown some of these dangers only too vividly. It is essential, therefore, for all those who are going to work with offenders, in whatever situation, to have endeavoured to come to terms with their own authority problems. In their training they need to be helped to see where their 'blind spots' may still arise. The informed and benign exercise of authority and enforcement has a number of advantages for those who are labelled as delinquent. Hunt (1964) has drawn attention to three of these:

(1) The offender cannot withdraw from the relationship if the situation becomes too uncomfortable. This in itself may provide opportunities for growth and change.
(2) The acceptance of the therapist or counsellor in an enforced relationship may well help the offender to begin to accept other figures of authority more readily (see above also).
(3) The enforced relationship may enable the offender to accept the fact that society has labelled him as a delinquent.

I drew attention to some of the disadvantages of labelling in Chapter 3. In the present context, however, the recognition of such a label through an enforced relationship may well have positive advantages. Because of its existence the offender may be motivated to begin to work on his own problems.

Having dealt with some issues of management in more general terms, we can now turn to discuss assessment and classification in a little more detail. In so doing, the emphasis is on work with offenders in the community, though much of what follows can be applied to the institutional situation. Having said this, it is also important to emphasize that institutions take on a life of their own. There is always the danger that they may come to serve their own ends rather than the persons they were established to contain or manage. Resistance to change in institutions is very powerful and it may well vitiate the introduction of more progressive regimes, such as those based upon the therapeutic community model. Jimmy Boyle, in his book *A Sense of Freedom* (1977), provides a personal and poignant account of the struggle to establish such a regime in a Scottish prison. Some of the more theoretical issues involved are discussed usefully in Hinshelwood and Manning (1979) and in some of the works listed as further reading at the end of Chapter 7.

## Assessment and classification

If we are to try and make sense of an offender's difficulties and his problems with society, it is essential to endeavour to make as accurate an assessment of his personal and social situation as possible. Indeed, the main thrust of the first part of this book was to demonstrate the complicated nature of the interrelated factors that may lead to antisocial behaviour. As we saw in Chapter 6, workers in this field are forced frequently to juggle with, or at least to hold in one hand, a number of possible conflicting explanations and remedies. Even more important, they may have to review and replace their early formulations as more information becomes available. It would be very easy to dismiss a disciplined approach to this task because of its ambiguity and complexity. That this need not be the case has been demonstrated very clearly by my colleagues Kathleen Curnock and Pauline Hardiker in their book on skills and methods in social assessments (Curnock and Hardiker 1979). In this work, they analysed rigorously some ninety social enquiry reports prepared by probation officers. Through this analysis they identified the acquisition, study, formulation, and goal-setting stages of the assessment process. Lest this disciplined attempt at assessment conjure up a picture of cold and impersonal detachment, it is important to emphasize that assessment and classification are concerned with the *problem*; such problem assessment can only be effective and humane if compassionate and informed understanding of the *person* is kept uppermost in the worker's mind. For the reasons advanced earlier in this chapter, this is not always an easy task in work with offenders, but such an approach is the hallmark of the caring professional as distinct from the mere voyeur or undisciplined amateur. Adequate assessment should therefore enable us to make some attempt at classification; such classification should than help us to choose appropriate models of management. The following classification must be regarded as somewhat idiosyncratic and arbitrary; it is merely advanced here in an attempt to pull together and focus some of the points made in earlier chapters of this book. Also, it needs to be remembered that not only do such categorizations overlap to a considerable extent, but that human and social problems do not always lend themselves to such neat classification.

(1) Those whose offending seems to be clearly associated with some kind of mental or physical disorder. In such cases, attention to the disorder *may* be accompanied by a reduction in the offence behaviour, but not *necessarily* so. The types of disorders and behaviours discussed in Chapters 4, 5, and 9 would come into this category. In these cases the person working with the offender will need to refer for specialist assessment and help with management.

(2) The young offender whose behaviour arises through faulty or crime-promoting parental example. The family backgrounds of these young people do not provide adequate social training or recognition of acceptable social standards; discipline is usually inconsistent, unpredictable, or even absent. The very fact that such a young person may be compelled to place himself in a relationship with a consistent and benign representative of authority (such as a probation officer) may in some cases serve as a useful corrective experience and enable him to absorb some reasonable standards of social behaviour. It may also help him to face his problems more realistically. In some cases it may also be appropriate to supplement this type of relationship with opportunities for involvement in non-delinquent outlets through the medium of intermediate treatment or similar schemes (see Chapter 8). Many of these young offenders outgrow their delinquency in early adulthood.

(3) The young offender whose delinquent behaviour is associated with a certain degree of restlessness and excitability. This restlessness is often accompanied by a degree of

surface charm that keeps the worker at a safe distance. Some years ago Stott (1950) identified such restless youngsters and their need to indulge in apparently pur- poseless activity as a means of dealing with stress. The following case illustrates this type of problem.

'A', aged 14, had a prior history of near delinquency over a two-year period. More recently he had been brought before the court for two quite serious offences of breaking and entering and stealing. His mother did not impress as being warmly maternal, and was also inconsis- tent in her handling. His father, a somewhat aloof man, found it difficult to come to terms with the warmer side of himself. He was decidedly uncomfortable with his two sons and, either unconsciously or by conscious design, allowed his work to preoccupy him. 'A's older brother had been unsettled since leaving school, and was subsequently before the court for various offences. 'A' was described by mother as a restless infant, with some history of wandering away from home, inattentive and unco-operative at school, and constantly flitting from one leisure activity to another. As his mother said, he was 'always on the go'. He was placed under supervision by the court. Although he was always bright and charming at interview, he never seemed to reveal his true feelings and succeeded in keeping the worker at a safe distance.

The outlook in such cases is not very favourable, but attempts to persist in the relationship, sometimes over many years, may pay eventual dividends. An interesting example of the difficulties involved and the eventual suc- cess derived from 'hanging on' can be found in a paper by Limentani (1981). Staffs of institutions will recognize the type of offender just described for he is the type who seems to go through his period of residence without effort, but with it making little impact on him.

(4) A smaller group of (mainly) young offenders, who seem to have been taught (unconsciously) by their parents to behave in delinquent ways in order to satisfy the parents' own unconscious delinquent needs. The theory which attempts to explain this kind of phenomenon has much in common with that which seeks to explain the development

of some types of mental illness. Writers such as Laing (1959), for example, have sought to explain some forms of schizophrenia by the family's need to maintain its own equilibrium and stability by projecting all its 'madness' on to one identified 'sick' family member. Similarly, with some families of delinquents, there is a need to present one family member as the 'bad' one and construct an environment where this can not only occur, but be maintained. An example of this type of behaviour would be where the parent gives an instruction or reprimand, but is unable to prevent his own uncertainty or ambivalence from creeping into his voice or gestures, so that the instruction or reprimand may be accompanied by a smile or hint of a counter-suggestion. The phenomenon has been clearly described by Johnson (1949) and by Strean (1968). Although such occurrences are rare, the problems presented by such behaviour may appear to be intractable at first sight. It takes much skill and confidence on the part of the worker not only to unravel the source of such behaviour, but to confront the parents with its true nature.

(5) Those who have been well trained to antisocial standards and who have been taught to get what they want without consideration for others. It seems likely that some so-called professional criminals come into this category. Such persons usually make conscious and calculated decisions to embark upon a delinquent career and are in most cases impervious to therapeutic or constructive management overtures. They may have to be detained for long periods (in as humane a way as possible) in order to protect the public from their depredations. Such offenders need to be distinguished from 'neurotic' offenders (Washbrook 1981) and those in group (6).

(6) Offenders who sometimes give the appearance of being 'professional' criminals. However, careful assessment will frequently reveal that these are a group of individuals who offend because of a need to compensate for some feeling of inferiority or hostility (imagined or real). Some serious sex offenders against women come into this category. Their sex offences may be a way of venting their hostility and aggression towards women for past wrongs they believe

have been committed against them. In such cases, a degree of 'uncovering' psychotherapy in a secure environment such as a special hospital or prison setting may be needed before any change in behaviour can occur. (See Cox 1978 a and b and West, Roy, and Nichols 1978.)

(7) The dull and retarded offender who lacks social relationships and social skills. The reason why such persons may offend were discussed in Chapter 5. However, it needs to be stressed in the context of this chapter that some workers tend to write off such an offender's capacity for engaging in any kind of therapeutic encounter because of his dullness. That this need not be the case is well demonstrated in a recent case study by Symington (1981). As Symington astutely suggests, the problem may lie more with the worker than with the offender/patient.

(8) The offender who, though not mentally retarded, seems quite socially inadequate and incapable of coping with the normal demands and expectations of society. Here, the key to successful management will depend upon working to limited goals. Such offenders will respond well if a probation officer or other worker assumes a semi-parental role. The aim of such work will be to foster growth and self-confidence rather than to promote any major personality change. The purpose will not be to free the person of any inner conflicts, but to seek to strengthen those parts of the personality that are intact or have a limited potential for development. The need is to build up controls and confidence rather than to uncover unconscious material (Schmideberg 1954, 1965, and 1981).

(9) Those whose offending seems to arise mainly because of feelings of lack of self-worth or a lack of social skills. In such cases, as already mentioned, the introduction of social skills training can be very useful.

(10) Those offenders whose behaviour is characterized by impulsiveness and unpredictability. Their offences may also be of an aggressive kind. Here, the causes of the behaviour may lie in a vulnerable constitution which is acted upon by an unfavourable or stressful environment. Such offenders will have much in common with those I have listed in group (1). The management of such offenders is best

tackled on a multi-disciplinary basis and medical help and oversight may be very important.

(11) Those whose offending seems to be the product of faulty learning patterns and where an element of compulsive behaviour may be discerned. In this category would be placed some offenders whose offending is associated with alcohol or other drug abuse, some compulsive gamblers, and car thieves. Such offenders may be helped by programmes of behavioural modification. Systems of behaviour modification are based upon learning theory. As a form of therapy it derives from a more 'scientific' approach than some other therapies, in that its application of laws of behaviour are derived more from the laboratory than from the inner world of the psyche. It lays great stress not only on determining clear objectives for management and treatment from the outset, but on monitoring these rigorously. Although behaviour modifiers make no extensive claims for success in the general treatment of delinquents, behaviour modification does seem to be a useful form of management in some of the specific cases mentioned above. Moreover, its emphasis upon the determination of clear objectives and the need to monitor change and results can be applied usefully in less behaviour-orientated interventions. Some of the critics of less goal-directed forms of psychotherapy may be justified when they state that such forms of therapy are frequently too vague and not sufficiently structured (see Fischer 1976).

## The need for control

A common theme running through some of the above classifications is the offender's need to be directed and controlled. Such offenders may include the unstable, unpredictable, aggressive delinquent who may sometimes offend quite without warning. On the whole, social workers in the penal field have not always applied themselves particularly well to this group of offenders, partly because there is a reluctance to be seen as a controlling 'agent' of society and a preference for being seen as a care-giver. This is to misunderstand the nature of 'care' and of 'control'. The two can coexist: indeed, they are both *essential elements* in the successful management of offenders. A number of workers have attested to this need for a careful combination of care and control (St John 1961, Allchin 1962, Winnicott 1962, Hunt 1964, and Treger 1965). It can be exemplified in the following short case extract.

> 'B' was aged 22 and on probation for housebreaking. He had previous convictions for taking and driving away and for malicious damage. He had experienced a poor relationship with father for many years, and more recently this had reached the point of open feuding. Father was at this time a very ill and 'ineffective' man. In interviews 'B' kept referring to his need for discipline, and how, in the past, he had got the better of most authority figures in his life. He expressed a great desire to be less impulsive. At various times, when he thought the probation officer was not taking this up with him, he would act provocatively and aggressively in an effort to get the probation officer to be more controlling. As supervision continued, it was possible to help 'B' to see this for himself and to help him to attempt to modify his behaviour.

A worker in the penal setting must frequently be more assertive in his approach than in some other contexts. He needs to act as an outside means of control when an offender is unable to effect control through his own unaided efforts. The worker has to intervene in what may sometimes be chaotic and critical situations by trying to halt or reduce expressions of destructiveness as a first step in what may eventually prove to be a prolonged relationship with the offender. As already mentioned, not all social workers, psychiatrists, psychologists, or other professionals are well suited to, or motivated towards, work with offenders. If this is not recognized and managed, they may make the problem worse for the offender/patient/client by pushing their reluctance and anxieties into the unconscious from where it could well menace any future constructive working relationships. This will merely serve to heighten the offender's feelings of rejection and isolation.

## Concluding comments

From the foregoing discussion it should be apparent that although we can make some rough kind of classification for purposes of analysis and assessment, every offender is an *individual* with different needs and problems. This presupposes that workers have to use a range of methods and approaches in their attempts at management. Some may espouse behavioural techniques, others prefer to help offenders develop their self-image and confidence through social skills training, through participation in therapeutic groups, or by involvement in the wider community. Since delinquent behaviour may have very complex origins, it follows that its management must be flexible and open-ended. In many cases various permutations and combinations of help must be offered at one and the same time. Practical forms of help may need to be combined with personal counselling. Perhaps one of the most important elements is to endeavour to provide opportunities for nurturing emotional and personal development, which may well have been lacking in the earlier life of the offender (Greene and Orman 1981). Thus much of the work is not only of a re-educational nature, but is also restorative in that it attempts to compensate for missed emotional and other experiences. A 'differential' approach is essential. For example, the inhibited and over-submissive offender may well need help to become more assertive in social situations and by so doing find more legitimate outlets for his feelings. The offender whose pattern of behaviour and life-style is to control and to exploit other people until they eventually reject him may well need to have a long-term relationship with someone who, whilst remaining well disposed and sympathetic, resists all attempts at manipulation. Above all, workers in the penal field need to recognize that the antagonism and ambivalence shown by society towards offenders also 'rubs off' on them. They must therefore also expect to share, to some degree, the alienation felt by those they are trying to help and control.

## References

Allchin, W.H. (1962) Some Positive Aspects of Delinquent Behaviour. *British Journal of Criminology* **3**: 38–46.

Bowlby, J. (1979) *The Making and Breaking of Affectional Bonds*. London: Tavistock Publications.

Boyle, J. (1977) *A Sense of Freedom*. London: Pan Books.

Cox, M. (1978a) *Structuring the Therapeutic Process: Compromise with Chaos. The Therapist's Response to the Individual and the Group*. Oxford: Pergamon.

—— (1978b) *Coding the Therapeutic Process. Emblems of Encounter. A Manual for Counsellors and Therapists*. Oxford: Pergamon.

Curnock, K. and Hardiker, P. (1979) *Towards Practice Theory: Skills and Methods in Social Assessments*. London: Routledge and Kegan Paul.

Fischer, J. (1976) *The Effectiveness of Social Casework*. Illinois: Charles C. Thomas.

Foren, R. and Bailey, R. (1969) *Authority in Social Casework*. Oxford: Pergamon Press.

Greene, M.J. and Orman, B. (1981) Nurturing the Un-nurtured. *Social Casework* **62**: 398–404.

Harris, R.J. (1977) The Probation Officer as Social Worker. *British Journal of Social Work* **7**: 433–42.

—— (1980) A Changing Service: The Case for Separating 'Care' and 'Control' in Probation Practice. *British Journal of Social Work* **10**: 163–84.

Hinshelwood, R.D. and Manning, N. (eds) (1979) *Therapeutic Communities: Reflections and Progress*. London: Routledge and Kegan Paul.

Hunt, A. (1964) Enforcement in Probation Casework. *British Journal of Criminology* **4**: 239–51.

Johnson, A.M. (1949) Sanctions for Super-Ego Lacunae of Adolescents. In K.R. Eissler (ed.) *Searchlights on Delinquency, New Psychoanalytic Studies*. London: Imago.

Laing, R. (1959) *The Divided Self*. London: Tavistock Publications.

Limentani, A. (1981) From Denial to Self-Awareness: A 20 Years' Study of a Case of Childhood Delinquency Evolving into Adult Neurosis. *British Journal of Medical Psychology* **54**: 175–86.

Priestley, P., McGuire, J., Flegg, D., Hemsley, V., and Welham, D. (1978) *Social Skills and Personal Problem Solving: A Handbook of Methods*. London: Tavistock Publications.

Prins, H.A. (1969) Casework and the Treatment of Offenders. *Journal of Applied Social Studies*. **1**: 181–87.

Salzberger-Wittenberg, I. (1970) *Psycho-Analytic Insight and Relationships*. London: Routledge and Kegan Paul.

Schmideberg, M. (1954) Is the Criminal Amoral? *British Journal of Delinquency* **IV**: 272–81.

—— (1965) Reality Therapy with Offenders. *British Journal of Criminology* **5**: 168–82.

—— (1981) Socialisation and Its Disturbances. *International Journal of Offender Therapy and Comparative Criminology* **25**: 114–21.

St John, J. (1961) *Probation the Second Chance*. London: Vista Books.

Stott, D.H. (1950) *Delinquency and Human Nature*. Dunfermline: Carnegie.

Strean, H. (1968) Casework with Ego-fragmented parents. *Social Casework* **49**: 222–27.

Symington, N. (1981) The Psychotherapy of a Subnormal Patient. *British Journal of Medical Psychology* **52**: 187–99.

Treger, H. (1965) The Reluctance of the Social Agency to Deal with the Offender. *Federal Probation* **29**: 23–8.

Washbrook, R.A.H. (1981) Neuroticism and Offenders. *International Journal of Offender Therapy and Comparative Criminology* **25**: 122–29.

West, D.J., Roy, C., and Nichols, F.L. (1978) *Understanding Sexual Attacks*. London: Heinemann Educational Books.

Winnicott, C. (1962) Casework and Agency Function. *Case Conference* **8**: 178–84.

FURTHER READING

*On measures and methods of supervision and control in the community see:*

King, J.F.S. (ed.) (1976) *Control without Custody*. Cambridge: University of Cambridge, Institute of Criminology.

Parker, H. (ed.) (1979) *Social Work and the Courts*. London: Edward Arnold. (especially Chapters 7 and 9)

*On various aspects of psychotherapy see:*

Bloch, S. (ed.) (1979) *An Introduction to the Psychotherapies*. Oxford: Oxford University Press.

Brown D. and Pedder, J. (1979) *Introduction to Psychotherapy: An Outline of Psychodynamic Principles and Practice*. London: Tavistock Publications.

Garfield, S. (1980) *Psychotherapy: An Eclectic Approach*. New York: Wiley.

Garfield, S.L. and Bergin, A.E. (1978) *Handbook of Psychotherapy and Behaviour Change: An Empirical Analysis* (second edition). New York: Wiley. (This is probably the most comprehensive manual available. It offers an in-depth survey of most theoretical models and psychotherapeutic methods.)

(The books by Brown and Pedder and by Bloch offer useful introductory over-views of various models of psychotherapy.)

*On applications of behaviour modification to the management of offenders in the community and penal establishments see:*

British Journal of Criminology (1979) *Special Number on Behaviour Modification*. Volume 19(4).

# PART FOUR
# The Effectiveness of Penal Measures

# CHAPTER TWELVE

# Assessing the results
# of management measures

But men may construe things after their fashion,
Clean from the purpose of the things themselves.
　　　　　　　　　　　　JULIUS CAESAR

Respect for observation as opposed to tradition
is difficult, and (one might almost say) contrary
to human nature.
　　　　　　　　　　　　BERTRAND RUSSELL

In this final chapter I shall attempt to examine the effectiveness
of some of the methods of management described earlier in this
book. The first part of the chapter is devoted to a brief consideration of some general issues concerning the measurement of
the effectiveness of social intervention; the second part is more
directly concerned with the measurement of the effectiveness of
penal measures and with the prediction of criminal behaviour.

## General issues

In the field of social and penal intervention it is notoriously
difficult to establish clear connections between cause and effect.
This is due in large part to the difficulty in controlling the many
variables that may impinge upon therapeutic encounters and
relationships. Not the least important of these variables is the
impact of the personality of the change-agent or therapist. The
history of medicine reveals how important the impact of 'charis-
ma' may be. We know that in biblical times the personal impact
of those endowed with the power of healing was considerable.
Jonathan Miller, in his book *The Body in Question* (1978), cites

Elijah and Jesus Christ as early examples of those who were endowed with such charismatic healing powers. He then goes on to show how the power of the 'Royal Touch' as a cure for the King's Evil (scrofula) seems not only to have been derived from this early charismatic healing force, but how it also had within it some of the origins of what we know today as counselling and psychotherapy.

Contemporary research attests to the importance of the therapist's belief in himself. For example, Truax and Carkhuff (1967) and others have shown that the most important components in the counselling relationship are not only the therapist's expressed genuineness and warmth but also his personal belief and confidence in the strength of his ability to offer help and produce change. Hundreds of research studies have been carried out into the effectiveness or otherwise of counselling, psychotherapy, and social work intervention. Many of them have tended to show that, at best, people tend to get no worse as a result of such intervention, but it is much more difficult to show that they get better in a clearly demonstrable fashion or to show precisely how any improvements have occurred. Sometimes this has been because the research designs have been inadequate or the intervention itself has been on too global a scale (see Brown and Pedder 1979: 193–200 and West 1980). It seems that the results have often been shown to be inconclusive because, as I mentioned in Chapter 11, *the aims and objectives* of the intervention were not adequately spelled out in the first instance. The importance of defining aims cannot be over-emphasized. Data on effectiveness are also frequently vitiated by the differing and imprecise meanings ascribed by various workers to such terms as 'cure' or 'improvement'. There can, of course, be many reasons for suggesting that an improvement in personal or social functioning has occurred. A person may be able to return to work; his marriage may no longer be so precarious; family members may no longer be at loggerheads with each other; anxiety may have been alleviated; specific symptoms may have abated. Such improvements might be summed up under the following three headings:

(1) Social adjustment of various kinds (which can of course include changes that have occurred in the environment).

(2) Relief from symptoms.
(3) Self-insight (i.e., a degree of self-awareness that enhances personal performance and integration).

To sum up this part of our discussion, strategies of social intervention might be improved if we:

(a) endeavoured to be much clearer about our aims and objectives,
(b) defined our populations more carefully and systematically,
(c) were clearer about the *specific* strategies of intervention to be applied,
(d) were more content with *small gains or improvements* and made attempts to *monitor these systematically*. Self and independent rating scales can be quite useful in this area, as Hamilton (1960) showed in the development of his rating scale for depressive disorders.

## The effectiveness of penal measures

Most research into the effectiveness of *penal measures* has made use of reconviction rates within a given period. In other words, management in the community and in institutions may be considered to have been 'successful' if offenders have remained conviction-free for a specified number of years. These rather crude criteria may have some merit, but their limitations become apparent when we examine them a little more closely. As West says 'a reconviction count is indeed only a rough index of continuing delinquency' (West 1980: 626). We may also ask whether *all* further convictions should be counted as indices of failure, or whether we should count only convictions for more *serious offences*, or for offences *similar in type* to the one for which the original sentence was received? Does the commission of another offence (major or minor) tell us very much about real success or failure anyway? Is it not quite conceivable that a person may have committed a further offence and yet have shown a considerable degree of improvement in other aspects of their social and personal functioning? Some of the more cynical detractors of the psychiatric prison at Grendon Underwood are said to have made capital out of the alleged semi-humorous statement made by a staff member that they may not have been able to make some of their inmates less criminal, but some of them were happier and better adjusted criminals! This apparent jest emphasizes the important point made earlier that mere reconviction rates tell us all too little about improvement, other than that they are a crude measure of what society may require. It is also important to remind ourselves of the observation made in Chapter 10 that *short-term* follow-up may also tell us little about positive improvement; only *long-term* follow-up may reveal an underlying propensity for re-offending. Thus, for most purposes, the reconviction rate is not a very precise means of measuring success or failure. It is not altogether surprising that management measures are not particularly successful for a variety of offenders, when one considers the adverse influences that are at work. West expresses the problem very succinctly and he also lends emphasis to some of the issues discussed in Chapter 11 of this book.

> 'The task of changing life-styles is more difficult than it once appeared. Histories of broken homes, faulty parenting, persistent truancy and erratic employment cannot be rewritten. Behaviour patterns developed in early life in response to adverse family circumstances, and reinforced in later years by immersion in a delinquent subculture, may be difficult to alter. Lack of work skills, alienation from mainstream society, the stigma of a criminal record and the absence of any rewarding prospects save those to be gained from crime are realities not easy to overcome.'
>
> (West 1980: 630)

With this realistic appraisal in mind we can now proceed to an examination of the effectiveness of different *types* of penal measures.

EFFECTIVENESS OF DIFFERENT TYPES OF PENAL MEASURES

There is a considerable literature which has examined different types of penal measures and which has endeavoured to compare the effectiveness of one with another (see Bean 1976 and Bottomley 1979 for summaries of some of these studies). One of the main difficulties that besets us when we wish to make comparisons between the effectiveness of different forms of sentence is that there is virtually no way in which such sentences can be randomized. For example, it would be virtually impossible to persuade courts to assign offenders to prison or probation on a random basis. I once tried to persuade a group of probation officers to assign young people randomly to 'straight' supervision or to a system of 'intermediate treatment'. Their defences against instituting such a procedure were wellnigh impenetrable and I had much sympathy with, and respect for, their views. We have to recognize that the ethical problems involved are no less considerable than they are for doctors when they seek permission to introduce comparative drug trials and other physical interventions for randomly allocated groups of patients (Samuels 1981).

A recent Home Office Research Unit study has reviewed the large amount of research that has been undertaken into the effectiveness of sentencing in the USA and elsewhere (Home Office 1976a). The conclusion reached in this survey is that most studies have, almost without exception, failed to demonstrate that one form of sentencing measure or type of management is more likely to be effective than any other. The results of most of the evaluative research that has been carried out can be summarized under the following broad headings. The format I have adopted follows that given in Part 6 of *The Sentence of the Court* (Home Office 1978).

(1) *Shorter or longer sentences.* No substantial evidence has been found that longer sentences or periods of detention produce better results than shorter ones (see Benson 1959, Dunlop and McCabe 1967, and Field 1969). In fact, much of the evidence points to the hardening and socially debilitating effects of long sentences (Richards 1978 and Flanagan 1980).

(2) *Effects of different institutional regimes.* Concerning young offenders, no research to date has indicated that any one institutional measure is more effective than any other. Although research into the former 'approved schools' suggests that some of these might have been marginally more effective than others, it is considered that this variation could well have been attributable to the idiosyncratic na-

ture of the regimes under which individual schools operated (Scott 1964 and Home Office 1975a).

(3) *Special institutional programmes*. Various experiments have been undertaken in running approved schools and other institutions for young offenders on a therapeutic community-type basis and in providing more individualized care (Miller 1964, Bottoms and McClintock 1973, and Home Office 1975b). Although such regimes may offer a more humane and caring approach, there is no hard evidence that they offer any improvement in reconviction rates over the more conventional methods of custody. (See also Weeks 1958, Adams 1961, Craft, Stephenson, and Granger 1964, Jesness 1965, and Warren 1964.) However, one piece of research has shown that when a group of adult prisoners were allocated randomly to receive more frequent and intensive care from prison probation officers, 57 per cent were reconvicted within two years of their release as compared with 76 per cent of men who did not receive such intensive work (Shaw 1974).

(4) *Custodial or non-custodial penalties*. Research reported on in the first edition of *The Sentence of the Court* (Home Office 1964) compared the effectiveness of fines, discharges, probation, and imprisonment. Although the research techniques used are now regarded as having been somewhat unsophisticated, the results tended to support the use of fines and discharges in preference to probation and imprisonment. In assessing the validity of the results it should be noted that the sample reported upon was an old one (i.e., for the year 1957). Despite this, some of the main points that emerged are worth noting:

(1) Fines were followed by the fewest reconvictions compared with those expected, for both first offenders and for persistent offenders of almost all age groups.

(2) Probation produced relatively better results when used for offenders with previous convictions than when used for first offenders. (The general conclusion that probation is at least as effective as institutional measures in preventing recidivism is also supported by evidence from some American studies – Hood and Sparks 1970: 187 and 248.)

(3) Imprisonment results were better for offenders with previous convictions than for first offenders, except for those aged thirty and over.

(4) Approved school results were also better for offenders with records of previous offences. (See also Scott 1964 above.)

(5) Fines and discharges appeared to be more effective than either probation or imprisonment *for first offenders of all age groups*. Fines were especially effective for those offenders convicted of theft.

Some of these findings require further comment. First, we should not necessarily conclude from the results that the particular method of disposal itself was necessarily helpful, since the absence of reconviction need not have had anything to do with the measure used; the offender may have simply escaped subsequent detection. As already mentioned, reconviction rates tell us comparatively little about possible improvements in social functioning in other aspects of an offender's life. It also needs to be emphasized that if the courts come to use non-custodial measures more than they do at present (as seems likely) this might in fact give rise to an increase in the crime rate, since there could be more offenders at liberty to commit crime (see also remarks in Chapter 2). This, in time, might lead to the introduction of more severe measures of crime reduction and have wide repercussions on the penal system. All these variables would thus have to be taken into account in assessing the system's overall effectiveness.

(5) *Variations in non-custodial measures*. Various research studies have endeavoured to demonstrate the effects of varying the quality and intensity of supervision of offenders on probation or parole licence. Such studies have, amongst other things, examined the effects of reducing the case-loads of probation officers, or of encouraging closer and more frequent contact. From most of these studies it seems likely that this does not have a significant bearing upon reconviction, though personal experience suggests that close surveillance may lessen the risk of further offending in some cases (Home Office 1976b and Prins 1980).

## Predictive devices

In Chapter 9 I suggested that there were no foolproof actuarial devices that would enable us to predict future criminality with any degree of accuracy. Two aspects of such prediction may be discerned. The first is relapse prediction (Walker 1968: 110), which is concerned with the prediction of further likelihood of reconviction. The second is delinquency prediction, which attempts to predict the likelihood of delinquent behaviour on the basis of other variables. I deal first of all with relapse prediction.

RELAPSE PREDICTION

This is based largely on an actuarial approach, described by Mannheim as follows:

> 'The basic idea common to all the various systems is to select a sample of case records representative of the type of offender for whom the prediction is made, for example borstal boys, and to abstract from them the information on a number of factors, perhaps 60 or a hundred or more – which might have some bearing on their criminal conduct . . . the sample is then divided into two groups, those who have been 'successes' and those who have been 'failures' over a period of discharge from the Institution, and only the factors showing the highest correlations with success or failure are used for predicting future conduct.'          (Mannheim 1965: 46)

Mannheim and Wilkins constructed their now well-known borstal prediction scales along these lines. They used such factors as history of drinking, number of previous offences, frequency of job changes, and so on. The boys were divided into groups or classes, A, B, C, etc., according to severity of risk. Boys in Group A would have the best chance of success. The tables they produced only predicted the *probability* of success or failure (Mannheim and Wilkins 1955). Although they demonstrated that the prognostications they made from the case records were more likely to be accurate than the subjective impressions of borstal staffs, they admitted that such tables, however useful, could never *replace* individual assessment. This is largely because predictions based upon retrospective studies of case records cannot take into account subtle factors that might have been highly relevant at the time of sentence. In addition, success or failure may depend on a range of variables entirely distinct from those upon which the tables are based. Furthermore, some tables may be based upon inadequate social and other background information. Although such tables may be of considerable value in developing *broad treatment policies*, they can never wholly take into account the enormous number of factors that influence individual behaviour (see also Simon 1971).

## DELINQUENCY PREDICTION

From the point of view of crime prevention, it would obviously be helpful if it was possible to spot at an early stage those young people who are at risk of delinquency. The literature on this subject contains many attempts to estimate delinquency-proneness and vulnerability. Glueck and Glueck (1960) conducted a very painstaking study of some 500 persistently delinquent young offenders matched with 500 non-delinquents. From the mass of information they collected, the Gluecks succeeded in producing five categories, each covering an area of the delinquent's life from which they said predictions could be made. These were: (1) discipline of boy by father; (2) supervision of boy by mother; (3) affection of father for boy; (4) affection of mother for boy; (5) degree of family cohesiveness. (See also Chapters 5 and 11 of this book.) Each of their categories headed a list of adjectives which could be used for qualitative rating, for example, lax, overstrict, firm and kind, fair, warm, indifferent, hostile, cohesive, and so forth. The Gluecks assigned various weightings to the five factors (categories) which, they suggested, could be used to predict the likelihood of future delinquency. In 1964, the Gluecks published a report by the New York City Youth Board on the use made of their tables on 244 boys. On 193 boys identified by the prediction instrument as having a very low chance of delinquency involvement, 96.4 per cent remained non-delinquent till the age of 17, when follow-up ceased; of 27 boys predicted as having a very high risk of delinquency, 85 per cent became serious or persistent minor offenders (Glueck and Glueck 1964). It is possible to make serious criticism of the Gluecks' work. For example, some critics have suggested that their original delinquent group was too highly selected, because it consisted of persistent and largely institutionalized delinquents. This must, therefore, invalidate some of their more general conclusions to some extent. However, the work is recognized by many as a brave venture into a complex and difficult problem at a time when little research on a large scale had been attempted in this field.

In this country a somewhat less ambitious attempt to predict delinquent behaviour was made by Stott. He devised a social adjustment guide, suitable for administration by schoolteachers and others. He claimed, on the basis of a small investigation of a Glasgow population, that his scale could have detected no less than 75 per cent of the children at high delinquency risk (Stott 1959 and 1960). We must now ask, if by the use of such predictive devices it were possible to predict which children were likely to become delinquent, what then could we do with this knowledge? As I have already shown elsewhere in this book, we can determine those conditions that are conducive to delinquency with a fair degree of certainty. (See particularly Chapters 3 and 5.) Even so, as I noted in Chapters 8 and 11, we have all too few effective resources for dealing with such young delinquents. Such management presupposes a 'take-up' of opportunities for social intervention. If, for example, a schoolteacher finds that a child is delinquency-prone, how is this to be got across to the parents and to the child in an acceptable fashion? The Gluecks maintained that delinquency should attract no more social stigma than did infectious disease. But the history of medicine shows that some infectious diseases have attracted a great deal of social stigma and, in any event, delinquency and antisocial behaviour are far more likely to produce an emotive response than many infectious illnesses. A sense of realism is therefore important if we are to deal with delinquency and crime both effectively and humanely. So far, this chapter has painted a somewhat gloomy picture of the effectiveness of penal and associated measures. There are, however, some helpful and forward-looking signs and these will now be touched upon in drawing this book to its conclusion.

## Some positive indications

In a recent paper, Jones (1981) has suggested that too many sweeping statements have been made about the ineffectiveness of correctional (penal) measures. He also suggests that the anti-correctionalists are guilty of one very serious over-generalization, namely the assertion that, because correctional measures have not been effective in the past, they cannot ever be effective. Jones puts the case very well when he says:

'Criminology unfortunately seems particularly prone to blanket pronouncements. A reduction in crime has been seen, at different times, as necessitating selective breeding, psychological treatment, community organisation, social reform, and even revolution. The protagonists of these various nostrums have seen little value in other points of view. Because of this lack of enthusiasm among theorists (though not among practitioners) for more modest formulations, one fashion in correctional method has succeeded another with a dreadful inevitability which might have bred scepticism in less flexible minds. The current preoccupation with anti-correctionalism is no less undiscriminating, and no less a fashion, equally destined to be superseded in its turn.

(Jones 1981: 3)

As indicated earlier in this chapter, those interventive efforts that are based upon the achievement of *modest* goals and which attempt to monitor the effects of these in a fairly rigorous fashion seem to hold out the best hope of success. West (1980) reports upon a number of such small-scale pieces of research that have been able to demonstrate small but significant changes in attitudes and behaviour. He suggests that 'treatments have not been invariably negative. Positive results might have been more frequent *if the necessity for scientific evaluation* had been more widely recognized' (my italics) (West 1980: 629). We also need to remind ourselves of the complex range of factors that may make intervention and management such unrewarding tasks. Success is likely to depend as much upon the motivation and enthusiasm of the penal worker as upon the theoretical model he or she espouses.

Although much evaluative research that has been carried out

does not lead one to be complacent or over-optimistic, the results have had some valuable implications. First, they lead us to raise important questions about the assumptions underlying present sentencing practices. They have shown that 'qualitative differences between different regimes or different styles of non-custodial supervision are often not as great as they are intended to be' (Home Office 1978: 88). Second, the fact that evaluative research has demonstrated that there is no single panacea for the crime problem is leading us to further review sentencing policies. It has also encouraged us not only to examine the cost of some more widely used measures which have been shown to be not very effective, but also to subject the need for custodial sentences to a good deal of critical scrutiny.

## Concluding comments

Those who have taken the trouble to read this book thus far may find many of the observations in this final chapter somewhat dispiriting. However, it would have been quite unrealistic and also academically dishonest to have left readers with the impression that we knew the remedies for the crime problem and how best to apply them. It *is* true that we have made some progress in understanding the phenomenon I have described as criminal behaviour and in understanding its multi-faceted origins. It is inevitable that some people will be attracted to one explanation in preference to another and this is as it should be. However, society's interests will best be served if those who hold divergent views continue to discuss these and share them one with another in an atmosphere of constructive debate rather than in one of polemical rancour, point scoring, and hostility. We need not only to learn patiently to collect and classify our *facts*, but to be clear in separating these from *opinions and feelings*. If the effect of this book is to have helped the reader in this process and to view the problem with what might be described best as dispassionate compassion, the efforts in writing it will have been amply rewarded.

# References

Adams, S. (1961) *Interaction Between Individual Interview Therapy and Treatment Amenability in Older Youth Authority Wards*. Monograph No. 2. Board of Corrections. State of California: California.

Bean, P. (1976) *Rehabilitation and Deviance*. London: Routledge and Kegan Paul.

Benson, G. (1959) Prediction Methods and Young Prisoners. *British Journal of Delinquency* **IX**: 192–99.

Bottomley, A.K. (1979) *Criminology in Focus: Past Trends and Future Prospects*. Oxford: Martin Robertson.

Bottoms, A.E. and McClintock, F.H. (1973) *Criminals Coming of Age*. London: Heinemann.

Brown, D. and Pedder, J. (1979) *Introduction to Psychotherapy: An Outline of Psychodynamic Principles and Practice*. London: Tavistock Publications.

Craft, M., Stephenson, G., and Granger, C. (1964) A Controlled Trial of Authoritarian and Self-Governing Regimes of Adolescent Psychopaths. *American Journal of Ortho-Psychiatry* **34**: 543–48.

Dunlop, A.B. and McCabe, S. (1967) *Young Men in Detention Centres*. London: Routledge and Kegan Paul.

Field, E. (1969) Research into Detention Centres. *British Journal of Criminology* **9**: 62–71.

Flanagan, T.J. (1980) The Pains of Long-Term Imprisonment. *British Journal of Criminology* **20**: 148–56.

Glueck, S. and Glueck, E. (1960) *Predicting Delinquency and Crime*. Harvard: Harvard University Press.

—— (1964) Potential Delinquents Can Be Identified: What Next? *British Journal of Criminology* **4**: 215–26.

Hamilton, M. (1960) A Rating Scale for Depression. *Journal of Neurology, Neurosurgery and Psychiatry* **23**: 56–62.

Home Office (1964) *The Sentence of the Court*. London: HMSO.

—— (1975a) *The Approved School Experience*. Home Office Research Study No. 25. London: HMSO.

—— (1975b) *Residential Treatment and Its Effect on Delinquency*. Home Office Research Study No. 32. London: HMSO.

—— (1976a) *The Effectiveness of Sentencing*. Home Office Research Study No. 35. London: HMSO.

—— (1976b) *Impact (Volume 2)*. Home Office Research Study No. 36. London: HMSO.

—— (1978) *The Sentence of the Court: A Handbook for Courts on the Treatment of Offenders* (third edition). London: HMSO.

Hood, R. and Sparks, R. (1970) *Key Issues in Criminology*. London: Weidenfeld and Nicolson.

Jesness, C.F. (1965) *The Fricot Ranch Study*. Research Report No. 47. California Youth Authority. Sacramento: California.

Jones, H. (1981) A Case for Correction. *British Journal of Social Work*: **11**: 1–17.

Mannheim, H. (1965) *Comparative Criminology (Volume 1)*. London: Routledge and Kegan Paul.

Mannheim, H. and Wilkins, L. (1955) *Prediction Methods in Relation to Borstal Training*. London: HMSO.

Miller, D. (1964) *Growth to Freedom*. London: Tavistock Publications.

Miller, J. (1978) *The Body in Question*. London: Cape.

Prins, H. (1980) *Offenders Deviants, or Patients? An Introduction to the Study of Socio-Forensic Problems*. London: Tavistock Publications.

Richards, B. (1978) The Experience of Long-Term Imprisonment: An Exploratory Investigation. *British Journal of Criminology* **18**: 162–69.

Samuels, A. (1981) Medical Research: Law and Ethics. *Medicine, Science and the Law* **21**: 295–98.

Scott, P.D. (1964) Approved School Success Rates. *British Journal of Criminology* **4**: 525–56.

Shaw, M. (1974) *Social Work in Prison*. Home Office Research Study No. 22. London: HMSO.

Simon, F. (1971) *Prediction Methods in Criminology*. Home Office Research Study No. 7. London: HMSO.

Stott, D.H. (1959) Spotting the Delinquency-Prone Child. *Howard Journal* **10**: 87–95.

—— (1960) The Prediction of Delinquent from Non-Delinquent Behaviour. *British Journal of Delinquency* **X**: 195–210.

Truax, C.B. and Carkhuff, R.R. (1967) *Towards Effective Counselling and Psychotherapy*. Chicago: Aldine Publishing Co.

Walker, N. (1968) *Crime and Punishment in Great Britain*. Edinburgh: Edinburgh University Press.

Warren, M.Q. (1964) *Correction in the Community: Alternatives to Incarceration*. Monograph No. 4. California: California Board of Corrections.

Weeks, A. (1958) *Youthful Offenders at Highfields*. Ann Arbor, Michigan: University of Michigan Press.

West, D.J. (1980) The Clinical Approach to Criminology. *Psychological Medicine* **10**: 619–31.

FURTHER READING

*On the evaluation of psychotherapy and allied interventions generally see:*

Garfield, S.L. and Bergin, A.E. (eds) (1978) *Handbook of Psychotherapy and Behaviour Change: An Empirical Analysis* (second edition) (*especially* Parts 2 and 5). New York: Wiley.

Reid, W. and Epstein, L. (1972) *Task Centred Casework*. New York: Columbia University Press.

Reid, W. and Shyne, A. (1969) *Brief and Extended Casework*. New York: Columbia University Press.


*On the evaluation of penal measures more specifically see:*

Bottomley, A.K. (1973) *Decisions in the Penal Process*. London: Martin Robertson.

Brody, S.R. (1976) *The Effectiveness of Sentencing: A Review of the Literature*. Home Office Research Study No. 35. London: HMSO.

Hogarth, J. (1971) *Sentencing as a Human Process*. Toronto: University of Toronto Press.

Home Office (1977) Advisory Council on the Penal System. *Interim Report. The Length of Prison Sentences*. London: HMSO.

Mathiesen, T. (1965) *The Defences of the Weak: A Sociological Study of a Norwegian Correctional Institution*. London: Tavistock Publications.

Sinclair, I. (1971) *Hostels for Probationers*. Home Office Research Study No. 6. London: HMSO.

Wilkins, L.T. (1969) *Evaluation of Penal Measures*. New York: Random House.

# Name index

# Subject index